Studies in Rhetorics and Feminisms

Series Editors, Cheryl Glenn and Shirley Wilson Logan

EVOLUTIONARY RHETORIC

Sex, Science, and Free Love in Nineteenth-Century Feminism

WENDY HAYDEN

Southern Illinois University Press
Carbondale and Edwardsville

Library of Congress Cataloging-in-Publication Data
Hayden, Wendy, 1977–
Evolutionary rhetoric : sex, science, and free love in
nineteenth-century feminism / Wendy Hayden.
    p. cm. — (Studies in rhetorics and feminisms)
Includes bibliographical references and index.
    ISBN 978-0-8093-3101-7 (pbk. : alk. paper)
    ISBN 0-8093-3101-2 (pbk. : alk. paper)
    ISBN 978-0-8093-3102-4 (ebook)
    ISBN 0-8093-3102-0 (ebook)
1. American literature—Women authors—History
and criticism. 2. Rhetoric—United States—
History—19th century. 3. Women and literature—
United States—History—19th century. 4. Free
love—United States—History—19th century. 5. Sex
customs—United States—History—19th century.
6. Feminism—United States—History—19th century.
7. Social problems in literature. I. Title.
PS217.W64H39 2012
810.9'928709034—dc23   2012018938

CONTENTS

ACKNOWLEDGMENTS

I am grateful to many people who supported me through the process of researching and writing this book. First and foremost, this project wouldn't exist without Jeanne Fahnestock, who encouraged me at every stage. She challenged me to dig deeper and brought me places I wouldn't have gone. Jane Donawerth also helped me work through my ideas and offered valuable feedback. Cheryl Glenn and Shirley Logan, editors of the Studies in Rhetorics and Feminisms series, gave helpful suggestions and guided me through the editing process. Jessica Enoch provided great ideas that helped me refine my argument. Kristine Priddy, Wayne Larsen, Barb Martin, and copyeditor Julie Bush at Southern Illinois University Press answered questions and offered invaluable support throughout the process.

Many people read earlier drafts of this work in different forms and gave useful feedback and suggestions. At the University of Maryland, I thank Leigh Ryan and Claire Moses for their support and enthusiasm. Marilee Lindemann and Zita Nunes had helpful research ideas. I thank my writing group colleagues, Lisa Zimmerelli, Andrea Dardello, Thomas Jody Lawton, Barbara Cooper, and Julie Strongson-Aldape. I also thank Jonathan Buehl, James Wynn, Linda Macri, Beth Colson, Damion Clark, and Scott Eklund. Nan Johnson, Patricia Sotirin, Cindy Griffin, Patricia Bizzell, Vicki Tolar Burton, and Carolyn Skinner offered feedback and support on other work that became part of this project. I am grateful to my colleagues at Hunter College, City University of New York, especially Cristina Alfar, Trudy Smoke, Barbara Webb, and Leigh Jones.

In researching this book, I owe debts of gratitude to scholars whose research pointed me in certain directions, particularly Joanne E. Passet and her excellent research. Grants from the University of Maryland English department helped fund research trips and gave me time to write. The support given to junior professors at CUNY helped me complete this project. I am grateful to the staff of librarians and archivists at the University of Maryland, the Library of Congress, New York Public

Library, Columbia University Library, Amherst College, the University of Washington, and Hunter College, CUNY.

Parts of this manuscript were previously published in the article "(R)Evolutionary Rhetorics: Science and Sexuality in Nineteenth-Century Free-Love Discourse" in *Rhetoric Review* 29.2 (April 2010): 111–28.

And finally, I thank my parents, Ron and Mary Hayden, and my sister, Nikki Best—and also my canine counterpart, Lily Mae, for telling me when it's time to stop working and go play.

EVOLUTIONARY RHETORIC

INTRODUCTION

The Unlikely Rhetorical Allies of Science and Free-Love Feminism

If you are in favor of science rather than Ignorance, Knowledge rather than Superstition; Fact rather than Tradition, Freedom rather than Slavery, Humanity rather than Bestiality, Reason rather than Dogma, Courage rather than Cowardice, Light rather than Darkness; if you are a lover of Justice, Honesty, Righteousness and Truth, then you should READ LUCIFER. Lucifer means the Light Bearer, is the name of an eight page weekly paper which is devoted to warfare on Superstition and Ignorance. Its piclasety is the scientific discussion Sexology, or Race Culture. It contends that the greatest right of all rights [is] to be born well. It is the pioneer paper of the Sexual Reform Movement. Price $1 a year. Three month trial subscription 25 cents. Sample copies free. Address, M. Harman, publisher, 507 Carroll avenue, Chicago, Ill.

—advertisement for *Lucifer*, 1900

On November 20, 1871, at Steinway Hall in New York City, a captivated crowd listened as the notorious Victoria Woodhull enumerated her views on sexual double standards, laws that made wives the sexual slaves of their husbands, and economic inequalities that exacerbated women's inferior position in sexual relationships until she proclaimed from the podium, "Yes, I am a Free Lover." In a century that had seen more women speaking in public for women's rights, abolition, and suffrage, a century that had seen crowds mob Angelina Grimke Weld for daring to speak to "promiscuous" audiences about abolition, Woodhull's "promiscuous" speech seems revolutionary for its time, but it was not an isolated critique of marriage and women's sexuality. "Free lovers" had been voicing the same concerns for decades, and many more women would do so before the century's end.

In Valley Falls, Kansas, on September 20, 1886, police arrived to arrest Edwin C. Walker and Lillian Harman for defying the laws by entering into a "free union," proclaiming in the presence of their families and friends their intentions to enter into a sexual relationship without the validation of church or state. The couple was promptly jailed "on the technical charge of living together as man and wife without being married, to the destruction of the peace and dignity of the State of Kansas" (L. Harman, *Marriage and Morality* 31). Walker was sentenced to seventy-five days in jail and Harman to forty-five. Their refusal to pay court costs extended their stay to nearly six months. Harman later admitted that they had been offered release if they would recognize the state's authority, but they refused to do so. The two believed the state had no authority over sexual matters and "practicalized" that belief in their "free union." In Harman's statement on their agreement, she insisted:

> I do not care to say much; actions speak more clearly than words, often. I enter into this union with Mr. Walker of my own free will and choice. . . . I retain, also, my full maiden name, as I am sure it is my duty to do. With this understanding, I give to him my hand in token of my trust in him and of the fidelity to truth and honor of my intentions toward him. (qtd. in "Autonomistic Marriage Practicalized")

Throughout the 1890s, women received their copies of free-love periodicals in bound volumes to hide the "obscene speech" from the post office and even from their husbands. One woman, who also wrote to the periodicals, struggled to conceal her subscriptions from her husband, until he found the contraband (L. Harman, "From My Point of View" [1899]). Many women were forced to end their subscriptions, but they found other women in their communities who shared the illicit material (Harman, "Freedom of Choice"). In defiance of their husbands and the post office's ban on "obscenity," these women continued to read and write to free-love periodicals, becoming part of a community of readers and writers that one woman called "a substitute for church membership" (Slenker, "Listen!").

These speakers, writers, readers, and practitioners represent just some of the rhetorical practices of nineteenth-century free-love feminists. These unexamined rhetors spent several decades, beginning in the 1850s until 1907, using the podium and the pen to denounce marriage, urge its abolition, encourage sex education, and promote an agenda that included women's sexual self-ownership—the defining features of free-love feminism. The "free" in the definition of "free love" emphasized the right for women and men to choose their sexual partners regardless of institutional sanction. Revealing marriage as an institution that fostered the degradation and inequality of women, free-love advocates rejected the ideologies behind marriage altogether. They pointed out how institutional marriage did not stop men and women from cheating, nor did it protect women from abuse. Furthermore, they revealed the inconsistencies in laws that punished certain sexual behavior outside of marriage but turned a blind eye to the same practices within marriage. Like the suffragists, free-love advocates objected to marriage laws that rendered a woman's legal identity obsolete. Unlike the suffragists, free-love advocates made sexuality the defining feature of their feminist calls for reform.

The women participating in what I am calling the free-love feminist movement spanned the breadth of the United States except perhaps for the South; as one opponent to free-love periodicals proclaimed of the South, "Thank God, if we have any vile demons in the form of woman in the south, such as those who write for that vile sheet, they hide themselves in brothels, or are ashamed to pollute the ears of the world with doctrines destined to fill lunatic asylums on earth, and the lower regions in eternity" (qtd. in Waisbrooker, "Wail of Ignorance"). Women promoting free love also came from different backgrounds and classes. In fact, many of them were born into the lower classes, setting themselves up as contrasts to the elitist suffragists.

Free-love feminists were, however, exclusively white. Though many black women speakers also critiqued the same structures demeaning women that free-love feminists did, they did not openly endorse an ideology of free love. Anna Julia Cooper, for example, criticized how the church "gave an inferior if not an impure character to the marriage relation, especially fitted to reflect discredit on woman" in an 1886 speech (56). Her critique was similar to the ways free-love feminists denounced church and state for their characterizations of women's sexuality. Cooper, however, stopped short of calling for the abolition of marriage and for the practice of free love since she was fighting against different institutional strictures. The institution of slavery had promoted black women's sexual availability rather than restricted their sexuality to certain frameworks; in contrast to the "passionless" white woman, institutional frameworks hypersexualized black women. Thus, black feminists did not endorse "free love" but nevertheless found ways to enter the conversation by also evaluating sexual practices. Free-love feminists also critiqued sexuality only within a heterosexist framework. In doing so, they reinforced some of the very ideologies they claimed to fight against, because this framework often relegated women's sexuality to maternity. Focusing exclusively on white middle-class heterosexist frameworks and often ignoring race would prove to be the undoing of free-love feminism.

Free-love feminists circulated their critiques of marriage and affirmations of women's sexuality through periodicals and lectures to other radical groups, which this project recovers in order to understand their contributions to feminist rhetorics. Misunderstood and often ignored in current scholarship, free-love feminists' rhetorical techniques help us to reconceptualize the topics and sources of nineteenth-century women's rhetorics. Scholarship on nineteenth-century women rhetors has related the many challenges women speakers faced. Susan Zaeske has highlighted the intricacies of the "promiscuous audience" charge that left any woman who dared to speak in public without the protection of their superior "womanhood." Seen as morally and sexually suspect, women combated these charges with what Zaeske calls a "gendered morality," emphasizing female moral superiority, thereby reinforcing gendered divisions (192). Merely listening to a woman speaking was enough to warrant a charge of immoral behavior (199), a charge that would be exacerbated if the woman whom an audience listened to spoke on the taboo topic of sex. Lindal Buchanan's work notes the effect of gendered conceptions of "women's place" on women speakers who often had to confront charges on their lack of "domesticity" and their increased sex drive when they spoke out against any injustice (108).

Despite these challenges, we can now view the nineteenth century as a prolific period for women rhetors, in both public and private spheres. Scholars of women's rhetoric have recovered the practices of women arguing for suffrage (K. Campbell), abolition, racial uplift (S. Logan), dress reform, and even the more conservative cause of temperance (Mattingly). They have found women both breaking taboos on women's speech and adhering to them in remaking the private space as a place for women's speech (Donawerth; N. Johnson). With all of this outstanding work on the time period, women speaking about sex in the free-love movement have yet to be examined. One explanation for the silencing of these women is their erasure from the histories of women's rights written in the nineteenth century; the suffragists wanted to distance themselves from these more radical (and problematic) women.

Another reason for the absence of free-love feminism in the recovery of women's rhetoric is that it could be considered a "failed social movement." Carol Mattingly relates how the temperance cause was long left absent from histories of women's rights, perhaps because of the idea that they in fact had failed in their aims (*Well-Tempered Women* 8). Free-love feminism can also be seen as a "failed" movement in this sense: women did not succeed in abolishing marriage or in ushering in an era of sexual freedom and often failed to change the "passionless" ideals they challenged. In addition, scholars have frequently struggled to make sense of their arguments. In 2005, for example, historian Michael Perry produced two anthologies of Victoria Woodhull's speeches, which he characterizes as "too weird and too mystical" (*Free Lover* 106). Others have dismissed the entire free-love movement as a "lunatic fringe" (Stoehr 3). The ways in which free-love feminists discussed sexuality might indeed seem "weird" to contemporary scholars, which also accounts for the lack of scholarship on them. Moreover, Mattingly observes that many twentieth-century feminists often ignored texts that did not adhere to their definitions of feminism, accounting for the long absence of the more conservative temperance movement from feminist scholarship ("Telling Evidence" 103). The ways free-love feminists argued about sexuality often seem removed from more (post)modern definitions of feminism, especially since their commitment to social justice often reinforced the very ideologies they spoke out against. As a result of their absence in discussions of feminist rhetorics, this study seeks not to examine their rhetorical accommodations, ethos, or agency to discuss sex in public forums but to understand the logic behind the often-perplexing statements contributing to their erasure.

The logic of their arguments certainly seems removed from contemporary discussions of sex and sexuality. Examining their logic, though, also reveals a surprising source of their arguments: science. Nineteenth-century women advocating free love found science an ally, rather than an enemy, to their aims. Closely examining their reasoning reveals warrants in the emerging scientific theories and disciplines of the nineteenth century, such as evolutionary theory, bacteriology, and embryology. While other women of the nineteenth century used natural rights discourse, religion, and even the "cult of domesticity" itself as the basis of their arguments, free-love feminists based their calls for women's sexual freedom in scientific warrants and language. We could read free-love discourse in the context of natural rights, "perfectionist," or Romantic ideals, but I find science the most helpful lens in understanding their logic.

Histories of women in the nineteenth century often portray science as the enemy to feminism. After all, nineteenth-century women had to contend with ideas that they were less evolved than men, that their bodily functions prevented them from doing the same work as men, and that their sex was inherently inferior. Many used science to support such claims, as documented by historians Carroll Smith-Rosenberg and Cynthia Eagle Russett. Both women find that the emerging sciences lent fuel to the antifeminist fire consuming feminist goals. Science helped to reinscribe female inferiority and, to some, even led to the failure of the women's movement since "men of science" "confer[red] the imprint of evolutionary science on traditional concepts of female difference and female subordination" (Erskine 117). This study does not dispute such findings. Rather, it shows another side of the story, where the same ideas could be used for women's liberation rather than for repressive restrictions.

That women were deemed "passionless" and "asexual" also dominates scholarship on nineteenth-century women. Historian Nancy Cott has examined the "passionless" ideology, one endorsed by many physicians throughout the century, which denied that women's physiology provided any sexual feelings. Other scholars have revealed how literature from the medical community resulted in defining women as "diseased," "hysteric," and controlled by their physiology, particularly their reproductive organs, and have analyzed how medical discourse was shaped by positions on women's social roles. Defining women as "diseased" served to limit their civic participation and keep them dependent on men. Furthermore, the treatment of female disorders formed a large and lucrative component of many physicians' practices (Fee 197).

However, other studies have revealed the complicated nature of these nineteenth-century debates. The free-love feminists discussed in this study were not the only ones challenging such views of women's sexuality. Physicians themselves often challenged it, countering our view of Victorian "prudery." One female physician, in particular, performed a study in the late nineteenth century that complicates "prudery" readings. Dr. Clelia Mosher, while working in clinics in the 1890s, initiated a survey that she gathered from at least forty-seven women. Questions on this survey included how many times per week these women experienced intercourse, how often they desired intercourse, and how often they experienced pleasure during intercourse (*Mosher Survey*). Long before Alfred Kinsey would ask the questions that made his examination of American sexual habits famous, Mosher studied the sexual habits of women in "Victorian" America—a place where, we are told, women were taught not to have sexual feelings. It would seem that Mosher had set out to abolish such myths about women; the collection of papers that she titled "Statistical Survey of the Marriages of Forty-Seven Women" provides a contrast to the middle-class ideals of the "passionless" angel of the home. But Mosher never published the study, and the reaction to Kinsey's review of American women indicates why. Mosher's look at sexual beliefs and practices, though, certainly paints a picture different from the chaste, passionless "Victorian" woman.

Clelia Mosher also represents the changing face of science in the nineteenth century. Once a study exclusively for men, women, in fact, began to assert a strong female presence in many different fields of science, such as botany and astronomy. Susan Wells and Carolyn Skinner have also recovered women physicians writing science, with Wells showing women participating in scientific discourse in the medical schools by writing anatomical treatises, textbooks, public health manuals, and research articles and Skinner analyzing the rhetorical accommodations of women physicians writing about sex for lay audiences. But women physicians were not the only ones participating in scientific discourse. Free-love feminists, who often had no scientific education at all, found science an "available means" to exhort free love.

In fact, we should not underestimate nineteenth-century women's knowledge of science, especially given the large market for scientific ideas in medical conduct books and mainstream periodicals. Science was "omnipresent" in mainstream periodicals (Dawson, Noakes, and Topham 1), including those aimed at women. Some free-love feminists, such as Victoria Woodhull, cited these mainstream scientific periodicals (*Popular Science Monthly*, specifically). They often quoted Charles Darwin, or referred to his theories, which would have been familiar to any periodical reader of the late nineteenth century. For others, we can ascertain their knowledge of science by reading their rhetoric alongside the popularizations of science found in medical texts aimed at laypersons. Popular fiction by women also engaged with scientific discoveries (Shuttleworth, Dawson, and Noakes 58; Tange). In addition, popular science journals often espoused more feminist ideologies because of women writers and subscribers (Fee iii). The language and theories of science, moreover, permeated public spheres of debate, finding their ways into free-love feminist arguments as warrants and as support.

Using science as a "terministic screen" to view the logic of free-love feminism and drawing on rhetorical theories from twentieth-century rhetoricians Stephen Toulmin, Lloyd Bitzer, Chaim Perelman and Lucie Olbrechts-Tyteca, and Kenneth Burke, this study reveals three major ways science influenced a rhetoric of women's sexuality in free-love feminist texts. First, science provided the language to discuss sexuality, more powerful than the language of Enlightenment rhetorics of natural law and individual sovereignty favored by male free-love advocates. Second, science changed the rhetorical situation of discussions of sexuality: rather than discussing sex as within the bonds of the marriage institution, free-love feminists discussed it as a key element of human evolution. Furthermore, free-love feminists responded to several exigencies provided by scientific discoveries, such as the discovery of the extent of venereal diseases in married women. Third, their logic reveals how they used warrants, or the assumptions linking the data to the claim, from science. Interestingly, science produced not only arguments that would later warrant feminist claims but also axioms that free-love feminists could use to warrant their existing arguments. That is, scientific discoveries produced arguments that would provide new warrants refreshing existing arguments and setting them in a new context. Looking more specifically at the logic of free-love feminist arguments also shows how these rhetors gave certain elements of scientific theory more presence than others. Thus, science provided new language, new warrants, and new urgency to discussions of sexual practices. Finally, stasis theory helps us understand how the premises of the arguments of free-love feminists changed from celebrating women's sexuality to promoting a much darker purpose.

This study traces free-love feminist logic from its basis in scientific discoveries, to the popularization of that science in medical texts written for lay audiences, to the scientific warrant in use in arguments for women's sexual self-ownership. To do so, the project looks closely at five scientific disciplines that affected discussions of sexuality: evolution, physiology, bacteriology, embryology, and heredity. The division of the chapters also serves another important purpose: to show how free-love feminism changed into something more sinister. Adherents' reliance on motherhood led to that darker purpose. Free-love feminists often relied on the benefits of free love to motherhood, the only acceptable outlet for women's sexuality. In doing so, they illustrate Mattingly's contention that "women thus found it necessary, as they broke some cultural restrictions for their sex, to 'yield to [the] audience's opinions in other respects.' . . . The careful negotiation between broken regulations and concessions to expectations defines the most successful women rhetors" (*Appropriate[ing] Dress* 6). These women positioned themselves not as "mothers-of-the-nation," as Nan Johnson reveals about women rhetors, but as "mothers of the race."

Thus, the story of free-love feminism does not end well. We may be tempted to celebrate the rhetorical practices of its adherents, when in fact their rhetoric reveals that they went down a dark path. In emphasizing the importance of motherhood as a benefit of women's sexual freedom, they initiated eugenic lines of argument that would eventually supersede their initial aims. By 1907, many women who supported free love now argued exclusively for eugenics, when once eugenics was a means to argue for women's emancipation rather than the end in itself. This study seeks to reveal how their revolutionary rhetoric devolved into a rhetoric of eugenics. We will see eugenic arguments emerging in all of the scientific disciplines examined here. This study seeks to understand how free-love feminists' logic brought them to eugenics as a solution. Looking at their rhetoric with science as a backdrop helps to illuminate their shift in focus.

Each chapter also looks at the progression of their warrants from the science to the mainstream. In looking at this progression, we cannot ignore the role of popular medical texts in the transition to reform. The medical conduct book aimed at lay audiences became a popular genre, particularly at midcentury. I chose to examine medical texts that represent the ways science was being parlayed into reform. But I also chose books that the women in this study were likely to have read. Books like Russell Trall's *Sexual Physiology* and John Cowan's *The Science of a New Life* were often advertised in free-love periodicals. Clelia Mosher's survey also asked women where they gained their knowledge of sex, and many named these types of books, even the book titles themselves. Some free-love feminists quoted from specific medical texts, so I tracked down the original sources to compare. Other medical texts I included were not explicitly used by free-love feminists but add to our conception of how the medical community conceived women's sexuality, how they explained the new scientific discoveries, and how they were part of a larger conversation on women's sexuality. These texts, however, have produced different readings by scholars. In fact, critics reading the same texts have often found differing advice on sexual practices within the same text, depending on what ideology of "Victorian sexuality" their research is supporting. For example, Ronald G. Walters's 2000 collection, *Primers for Prudery: Sexual Advice to Victorian America*, uses some of the same physiology texts that I examine, such as Russell Trall's and John Cowan's texts. While he finds evidence supporting a view of Victorian prudery, my analysis reveals more liberating views of women's sexuality in these medical "primers," which reformers used to support women's rights. Rhetorical analysis of these texts confirms that the debate over women's sexual physiology in the nineteenth century was multivoiced and multifaceted. If we look for the prudish view of sexuality in these texts, we will find it. If we look for more liberating views, we will find them as well. Placing a different screen on what we are reading reveals the complicated nature of these debates.

The main texts in this study, free-love feminist arguments, came from pamphlets, texts of speeches, and books written by women. I also initially wanted to include more articles from free-love periodicals edited by women. (I thus did not concentrate on the periodicals exclusively edited by men.) These would seem to include *Woodhull & Claflin's Weekly*, edited by Victoria Woodhull and Tennessee Claflin; *The Word: A Monthly Journal of Reform*, whose editorship is solely attributed to Ezra Heywood, but Angela T. Heywood played a large role; and *Lucifer, the Light Bearer*, which had several female editors in its longer run. I found, however, that *Woodhull & Claflin's Weekly*, while including the voices of its two female editors and other women of the movement, still seemed largely male-dominated due to the influence of Stephen Pearl Andrews. Women's voices were included, but not in as prominent a role as I initially thought. Since the more radical versions of free-love feminism I have charted were in their infancy during its run in the 1870s, I therefore concluded that it was less of a forum for free-love feminism than it first seemed. *The Word* also included the voices of the emerging movement but can also appear male-dominated. It does, however, allow us a glimpse into the rhetoric of a singular free-love feminist whose works are available only in its pages—Angela Heywood. While *The Word*, *Woodhull & Claflin's Weekly*, and other free-love periodicals included the voices of free-love feminists, it was in *Lucifer, the Light Bearer* that these voices were more prominent. *Lucifer* also allowed a broader view of the debates among male free lovers and free-love feminists. I therefore include more texts from *Lucifer* than from other equally radical periodicals.[1]

I also made specific decisions on the chronological scope of this project based on my definition of free-love feminism as a social movement. While free-love arguments emerged as early as the 1830s, I highlight the 1850s, particularly in the work of Mary Gove Nichols, as the inception of free-love feminism. The last three decades of the nineteenth century saw such arguments proliferate and also turn into something quite different. I therefore chose 1907 as the end of free-love feminism, not only because fewer texts were produced at this time but also because it was the year in which free-love feminist Lois Waisbrooker produced a book called *Eugenics* and the year where the important venue for free-love feminism, *Lucifer, the Light Bearer*, changed its name to the *American*

Journal of Eugenics. Several free-love feminists discussed in this study continued to publish their ideas in the *American Journal of Eugenics*, but 1907 marks the end of a feminist movement, an end that had been building for some time.

This study focuses on analyzing logic in looking at this specific group of feminists because their arguments can seem so wild and incomprehensible to modern readers. In addition, an analysis of their logic can help us understand how science informed a turn from a rhetoric of silence on sexual matters to a rhetoric of resistance, and finally back to a more conservative aim. It focuses on the scientific roots of their logic but acknowledges that science is not the only lens with which to view their rhetorical practices; it is simply the most helpful in initiating the recovery of these often ignored rhetors. However, the "science" described here doesn't always seem like science. Some ideas, like those of spiritualists, are clearly not science. Thus, the science of these texts often seems spurious. Most of what we know today seems obvious—we learned it in high school biology. My own challenge was to see what scientific thought was and how laypersons interpreted it before we knew what we now know. Several scientific theories would seem to have no connection to the points made in medical and reform texts, but these theories were related and synthesized in the minds of the public. Medical popularizations show how that synthesis occurred. Finally, to answer the question of how such a revolutionary rhetoric of women's sexuality turned into a problematic rhetoric of eugenics, looking at mainstream interpretations of science is essential.

The professionalization and specialization of science throughout the nineteenth century yielded many discoveries and even new disciplines that produced greater understanding of the human body and its sexual functions. While some of that knowledge has since been refuted, the new theories often provided the germ for later breakthroughs. It was not until the twentieth century that major discoveries came by way of endocrinology and genetics. There was much that nineteenth-century scientists did not yet know in relation to sexuality, but there was also much that they did know. In the beginning of their history of sexuality, John D'Emilio and Estelle B. Freedman caution against viewing the history of sexuality as one of "progress from repression to liberation, ignorance to wisdom, or enslavement to freedom" (xii). Likewise, the history of scientific breakthroughs cannot be viewed as a story of ignorance yielding to illumination. At times, nineteenth-century science was radically wrong in its conception of the body. At times, discoveries produced the wrong conclusions. Yet, the making of scientific knowledge can be found even in theories that have since been refuted.

Chapter 1 recovers free-love feminism as a social movement, diverse in its adherents and arguments but unified in its goals to critique the sexual status of women. Many historians have failed to recognize free love as a movement, or even as a feminist movement, because of its disparate ideas and seeming lack of consistency. This chapter argues that there was a movement, especially if we look at it from a rhetorical perspective. For the purposes of this project, a social movement is defined as a collective endorsing a shared political goal, with members conversing with each other to define that goal. Free love was a small social movement with various incarnations, which often included feminist goals or goals to assert social justice for women in a time where legal marriage meant that they surrendered their legal identities and lost all rights, including the right to control their bodies, to their husbands. However, free love was not a predominantly feminist movement until after the Civil War. Drawing on the pioneering work of Mary Gove Nichols in the 1850s, women supporting free love in the late nineteenth century made feminist goals the main focus of their calls for reform. This chapter thus shows how a feminist rhetoric of free love emerged by recovering the experiences and rhetorical strategies of a group of women we can call free-love feminists. While not a traditional social movement, their practices enable us to trace a movement made cohesive by its shared rhetoric.

Chapter 2 begins the study of how science influenced free-love feminism by finding the basis of adherents' logic in evolutionary science. Relying particularly on the works of Charles Darwin, it shows how free-love feminism received three integral warrants from evolutionary theory. First, free-love feminists appropriated the focus on nature to define marriage as an outdated institution that perverts nature. Since similar arrangements are absent in the natural world, they argued that the man-made institution had a negative influence on human sexual practices. The second warrant came from Darwin's theory of sexual selection, outlined in *The Origin of Species* and *The Descent of Man*, which led to a new emphasis on female choice in mates. Free-love feminists extended the provenance of female choice to make Darwin's theory a central tenet of their ideology. Finally, this chapter uncovers the warrant that would later prove to be the undoing of free-love feminism: that free love would lead to progress in the race. Thus, this chapter serves as a starting point to view the ascendance of eugenic rhetoric, also traced through the other chapters.

Chapter 3, discussing the field of physiology, and chapter 4, discussing bacteriology, examine the redefinition of certain sexual mores. Chapter 3 looks at free-love feminist claims on the nature of women's sexuality against the backdrop of a larger conversation occurring in the medical field. Free-love feminists actually accepted the premise from physicians that women's sexual organs controlled their bodies and minds but used it to argue that women were therefore entitled to pleasurable sex to maintain a healthy physiology. They also claimed that women's sexuality was more evolved than men's and factored that belief into their calls to reform sexual practices. Chapter 4 shows how the new discovery of disease causation and transmission through bacteria created a new rhetorical situation for these calls. The frequency of venereal disease transmission in marriages and the effects on fertility also sparked more interest in eugenic arguments. Thus, bacteriology gave free-love feminists both a new urgency and a new warrant that literalized their characterization of marriage as a "diseased institution." The "bacteriomania" resulting from scientific discoveries not only created arguments for the protection of the home and the body but also transformed discussions of sexuality into a rhetoric of responsibility.

The discipline of embryology provided a case of new warrants reviving older arguments, and in some cases superstitions, about sexuality and pregnancy. Chapter 5 shows how free-love feminists had argued for the special circumstances of the potential mother in sexual relations; new findings on fertilization and the development of the embryo then refreshed and reframed these arguments. It also shows the emergence of the concentration on producing "better children" when women started arguing for rights using improvements to the next generation as support. The "Republican motherhood" arguments popular with earlier feminists regenerated into a different kind of rhetoric of responsibility: women needed rights to secure the most helpful conditions for molding new life while pregnant.

Finally, chapter 6 elaborates the rhetoric of eugenics in free-love feminism. Looking at adherents' logic in the context of scientific debates on heredity reveals one possible reason for eugenics conquering feminist aims: the loss of the warrant that acquired characteristics could become hereditary, based on Lamarckian conceptions of evolution. This warrant allowed feminists to argue for reforms on the basis of their benefits to future generations. But the refutation of Jean-Baptiste Lamarck's theories in the late nineteenth century caused the reform warrant to disappear, and arguments that used eugenics as a means to the end of women's rights became purely eugenic arguments. The conclusion of this project examines the implications of recovering this movement in light of what it devolved into.

Although each chapter begins with science to trace the logic of free-love feminist arguments, I should point out that this relationship was not strictly linear. Feminist ideas influenced science as much as science influenced feminist ideas. The emergence of sexology in the beginning of the twentieth century provided a backlash against feminist ideas, culminating in the work of Sigmund Freud and Havelock Ellis becoming the predominant doctrine of women's sexuality. Scientific and medical communities, aware of the "agitation" provided by feminists, reacted to it with further reinscribing of women's bodies. The efforts of free-love feminists to resist such inscribing illustrate Michel Foucault's contention that the Victorians spoke "verbosely of [their] own silence" (1.8). In examining "the way in which sex is 'put into discourse'" (1.11), Foucault shows that discourse itself helps to shape our experiences of sexuality. In contrast to a "Victorian" view of discussions of sexuality, we see that free-love feminist rhetors spoke verbosely about sex and broke the last taboo on women's speech.

1

The Season of Battle: The Rhetoric of Free-Love Feminism in Nineteenth-Century America

The season of love is that of battle.
—Darwin, *The Descent of Man*, 1871

In 1889, after the male editors of a small, radical paper titled *Lucifer, the Light Bearer* were arrested for distributing "obscenity," a letter signed by eleven women, including Lucinda B. Chandler, Celia B. Whitehead, Juliet H. Severance, M.D., Elmina D. Slenker, Lillie D. White, and Lois Waisbrooker, began to circulate. This letter protested the arrest but also presented an appeal to "women, wives, and mothers, everywhere" to seek justice for women under the law. Viewing the arrest as an attempt to silence arguments for women's sexual equality, they pled, "This is a woman's battle" (Chandler et al. 1):

Free speech, free press and free womanhood ought not to lack valiant defenders among our sex in this case. Now is our opportunity. We can at least try to prove whether woman has any protection from legal lust in the higher civilization. We can testify on paper if we cannot before the court, that we consider the mutilation of a wife's body "a great and flagrant wrong." . . . We can protest against the conviction of the defendants because they published a fact of outrage upon a legal sex slave, containing a plain physiological term. . . . We can pronounce that the man who forces himself upon a lawful wife commits rape, precisely as a man who forces himself upon woman not his wife is held to have committed rape. . . . Every woman who realizes the bondage and degradation of thousands of her sex, married and unmarried, ought to feel herself individually responsible to protest against the misdirected and invasive proceeding that seeks to keep under cover in the name of protection of public morals, such enormous crimes are perpetrated upon wives. . . . Send your best and strongest words, my sisters, to Judge Foster. . . . Protest against the

action of Comstockism in prosecuting the defenders of womanhood. . . .
Send your most vigorous denunciation of the barbarous statutes and the
barbarous treatment of wives. . . . Prove . . . that American womanhood
is worthy to be free because she is herself ready to strike for freedom. (1–2)

This letter defines several tenets of free-love feminism, a distinctive
offshoot of nineteenth-century agitation for free love. We can define
free-love feminism as an attempt to redefine women's sexuality and to
critique the social and legal systems that attempted to regulate it. Believing that love in freedom was the only way to achieve women's full
equality and that sex in legal marriage equated to "legal lust," free-love
feminists advocated the abolition of marriage so woman could "own
herself." This letter from several prominent free-love feminists also illustrates the battles occurring over nineteenth-century sex speech: the battle
between the prudish and vigilant Anthony Comstock, armed with his
own position in the post office to weed out "obscenity," and those seeking
more frank discussion of sexual matters; the battle between the courts
and those defending freedom of speech; the battle between women and
men for women's sexual rights; and the battle between males exhorting
the cause of free love and the feminists who began to champion it, thus
transforming this often ignored "lunatic fringe" movement into a space
for women to create a rhetoric of sexuality.

The Emergence of Free-Love Feminism in
Nineteenth-Century America

The story of free-love feminism has remained unexamined, particularly
from a rhetorical lens. The valuable historical studies recovering this
movement often depict it as male-centered, such as John C. Spurlock's
1988 study, *Free Love: Marriage and Middle-Class Radicalism in America,
1825–1860*. Spurlock focuses on earlier incarnations of the movement,
where males featured more prominently, and ignores its later evolution
into a feminist movement. Both Hal D. Sears's earlier study, *The Sex
Radicals: Free Love in High Victorian America*, and Taylor Stoehr's anthology, *Free Love in America: A Documentary History*, discuss both male
and female free lovers but more prominently feature men. Stoehr also
limits his definition of free love to those who were actually practicing
it in the communes and portrays arguments for free love as individual
acts of radicalism rather than as a social movement. Linda Gordon,
historian of birth control in America, also rejects the idea of a movement
for free love, and she too views the groups advocating free love as "small
and sectarian" and "male-dominated" ("Voluntary Motherhood" 5).

Only Joanne E. Passet's important work of recovery, the 2003 book *Sex Radicals and the Quest for Women's Equality*, primarily focuses on the role of women. These studies illustrate the main problem with tracing a cohesive movement for free love in nineteenth-century America: there wasn't one. A cohesive movement did not exist because those calling themselves free lovers often disagreed on the definition and ideal practice of free love. Reading their acts from a rhetorical perspective, however, enables us to view these rhetors as participants in a social movement, often feminist in its various incarnations, made cohesive by its rhetoric.

Agitation for free love began as early as Fanny Wright's claims in the 1830s, though it did not become more widespread until the 1870s, when the movement began its more feminist leanings. In the 1850s, communes such as Berlin Heights in Ohio, Modern Times on Long Island, and Oneida in New York emerged as places where "perfectionists" could practice the values of free love. This incarnation of the movement found its basis in Fourierism and perfectionism and aimed to produce children in freedom, meaning freedom from church or state control. John Humphrey Noyes's community of Oneida was the most radical, as he encouraged the practices of stirpiculture, an early form of eugenics that matched the "best" women to the "best" men to produce "superior" children, and male continence, emphasizing the woman's pleasure over the man's in sexual intercourse, as men would refrain from climax. Berlin Heights and Modern Times also recognized women's rights to choose their sexual partners, but these communities were male-dominated in their leadership and often ignored more feminist goals. The 1850s also saw the emergence of several free-love organizations, such as the Free Love League in New York City, where philosopher Stephen Pearl Andrews led groups meeting in his home in informal salons, debating issues related to sexual matters and individual rights. Andrews, though he had feminist ideas, focused more on the sovereignty of the individual in his philosophy of free love, applying Enlightenment philosophies to contemporary sexual relations. It would be up to the women of the emerging movement to provide a feminist focus.

Periodicals played a major role in coalescing the disparate free lovers into a cohesive movement. The communes produced several periodicals, but as the movement began to spread beyond perfectionist communities, more periodicals began publication, the most notable of which were *Woodhull & Claflin's Weekly* (1870–76), published in New York City and edited by the Claflin sisters, Victoria Woodhull and Tennessee Claflin; *The Word: A Monthly Journal of Reform* (1872–93), published in Princeton, Massachusetts, by Ezra and Angela Heywood; and *Lucifer, the*

Light Bearer (1883–1907), published in Valley Falls and Topeka, Kansas, and Chicago by Moses Harman. While the latter periodicals were the most widely read, several free-love advocates briefly started their own periodicals. These periodicals shared readers, authors, contributors, and radical philosophies. Free-love periodicals and lectures helped to create a "counterpublic," where women were empowered to challenge the dominant ideologies constructing their bodies through telling their own stories. Women also played larger roles in the leadership of the periodicals. The most widely circulated, *Lucifer, the Light Bearer*, boasted several female editors during its run, such as Lillian Harman, Lois Waisbrooker, and Lillie D. White. Moses Harman, an anarchist feminist and chief editor of the periodical throughout its run, made *Lucifer* a space for open discussion, and his policy was to print all signed letters, whether from supporters or detractors, which enables us to discern the movement operating behind those arguing the cause of free love, conversing with each other for a common goal.[1]

In addition to the periodicals, free-love advocates also formed organizations, both small and large, so that participants could read papers to each other and engage in debates on social issues. Some of these organizations included the aforementioned Free Love League of New York City as well as the New England Free Love League, the Free Love Bureau, and the National Liberal League. Furthermore, free-love advocates met in informal settings to read papers to each other, such as one known as the Lucifer Circle, and they later published these essays in periodicals or as pamphlets.

Another reason for the difficulty in tracing a cohesive movement for free love is because the advocates came to exhort it from a variety of other radical viewpoints. Some identified primarily as anarchists, others as spiritualists, and some as labor reformers. The utopian perfectionists in the mid-nineteenth century incorporated free love into their ideals but focused more on transcendental values and often ignored the roles of women, though they did apply their individualist doctrine to both men and women.[2] In the later part of the nineteenth century, many labor reformers seeking better working conditions also focused their attention on the conditions of women within the home, viewing them as laborers without a wage. They turned to free love as a solution for the inequalities of women within the labor system, which they attributed to restrictions on married women working outside the home.

One philosophy that brought many to exhort the cause of free love was spiritualism. Spiritualists, often portrayed as "cranks," despite the devotees of spiritualism in "respectable" society, emerged in 1848, claiming to be able to channel the spirit world through mediums. This belief led to reconceptions of the relationship between heaven and earth, and their views of heaven captured the attention of the perfectionists. Spiritualism appealed to those who wanted to "conquer death" and bring heavenly values to their lives on earth. It found a theology in the writings of Andrew Jackson Davis, who revised the Swedenborg idea of a multilayered heaven, where beings could ascend to different levels. Spiritualism, then, incorporated democratic values since it envisioned a heaven where all people could ascend (Gutierrez 190). Many early feminists were also drawn to spiritualism since women frequently acted as mediums. It took on even greater appeal in the face of technological changes that caused some to feel disconnected from their spirituality.[3] In spiritualist discourse, free love became one of the ways to achieve higher ascendancy. However, not all supporters of spiritualism supported this focus, and many, in fact, chose to distance themselves from free love, often canceling speakers who promoted it. These devotees followed spiritualism as a religion, differing from the social reformers who used spiritualism as part of their platforms (Passet, "Power through Print" 235). Other spiritualist camps often granted large audiences to free-love speakers.

The perfectionists, anarchists, and spiritualists promoting free love included feminist thought in their philosophies, but women's rights did not dominate their ideals. Within each movement, though, we find women exhorting what I am calling free-love feminism. Free-love feminists brought their philosophies out of the communes and into a public conversation; they applied "perfectionist" ideals to the lived experiences of women. Whether they came to support free love from a perfectionist, anarchist, or spiritualist background, women exhorting the cause created a feminist discourse community and social movement.

Free-Love Feminism as a Social Movement

Another complication to analyzing free love as a social movement stems from the ambiguity of the term "free love" itself. Not only did it change in the last decades of the nineteenth century, but different theorists also promoted different applications of "free love." Some applied the term to chaste relationships and some to "variety" or having multiple partners, while others championed its more popular association as a kind of serial monogamy (Passet, *Sex Radicals* 2). Whether they advocated chaste relationships or the freedom to practice promiscuity, all who endorsed free love coalesced around the ideology that for love to be "free," it must be an agreement between partners, not a compulsory activity validated by church or state. At its basis was the right of women to choose their sexual partners based on love, not economic necessity or social or family pressure. That is, we might read their calls for sexual freedom as "freedom from" church and state influence rather than "freedom to." They called such freedom "social freedom," with free love being one of the practices under its mantra. For free-love feminists, it was the nature of the relationship and the involvement of sexist social mores, church, or state that differentiated "free" love from compulsory love. However, many supporting free love were married; some several times. While it may seem contradictory to preach the values of free love while married, many women married partners who shared their values. Thus, since the men recognized their wives' self-sovereignty, their marriage could still be called "free love." Victoria Woodhull and the equally radical Juliet H. Severance espoused definitions of free love shared by many free-love feminists. Woodhull proclaimed in her 1871 speech at Steinway Hall, "Yes, I am a Free Lover. I have an *inalienable, constitutional* and *natural* right to love whom I may, to love as *long* or as *short* a period as I can; to *change* that love *every day* if I please, and with *that* right neither *you* nor any *law* you can frame have *any* right to interfere" (*"And the Truth"* 23; emphasis in original). Writing in 1891, Severance defined "free love" by differentiating it from "legal lust":

> There is really but one question in the matter, which is this: "Shall mutual love (as is proposed by Free-lovers) or selfish lust (as it exists to-day in and out of marriage) be the basis of the relations of the sexes?" If you reply that mutual love should be the basis, then you are a Free-lover. If you reply that it should be lust, you are in sympathy with the present laws and customs of society, in which purity of life for woman becomes an impossibility. (*Discussion* 16)

Severance believed that whether someone practiced "free love" depended more on the ideologies behind their unions than with legal definitions (thus, free lovers could be married and still be practicing free love). Angela Heywood, writing in 1881, supported such a definition in her conception of free love. She insisted, "One is not a Free Lover because she cohabits with one or more men, or with none at all, but rather by the import and tone of Association" ("Ethics of Sexuality" 40). Both Severance and Heywood emphasized love, rather than economic necessity or social pressure, as the basis of free-love unions. Tennessee Claflin highlighted the distinction in 1871, differentiating between "free love" and "forced love" (*Constitutional Equality* 75). To free-love feminists, women were too often led astray by their upbringing, believing marriage a necessity. Such relationships equated to "forced" love in free-love feminist thought, though the "force" was not physical but applied by social pressure.

In their advocacy of free love, these feminists had to fight accusations of promiscuity, causing them to clarify that practicing free love did not necessarily mean practicing promiscuity. Juliet Severance responded to such an accusation, questioning why a man who would make such an accusation "assumes that if a woman owned her own body she would be ready to offer it to every man she met, and that without 'fencing in' she would riot in excesses" and exclaiming, "That is a libel on womanhood" ("Dr. Severance on Ownership"). Lillian Harman, in a speech delivered in 1898, asserted a similar criticism when she proclaimed, "In a recent lecture this society was told . . . that freedom in love is impracticable, because no man can love and respect a woman who is the 'common property of the herd,' the inference being that a woman who is not the property of one man must inevitably be the property of all men; that she can never by any possibility be the property of herself" ("Some Problems" 121). Harman and Severance attacked those who would call free lovers promiscuous by pointing out their limited definitions of free womanhood. These free-love feminists may have disdained promiscuity, but they stressed the rights of women to practice it, should they wish to do so. Lois Waisbrooker, for example, criticized proponents of variety but clarified that while "permanent love" was preferable, it should not have to be validated by a legal bond. She championed the right of a woman to practice promiscuity, because she "should have the right to bring one or a dozen men to her home if she wanted them," believing few women would choose to do so ("Rainstorm Duck"). In fact, many free-love feminists rejected interpretations of free love as variety, preferring instead to endorse what we would call serial monogamy.

Many free-love feminists embraced the term "free love" itself, believing it encapsulated their ideologies. Some males, however, rejected the negative associations of the term. Moses Harman, for example, who published many works advocating "free love" and whose newspaper was the most popular venue for those espousing free love, rejected the term, denouncing any who would call him a "free lover" as a "defamer":

> Its etymology is innocent enough but by common usage it has a decidedly sinister meaning. As defined by the defenders of marriage morality . . . free love means "gross sensualism," "promiscuity in sex relations," "irresponsible sexuality," "the sum of all that is vile in human conduct,"

etc., etc. To be introduced to an average audience, or to the readers of a popular journal, as a free lover is nearly if not quite tantamount to being labeled a miscreant, a "vile wretch," an "unprincipled person," etc. ("Freedom versus Marriage")

Fellow anarchist Voltairine de Cleyre refuted him, saying she would embrace the term no matter what its intention since it encapsulated her protest against marriage ("Love in Freedom"). Tennessee Claflin also championed the term, claiming that women needed to rise above any "epithet intended to degrade" and that only when they did so could they truly be free ("Virtue"). Thus, a truly "free" woman would embrace the term "free love" rather than reject it, and in doing so, she would reclaim her freedom from social standards of morality and "own herself." Many historians have questioned the term, since not all who advocated free love explicitly used the term to define their philosophies. Some historians, such as Sears and Passet, prefer the term "sex radicalism" to "free love." I, however, prefer "free love" since it was the term free-love feminists used themselves. It also helps to show how free-love feminism differed from male free-love philosophies. Claflin's protest says it all: women who were truly "free" would not be intimidated by the term.

Free-love feminism differed from male free-love philosophies because it placed women's emancipation as its central tenet. Male free-love philosophies championed the rights of the individual, but free-love feminists distinguished women's specific oppression from the more general oppression people faced under government strictures on marriage and family. Therefore, free-love feminism foregrounded the role of women, whereas "free love" itself merely included the emancipation of women under its mantra. In fact, the pages of *Lucifer* often featured debates divided along gender lines. Under Lillian Harman's editorship in the 1890s, letters from men criticizing the focus on the "woman question" proliferated, but Harman took a strong stand, continuing to include an emphasis on women's sexual rights ("From My Point of View" [1899]). In fact, Harman questioned which faction was more radical in one of her columns published in 1900: "Are women becoming the radicals and men the conservatives?" ("From My Point of View" [March 1900]). Many males, including former leaders in the movement, expressed a desire to hear less from more radical women, such as Lillie D. White (Barry, "Crudities Criticized—No. 8"). The women who emphasized "women's issues" in free love came under attack from their male cohorts, even though the same men had purported women's freedom under "free love." Consequently, free-love feminism became a distinct philosophy and set of rhetorical strategies.

Who Were the Free-Love Feminists?

The ways that women came to support free love also provide insight into how free love became feminist. Many of the free-love feminists who advocated their views in books, pamphlets, lectures, and periodicals became the more public faces of the movement. Some women began advocating free love after disastrous first marriages. Some later turned their backs on free love, finding more conservative causes. Whether they came from the more conservative or more radical factions of the movement, they conversed with and cited one another to redefine free love to include feminist goals, and their similar rhetorical strategies enlarge our view of nineteenth-century women's rhetorical practices.

Mary Gove Nichols: Rewriting "Disease"

Mary Sargeant Neal Gove Nichols (1810–84)—novelist, speaker, and physician—participated in both medical and free-love discourse communities, and her pioneering free-love feminism combined ideas on women's moral influence on sexuality with ideas of women's right to choose when to exercise that sexuality. Born in Goffstown, New Hampshire, to the freethinker William Neal and his Calvinist wife, Rebecca Neal, Mary Neal asserted her independence from her family by becoming a Quaker and later a schoolteacher during the 1820s. As a young woman, she expressed interest in her brother's anatomy textbooks and read them secretly. Her brother's discovery of her medical knowledge prompted him to rebuke her for studying inappropriate subjects (Gove Nichols, "Mrs. Gove's Experience"). She nevertheless continued her secret study, though she knew she could not pursue a medical degree; no school was granting women medical degrees in the 1820s (Silver-Isenstadt 22). Gove disdained early marriage prospects until a relative introduced her to a fellow Quaker eleven years her senior, Hiram Gove. After their union, Mary discovered the sad fact that Hiram Gove was a frequently jealous and unambitious man. She provided the only monetary support to the family by lecturing to women on anatomy and physiology. During her acrimonious marriage, she endured five pregnancies with only one child surviving and consequently suffered ill health. Her interest in improving medical care for women increased, and she discovered an ally in the alternative medical movement known as the "water cure."

The water-cure movement began with the philosophies of health inspired by Austrian Vincent Priessnitz in 1826.[4] This homeopathic medical movement stressed preventative medicine and hygiene rather than harsh surgeries or drugs. American water-cure practitioners also added the philosophies of Sylvester Graham, who preached abstinence from stimulants like coffee and tea, and advocated a vegetarian diet. Water-cure adherents prescribed a regimen of cold-water bathing and drinking. These physicians believed that disease and illness were caused by lack of "vital energy" and that water would restore that energy, since it was a "vital power." Prior to the germ theory of disease, such explanations were widely accepted. In 1837, after hearing Graham speak in Lynn, Massachusetts, Mary Gove embraced his philosophy of natural healing, along with vegetarianism and dress reform (Passet, *Sex Radicals* 21). She became a water-cure physician herself after self-study and apprenticing. Many early water-cure physicians had obtained their degrees at regular medical schools and then turned to water cure in their practices. By the 1850s, several medical schools existed to train water-cure practitioners, one established by Gove. At the time she sought medical study, how-ever, she lacked such opportunities and became one of many women to overcome these challenges. In 1845, she apprenticed at Dr. Robert Wes-selhoeft's water-cure medical school in Brattleboro, Vermont, and then served as a resident physician at Dr. Joel Shew's New Lebanon, New York, water-cure establishment (Silver-Isenstadt 72–73). As a reformer and then a physician, Gove lectured to women on health and physiology in the 1830s and 1840s.

Gove's own health continued to suffer from the strain of her mar-riage, and in 1841, she took the drastic step of taking her nine-year-old daughter, Elma, and leaving Hiram Gove. Though she had left him, she was forced by the laws of coverture to support him financially, since he would not give her a divorce. Their separation proved as acrimonious as their marriage. Hiram kidnapped his daughter in 1845, beginning a battle between the couple that ended with Mary illegally reclaiming her and living in fear of another separation from her. She fled to New York City, where she lived and worked with the Shews, prominent members of the water-cure medical sect. During this time, her lectures also included a focus on women's rights, particularly on the lack of women's rights within marriage. Her critiques of institutional marriage had begun, but she was not introduced to the philosophy of free love until after she met her second husband, Thomas L. Nichols.

In Nichols, Gove found a like-minded soul on both a personal and professional level. Nichols had left medical study but returned to it after he became involved with Mary; it was she who introduced him to water cure. They hit some legal blocks to their relationship because of Mary's marriage to Hiram Gove but were able to wed after Hiram sought a divorce to marry a new wife. Mary's experience had soured her on traditional marriage, but she wed Nichols expecting and receiving a different kind of marriage: an equal partnership. Together, they edited several periodicals and briefly operated a water-cure medical school. They had also become aware of perfectionist free-love theories, which appealed to their ideals of reform. They briefly joined a free-love commune, Modern Times, but later converted to Catholicism, moving away from their free-love roots.[5]

Mary Gove Nichols's early contributions to free-love feminist rhetoric blended medical reform with women's rights. Her lectures to women and writings on anatomy, physiology, and water cure not only provided information but also incorporated her women's rights agenda, an agenda that had become central to the water-cure philosophy. Many women found the philosophy more conducive to their health and the health of their families. Water-cure physicians like Gove Nichols treated patients at their practices and homes but also established facilities (much like spas or retreats) where patients could spend weeks or months living the water cure. Many women attended these facilities (and some led the facilities), and they became, in one scholar's estimation, a female enclave for homosocial bonding (Cayleff 161), popular among women's rights activists. At a time when some in the medical establishment defined women as inherently diseased, hysteric, or unfit for public roles, water-cure physicians redefined women's bodies and capabilities. Gove Nichols pioneered some of this work, as her own lectures stressed the need for healthy, competent women. Insisting that "health is the basis of all education. All learning is useless without it" ("Letter from Mrs. Gove Nichols"), Gove Nichols viewed women's health as the first prerequisite to women's rights, whether to education or legal rights. Women could not achieve their full capabilities without the first step of perfect health.

Gove Nichols also applied this line of argument to sexuality, later incorporating her new rhetoric of free love. Taking the next step from arguing the right of a woman to a healthy body, she then argued that a woman had the right to share that body with whomever she chose. Her support of free love, however, led many water-cure leaders to shun her. In addition, Thomas Nichols composed a book on sexual matters, *Esoteric Anthropology*, that competed with Russell Trall, a leader in the water-cure movement, and his book on sexual physiology. Since Trall had become the editor of the *Water-Cure Journal*, the Nichols then lost an important forum. They began their own journals but found resistance from previous allies, such as physician Dr. Harriet Hunt, a former friend of Mary's who praised her as a lecturer on physiology but rejected her free-love ideals (Silver-Isenstadt 184–85). Her advocacy of free love suddenly left Gove Nichols without students at her medical school, but it did not muzzle her convictions. She continued to publish and lecture on health reform, even after later turning away from free love.

Gove Nichols was a more conservative theorist among free-love feminists. While she acknowledged the presence of women's sexual feelings, she often spoke against their "abuses," writing anti-masturbation tracts and attributing many female illnesses to masturbation. She advocated temperate sexual relationships based in love. In her advice on women's health, she warned that, like sweets or coffee, sex should not be indulged in excess. However, she did not explicitly urge women to deny their sexual feelings but rather to recognize overindulgence as harmful to their health. Her later work on marriage, cowritten with her husband, provided a critique of the marriage system that depicted the harms to women's health as a result of husbands' demands and wives' excessive childbearing. She attributed "hereditary evils to children born in a sensual and unloving marriage" and illness, weakness, and crime to the conditions under which children were born to tired, ill mothers suffering because of marriage ("Murders of Marriage" 305), thus foreshadowing the eugenic shift in free-love feminism. Gove Nichols was radical for her time and a precursor to the more extreme free-love feminists who followed her decades later. Her key contribution was her "rewriting" of the "diseased" institution of marriage (Keetley). As a physician, Gove Nichols brought the issue of women's health to the forefront of the debate over sexual practices, an important step in using contemporary science to promote free love. Later free-love feminists were in debt to the rhetorical strategies she initiated.

Victoria Claflin Woodhull: "Notorious Victoria"

Victoria Claflin Woodhull (1838–1927) was perhaps the most notorious free-love feminist of the nineteenth century, and her arguments reached larger audiences, thus making her one of the faces of the movement to the general public. Lampooned by cartoonist Thomas Nast as "Mrs. Satan" and satirized in works of fiction such as Henry James's *The Bostonians*[6] and Harriet Beecher Stowe's *My Wife and I*—as the provocative character Audacia Dangyereyes—Woodhull became a scapegoat for the problems of both the free-love and suffrage movements. Her often flamboyant and sometimes volatile rhetoric contributed to her negative reputation. Yet, her notoriety gave free love more attention than it would have received otherwise. Even her opponents often agreed with her critiques of marriage, making her one of the most influential free-love feminists. Born in Homer, Ohio, she was the seventh of ten children. Her mother, Roxanna Hummel Claflin, remained illiterate throughout her life, and her father, Reuben "Buck" Claflin, ran fortune-telling and palm-reading shows. Woodhull and her siblings participated in these shows as teenagers, which led to Woodhull's brief stint as an actress (Passet, *Sex Radicals* 96). After marrying the older Canning Woodhull, an alcoholic, Woodhull bore two children, a mentally challenged son, Byron, and her daughter, Zulu Maud. Her early experiences with her father's shows, her experience as an actress, and her hardships during her first marriage all influenced her rhetoric of free love.[7]

After leaving Canning Woodhull and moving to New York, Woodhull made a career out of breaking gender conventions as the first woman to address a congressional judiciary committee, the first woman stockbroker, and the first American publisher of Karl Marx's *Communist Manifesto*. She was also the first woman to run for president. Nominated by the Equal Rights Party in 1872, along with Frederick Douglass for vice president—a nomination he neither acknowledged nor endorsed—Woodhull's run was more symbolic than serious, though probably not to her. Historian Amanda Frisken suggests that the Equal Rights Party nominated Woodhull "more to express [its] support for race- and sex-blind equal rights than with any concrete plan to get them elected" (*Victoria Woodhull's Sexual Revolution* 67). Woodhull, whether seriously running for president or not, nevertheless actively campaigned for the position and found it useful to her goals.[8] Having addressed a congressional committee arguing that the Constitution already granted women the right to vote, an argument later employed by Susan B. Anthony after her own arrest for voting, Woodhull used the nomination to disseminate this argument to wider audiences. Her presence on the lecture platform would continue for several years, and free love became part of that presence.

Woodhull's second marriage to Colonel James Harvey Blood and her association with Stephen Pearl Andrews exposed her to the new radical views at the time occupying only small groups. Andrews, who had authored several tracts on free love, found in Woodhull a more attractive and provocative mouthpiece for his views. The extent of his authorship of Woodhull's earlier speeches is unknown and has caused much speculation among historians.[9] The speeches that Woodhull delivered, which historians often attribute exclusively to Andrews, contain differences from his other work and a stronger feminist sensibility than what appeared in his earlier writings, implying a contribution by Woodhull. Furthermore, her speaking career did not end when her relationships with Blood and Andrews ended. Woodhull's speeches on free love during the 1870s both epitomized and influenced the free-love feminism of the time. During her lecturing career, including for-profit lecture tours throughout the 1870s, Woodhull spoke to large audiences who seemed drawn by her notoriety rather than by her speech, expecting to hear scandalous talk from a scandalous woman.[10] Instead, as some reviews of her speeches suggest, these crowds found a woman who "advocated free love; but in a sense so high and language so pure that the very personification of chastity could not *justly* find fault with it" (qtd. in Woodhull, *Human Body* 425; emphasis in original).

Already a controversial figure due to her advocacy of free love and sense of sensationalism, Woodhull found her notoriety increased after her arrest for exposing Henry Ward Beecher's extramarital affair in *Woodhull & Claflin's Weekly*. She continually tested the patience of Anthony Comstock, and her acts influenced the obscenity laws he established in 1873.[11] The issue of the *Weekly* detailing Beecher's affair with the wife of his protégé, Theodore Tilton, led to Woodhull's arrest for obscenity; she spent the election night of 1872 imprisoned. Woodhull framed her exposure of Beecher as a public service, displaying the hypocrisy of a man who had denounced free love but, in Woodhull's mind, practiced it. In her 1874 speech, she even justified this exposure as an important step in securing more discussion of sexuality:

> My purpose was accomplished. Whereas, before, none had dared to broach the sexual question, it is now on everybody's lips; and where it would have been impossible for a man, even, to address a public, promiscuous audience anywhere without being mobbed, a woman may now travel the country over, and from its best rostrums, speak the last truth about sexuality and receive respectful attention, even enthusiastic encouragement. (*Tried* 7)

Woodhull spun her actions as a necessity, but her actions implied a more selfish motive. Beecher had refused to introduce her at a lecture, which fed her fury on his hypocrisy.

In addition to exposing Beecher, she also attacked prominent men such as Luther Challis and editor S. S. Jones in actions that equated to blackmail. Others have interpreted the exposures as acts of civil disobedience, since Woodhull knew there would be legal repercussions for publishing the accounts in her paper but did so anyway, saying she was prepared to take responsibility for it (Frisken, *Victoria Woodhull's Sexual Revolution* 94–95). In addition to landing her in court, these incidents earned her censure, not only from public figures but also from those within free-love and spiritualist communities. Some radicals supported her, such as Angela Heywood, who viewed the critics of Woodhull as illustrating a double standard in questioning Woodhull's reputation but not Beecher's (109). Her increasingly radical rhetoric and notoriety led to the cancelation of several lecture engagements, including one in Boston immediately following her arrest (Blatt 79). The public also found her living arrangements questionable, when they learned that her first husband, the ailing Canning Woodhull, resided in her household along with her second husband, Colonel Blood. Woodhull's support of free love and reputation also led to a split within the suffrage movement. While suffragists such as Elizabeth Cady Stanton had initially praised her, others were reluctant to do so and had their suspicions confirmed by her actions. Within the free-love movement, some felt that Woodhull's notoriety hurt their cause more than her visibility helped it. Some historians have even blamed Woodhull for decreasing the legitimacy of both the suffrage and free-love movements.[12]

Woodhull's radical rhetoric, however, gains more importance when we look at her in the context of free-love feminism as a social movement. In her arguments for free love, she often employed redefinitions of cherished ideals and terms, and, like Gove Nichols, Woodhull attempted to expose the hypocrisy of "virtue" by presenting new definitions of "virtue" and "vulgarity" in relation to women's sexuality, allowing women who embraced sexual feelings to be called "virtuous" and denying that term to those who ignored such feelings (Woodhull, *Tried* 24–25). This rhetorical strategy of inverting a cherished belief by juxtaposing it with negative terms continued through much of her writing and acted as a basis for later arguments by Waisbrooker and de Cleyre. Though her career as a free-love speaker was considerably shorter than these women's, Woodhull left her mark on free-love feminist rhetoric.

In 1877, after the death of Cornelius Vanderbilt, who had set up the Claflin sisters' stockbroker business, Woodhull and her family fled for England, amid allegations that Vanderbilt's son paid them to leave. In England, Woodhull renounced free love and started writing more works on government, economics, and eugenics. These arguments did not reject the critiques of marriage of the free-love movement but the solution of free love. Woodhull found respectability in England, marrying a wealthy banker, Joseph Biddulph Martin. Her prolific writing makes Woodhull a key figure in free-love feminism. In fact, some historians view Woodhull as a "bridge connecting the utopian free love theories" of the communes to the anarchist free lovers of the late nineteenth century (Passet, *Sex Radicals* 91). Woodhull's shift into more explicitly eugenic rhetoric also illustrates the changing focus of the movement, though her eugenic theories arrived much earlier than the movement's more explicit shift. Like Gove Nichols, Woodhull later renounced free love, but her rhetorical strategies made an impact on the free-love feminists of the 1880s and 1890s (and on later birth control advocate Margaret Sanger).

Tennessee Claflin: The Other "Vixen"

Woodhull's younger sister, Tennessee Claflin (who also published as Tennie C. Claflin and as Lady Cook, her later married name), receives less critical attention but was as radical and prolific as her more flamboyant sister. Tennessee Celeste Claflin (1845–1923), the youngest of the ten Claflin children, endured the same erratic childhood as her sister, and her father put her good looks to use as a child faith healer,[13] clairvoyant, and fortune teller. Their actions stirred interest from authorities, prompting frequent moves throughout Ohio and Illinois. Separated from her sister during Victoria's marriage to Canning Woodhull, they reunited in New York City after Victoria's second marriage to Colonel Blood. Claflin then claimed the attention of the wealthy spiritualist Cornelius Vanderbilt. She became his mistress, fortune teller, and magnetic healer, and he educated her about the stock market during their long relationship. Vanderbilt helped finance the first of the sisters' radical ventures: their stockbrokerage firm.[14]

During the early 1870s, many in the press seemed obsessed with reporting the Claflin sisters' exploits, contributing to their unsavory reputations.[15] Not to be outdone, when Woodhull announced her candidacy for president, Claflin declared her candidacy for Congress, a move that did not garner as much attention. After the murder of Colonel James Fisk in 1872, Claflin lobbied for and won the position of colonel of the African American Eighty-Fifth Regiment. The sisters' actions continued to shock the media, especially when their dirty family laundry was aired in the courts. In addition to the obscenity trial for the Beecher-Tilton scandal and the libel suit from Luther Challis, the sisters found themselves in court when their mother, Roxanna, sued Colonel Blood for what she deemed control over her daughters (Frisken 30–31), and the press became obsessed with the scandalous family. In the press, Tennessee was an actor in her own right, though history has relegated her to a devoted follower of her sister. They were more of a collaborative act, working together on speeches, sharing a prison cell for their arrest for obscenity, touring together, and moving to England together. They both found a measure of respectability in England, with Tennessee marrying the wealthy widower Francis Cook, becoming Lady Cook. Claflin's personal journey often mirrored her sister's, and their arguments for free love shared similarities as well. They both condemned marriage for relegating women to subservient positions, though Claflin never proclaimed a "war against marriage" as her sister did (Woodhull, *Tried* 7). Like Woodhull, who argued in her *Elixir of Life* speech that all of women's health problems stemmed from inadequate sexual conditions, Claflin also highlighted women's improved health as a result of free love, explaining that she never knew "a woman suffering from 'weakness' who was perfectly content—who was happy and suitably married" and never knew "a perfectly healthy woman who was unhappily mated" (*Ethics* 11). Thus began the arguments that later become eugenic: Claflin contended that marriage detrimentally affected the health of women suffering from excessive childbearing and sexual diseases, which led to unhealthy children. These arguments later shifted their focus to the health of the children, starting the eugenic turn in her rhetoric. At this time, however, she emphasized diminished health as just one of the harmful effects of marriage. She critiqued the laws and customs of a society that attempted "to compel all sorts of people to conform to the same rules of life" (5). Consequently, she offered free love as the solution for these restrictions.

Claflin's rhetorical strategies concentrated on redefinition; as she believed, "It is unfortunate that terms should have such sweeping application, and in reality so little real meaning, and still be so freely used by those who know not what they are saying" (*Constitutional Equality* 75). Throughout her prolific essay writing career, she composed essays redefining virtue, purity, modesty, and seduction. For Claflin, too many words existed to apply to women who chose to deny restrictive ideologies. She attacked definitions of "purity" that would connote only chastity as purity. Instead, she argued, purity could be applied to women who indulged their sexuality and thus reached what she believed to be their highest purpose—motherhood ("Woman's Purity" 113). Claflin acknowledged the sexual appetites of women and endorsed their indulgence, in or out of marriage, but made her argument more palatable to wider audiences by focusing on motherhood as the consequence of such indulgence. Her later arguments, after her move to the respectable classes of London, shifted their emphasis to these exaltations of motherhood. Though she does not receive the same critical attention from historians, Claflin's rhetorical strategies and critiques of sexual inequality are just as important as her sister's in the recovery of free-love feminism. Together, Woodhull and Claflin left their mark on free-love feminist rhetoric. When frequent financial difficulties after their arrest forced them to suspend publication of the *Weekly* in 1876, radical women turned to *Lucifer, the Light Bearer*, and to the women of *Lucifer*, such as Juliet Severance, to continue the conversation on free love.

Juliet Severance: The Woodhull of Wisconsin

Referred to as the "Woodhull of Wisconsin," Juliet Hall Worth Stillman Severance (1833–1919) also left her mark on the lecture circuit. Like Woodhull, Severance brought the values of spiritualism to her free-love feminism, believing that only free love could help humanity attain higher evolution. And like Gove Nichols, Severance bridged the gap between the medical and free-love communities as a physician. Severance, born in Madison County, New York, the thirteenth of seventeen children, was a distant cousin of another prominent feminist reformer, Lucretia Mott. Severance's family worked in dairy farming, and her daily contact with animals led to her interest in medicine (Passet, *Sex Radicals* 121–22). As devout Quakers, the Worth family believed in educating females, and Severance was well-educated, taking classes at the De Ruyter Seminary. In 1857, she attended the Hygeio-Therapeutic College in New York City, a water-cure medical school whose program stressed the naturalness of women's bodies (123). These values attracted Severance, who favored "scientific notions" over popular, superstitious ones. Severance became a voice for many causes, having also aided in the Underground Railroad and joined labor parties working to improve job conditions. As a physician, Severance counseled patients on sexual matters and provided information on contraception and abortion (126).[16]

Like Gove Nichols, Severance used her ethos as a physician to argue the benefits of free love in helping women improve and maintain their health and believed that her duty included being a teacher of hygiene. She compared how the medical establishment had kept certain information from women to how the church historically had kept the public in ignorance (Severance, *Lecture on the Philosophy of Disease* 3). For Severance, empowering women meant providing them with the information they needed to maintain their health, which included the principles of hygiene and diet and advice on birth control. While it is unknown if Severance encountered the same problems as Gove Nichols in her progressive approach to medicine, she did recount an incident at a medical convention she attended in the early 1870s, where she challenged the attendees to explore the issue of sex slavery as detrimental to women's health. After her proclamation, two doctors left the conference because "they did not wish to endorse free love" ("What They Think").

Severance had harsh words for the laws that maintained wives' status as "sexual slaves" of men. Her arguments often indicted the laws of the land as the chief oppressor of women and pointed out how the laws of coverture allowed the husband to own the wife but did not extend any ownership rights to women (Severance, "Dr. Severance on Ownership"). Since Severance maintained that the laws should protect individual rights, she condemned marriage for violating women's rights. Her arguments highlighted the issue of marital rape, condoned by the laws, and made analogies between the condition of wives and the conditions of slaves in the South, a popular, if troubling, feature of free-love rhetoric. Severance's critique of these laws became a prominent feature of free-love feminist rhetoric, also employed by Lillian Harman in the 1890s. Severance's condemnation of marriage laws included those who defended them: "Every man who advocates our marriage system virtually claims that right, and if he does not abuse his wife he is better than the laws he advocates. When any man calls Free Love prostitution, he writes himself down an ignoramus" ("Dr. Severance on Ownership"). She defended the practice of free love, believing it granted women freedom, not to be promiscuous but to ignore the laws that condemned them to servitude.

Severance also participated in the redefining of "virtue," as when she stated, "We should insist that virtue is not necessarily feminine, but that men as well as women should be expected to be pure in their lives and that virtue consists in living true to organic law in every department of being; that a person may be 'not virtuous' just as truly as by unnatural repression as by excessive indulgence, that both should be avoided" (*Lecture on Religious, Political, and Social Freedom* 15). While her insistence that men and women should be held to the same standard here seems closer to more conservative ideals, her definition of what was "virtuous" was more radical: a virtuous woman could indulge her sexual feelings. Severance championed free love as a panacea for all economic, social, and health problems facing women, since under free love, "*The woman will be free, which means neither owned nor rented*" ("Dr. Severance on Ownership"). A voice for health reform and dress reform, Severance did not attract scandal to the same extent as Woodhull. She did raise eyebrows when she married Anson Severance shortly after his divorce, prompting some to call her a "practical" (versus theoretical) free lover (Passet, *Sex Radicals* 127). Yet, Severance continued her advocacy of free love and never renounced it, as Gove Nichols and Woodhull did. Her 1901 book *Marriage*, originally an address to the International Congress of Freethinkers in Chicago in 1893, earned her acclaim beyond the free-love community as "an eloquent pleader for personal freedom" ("Says 'Boston Ideas'—").[17] Many viewed Severance as a voice for all radical reforms. One male leader of the free-love movement characterized her as "a life long defender of every phase of freedom and right" (Barry, "Has Frank Barry Gone Back?").

Angela Heywood's Language Revolution

While Woodhull was the most notorious, Angela Fiducia Tilton Heywood (1840–1935) was in fact the most shockingly outspoken free-love feminist. Born into a poor family of farmers in Deerfield, New Hampshire, Angela Fiducia—whose name means "angel of fidelity," which she would call "an awful load to carry" (Heywood, "Woman's View of It—No. 2")—worked as a domestic servant, cook, and factory worker, which stimulated her interest in labor reform (McElroy, *Individualist Feminism* 22). Like Woodhull, Heywood had little formal education but was self-educated. While it would seem that her radicalism stemmed from her relationship with her anarchist husband, Ezra Heywood, in fact her influences came earlier. Her mother, Lucy M. Tilton, had joined movements for abolition, labor reform, and earlier incarnations of free love (Blatt 67). What many would come to view as Heywood's bitterness also came from her mother, who disdained "intellectual culture" and refused to raise her children with false values of modesty (68). In one letter from prison, Ezra Heywood praised his mother-in-law as a "Grand Mother . . . a radical who taught and wrought anarchism long before the meek conservatives who now mouth the noble word were born. She says 'learned' men and 'refined' women who don't even know the names of their sex organs are so ineffably idiotic that she has to keep herself hid for disgust of them" (qtd. in Blatt 68). He also noted Tilton's influence on her children, and Angela, too, credited her mother with nurturing their radical views. Angela, in fact, attributed her views on sex to her mother's open discussion of it in their home. She even remembered how her mother would call the children to watch the horses mating on their farm and explained what they were seeing (Heywood, "Penis Literature"). Angela's sisters, Josephine and Flora, also became activists as a result of their mother's influence, with Josephine working more closely with Ezra and Angela's radical causes.[18]

Ezra Heywood (1829–93) has often inexplicably overshadowed his more radical wife in historical accounts. He began his career in the labor reform movement and credited several women mentors with moving him to include women's rights in his agenda (Blatt 15), but it was Angela who helped him move further into radicalism, particularly sex radicalism. Heywood's book *Cupid's Yokes* earned Comstock's ire for giving explicit details on birth control. He also began *The Word* to bring together the sex radical and labor reform communities. Ezra and Angela had four children together, who would later become part of their reformist exploits. During most of their career as reformers, the Heywoods operated the Mountain Home resort in Princeton, Massachusetts, where they also began publication of *The Word*. By 1883, they had lost Mountain Home because of the financial burdens of Ezra's arrests for obscenity.

Angela Heywood's writings proved more attention-grabbing and readable than Ezra's. Historians Hal Sears and Martin Blatt both note that Ezra's writing often came across as too "scholarly" and therefore inaccessible.[19] Angela, however, produced passionate and readable prose; thus it is no surprise that her articles in *The Word* were the ones targeted for obscenity. In fact, Angela not only helped to define her husband's free-love tenets but also defined the "plain speech" policy of *The Word*, both in theory and in practice. Heywood insisted on "plain speech," and the tone of much of her writings has led some scholars to label her as "ill-tempered" and bitter (L. Gordon, *Woman's Body* 104). Referring to marriage as "The Penis Trust," Heywood's insistence on plain speech led to her characteristic forthright tone in her contributions to *The Word*, and she took on a new crusade to write the word "penis" as many times as she could to test the obscenity watchdogs. In Angela's theory of language, "penis" represented all that was wrong with language; men could write about any part of a woman's anatomy and not earn an obscenity label, but a woman writing "penis" would be deemed both "obscene" and "unchaste." She highlighted a language double standard in pointing out how many words existed to condemn women's sexual practices:

> Words like "prostitute," "harlot," "whore," "strumpet," "fancy-girl," "mistress," "fallen-women,"—all these popularly used . . . while "libertine," "wild-oats-ism," gently disclose man's aberrations. Why are the "cultured" so satisfied with savage criminations flung at woman, yet so sensitive about definite expression relative to man's penis and his generative sexhood? (Heywood, "Sex Service").

She then used the word "penis" as a clever synecdoche, when she insisted, "An *irresponsible* penis manufactures 'prostitutes,' 'harlots,' 'whores,' 'strumpets,' 'fancy-girls,' mistresses,' 'fallen-women,'—furnishing material for 'written histories' of negation side of girl-life; a conscientious penis *glorifies* woman, builds homes, assuring that all that is worthy in school, church, state and society" ("Sex-Symbolism"). "Penis" also became her adjective for certain literature, ideologies, and sexism. She coined the words "manism" and "heism" to describe sexism and decried the "heistic state" that denied sex speech to women ("Sex Service"). Some of her writings are almost odes to the penis, idealizing and celebrating its functions in both sex and reproduction. Thus, her writing of the word "penis" began to encapsulate her free-love philosophy, as she insisted, "As long as the penis is *known about* as a pleasure-seeking, race creating instrument, by men who possess it and by women who require it, and yet *is not spoken out about*, in the mental, social, and literary world, so long will disaster mar sex-experience" (2). For Angela, speaking about sex would help to free women from sexual slavery.

Angela's speech earned Ezra several arrests, for which other free-love feminists criticized her, but she refused to be deterred from her crusade.[20] Ezra's imprisonments strained the family's finances until they lost both their home and the means to publish their periodical. After Ezra's death in 1893, Angela contributed sporadically to other periodicals until her voice faded away. Presumably, she found herself overwhelmed with the care of her children and retreated from the public stage and page. Little is known of her later life, but she left her mark on a movement that often shunned her increasingly controversial philosophies, and her spirit certainly lived on in the second-wave feminists of the twentieth century.

Rachel Campbell's Prodigal Daughters

Another rhetor indulging in "anti-male" free-love feminist rhetoric, though, admittedly, less acerbic than Angela Heywood's, was Rachel Campbell (1834–92), well known in the free-love community, who considered her "one of the best thinkers on sex ethics" ("An Appeal") but nowhere else. Campbell's story, told by longtime friend and correspondent Mary Florence "Flo" Johnson, revealed the sad truth about what happened to radical women outside their free-love communities but also showed how these communities rallied together to support their sister. Rachel Campbell was born in Hinchinbrook, Canada, and moved to St. Lawrence County, New York, in early childhood. Her family endured financial difficulties after the death of her father, and with her mother's urging and support, Rachel married "to leave an unhappy home" (M. Johnson 32). The husband, who became abusive to Campbell during their marriage, was never named by Johnson or Campbell during their correspondence. Johnson related that the problems with the marriage began on their wedding day, retelling the stories Campbell told her about her ignorance of sexual matters and her husband's lewd humor and brutish actions on the evening of their wedding (32). Her husband became physically abusive, and she lost several pregnancies as a result. The one child she bore was too weak to survive infancy, which Campbell also blamed on the treatment she received when pregnant. Campbell's strong will won out, however, and she left her husband in Wisconsin, despite the criticism she received from her family (34), and moved to Manchester, New Hampshire, where she worked for many years in a cotton factory to support herself. Though she left her husband to be on her own and did not seek another man, she later found companionship in a man with whom she had a long affair, but her first marriage had soured her on that particular state.

Campbell's disastrous marriage and subsequent hard life as a factory worker influenced her free-love feminism. While living in New Hampshire, she converted to spiritualism, worked with Moses Hull on his free-love paper, *Hull's Crucible*, and lectured to free-love circles throughout the 1880s. Campbell never found material prosperity. After becoming an invalid because of her factory work, she lived with a man named S. G. Lewis, who cared for her while she was ill. However, after he died, she was left with no support and no home. Readers of *Lucifer* rallied together, donating money to Campbell to give her the fare to go to Iowa to live with her sister ("An Appeal"). However, Campbell's sister had a change of heart upon learning of her spiritualism and refused to have her in the house; Campbell then hired someone to take care of her with the money collected by *Lucifer* readers and died shortly afterward (M. Johnson 41).[21]

Campbell's most prominent and influential work was her 1888 pamphlet, *The Prodigal Daughter, or The Price of Virtue*, which received accolades from free lovers, both male and female, who continued to cite, reprint, and circulate her work after her death in 1892. Originally a paper she read in 1881 at a meeting with the Heywoods, Campbell sent it to the anarchist periodical the *Truth Seeker*, and while she was promised publication, her piece never appeared in that paper. Campbell then printed and distributed it herself, until it came to the attention of Moses Harman, who reprinted and advertised it in the pages of *Lucifer*. *The Prodigal*

Daughter examined the "social evil" of prostitution from a new perspective. Much of the discourse on prostitution had focused on "saving" prostitutes, especially in feminist circles, or blaming them for the spread of venereal disease. Free-love rhetors had also given them little attention, except to compare the conditions of wives, whom they defined as legal prostitutes, to the conditions of illegal prostitutes. Campbell revised these critiques, noting the inequalities that produced prostitution and calling for legal and illegal prostitutes to work together to break free from their common bondage (*Prodigal Daughter* 28–29). Attacking both the social and legal systems that produced inequality in sexual relations and the economic systems that precluded women's independence, her conclusions blended labor reform principles with free-love feminism. Campbell also contributed to the free-love feminist conversation about "virtue," blaming the ideals of women's "virtue" for the unequal conditions of wives and prostitutes and calling ideals of womanly virtue "too huge a price for virtuous monogamy" and "a terrible waste of womanhood" (9–10). She then pointed out the limited options for women in sexual relations: "A woman, to be virtuous, must live celibate or else become a legal wife" (10). Campbell's rhetoric then became more volatile, even pondering a masculine conspiracy for the plight of women and proclaiming that men both create and maintain the conditions that lead women to prostitution, with "the pursuit of sexual pleasure being their only end and aim" (24). She poked holes in the common justifications for the laws regulating prostitution and marriage, concluding that marriage laws existed not for "protection of the wife" or children but to protect men's sexual property (26–27). Campbell thus created a new reasoning for separate spheres ideology and Republican motherhood: all served to sustain the sexual conquests of men. Arguments that such laws and ideologies "protected" women and the home carried no weight with Campbell. Consequently, she turned to a more moderate version of free love as the solution.

Campbell's free-love feminism echoed Mary Gove Nichols's, since she rejected broader interpretations of sexual freedom and instead endorsed a more conservative version where men and women lived equally chaste sexual lifestyles. Though she viewed women as less sexual than men, she did not attribute it to women's nature but to social constructions. She asserted that men and women must be held to the same standard, whether moral or sexual, and encouraged monogamy in sexual relations, but only if the woman was given "the ownership of herself and the emancipation from sexual bondage" (*Prodigal Daughter* 27). She argued that any marriage reform would fail "if it does not recognize as equally clean, equally chaste and equally respectable every phase of human love, prompted by mutual attraction, it is not fitted for human needs and is no better than the straightjacket of orthodox marriage" ("Sex Ethics No. 2"). She defined free love as a sexual relationship free of coercion and the influence of sexist laws. For Campbell, "free love, freely given, always blesses and never causes sorrow" (qtd. in M. Johnson 37).

Campbell's life illustrates the hard life of the independent woman of the nineteenth century. Other free-love feminists, such as Gove Nichols, Woodhull, and Severance, found supportive partners after their acrimonious first marriages, but Campbell never again married. Instead, she found a community of women who admired and supported her, and she mentored a generation of free-love feminists, including the younger Johnson, who would celebrate Campbell's life lessons in their own work. Johnson admitted that her "teacher and counselor" was not "as radical as some" (42), but though Campbell's ideas seem less radical, she was influential to free-love feminist rhetoric.

Lois Waisbrooker: "The Female Abraham Lincoln"

When Moses Harman polled *Lucifer*'s readers on suggestions for a woman coeditor, one male reader cautioned against choosing a "respectable woman" who would dilute *Lucifer*'s radicalism. He suggested a free-love feminist whose work would foreshadow the radical second-wave feminist rhetoric of the late twentieth century as the ideal editor, saying, "I regard pugnacity as a desideratum and Lois Waisbrooker has it. . . . Don't call a 'respectable' woman to your aid" (qtd. in Sears 229). An anarchist feminist and spiritualist, Waisbrooker (1826–1909), born Adeline Eliza Nichols (no relation to Mary Gove or Thomas L. Nichols), was raised in Catharine, New York. Her father was a day laborer, and her mother died of consumption at the age of thirty-six. Waisbrooker often referred to herself as being from "the lower strata of life" (qtd. in Sears 231) and started her career as a domestic servant. She noted of her beginnings, "My early advantages were few. I did not come of a literary stock of ancestry. My parents worked hard for daily bread, had but little education, and less time to use it; consequently I grew up with . . . little idea of the world's greatest literary riches" (Waisbrooker, *Suffrage for Woman* 12). She was widowed before she was twenty after marrying George Fuller at seventeen, a union her father had pressured her into because she was pregnant. The birth of her daughter five months after her marriage produced a stigma that would influence her advocacy of free love.

Waisbrooker, as she renamed herself in the 1860s, became an activist for many causes, promoting abolition and teaching African American children in Muskingum County, Ohio, during the 1850s until she was forced to quit in 1856 because her father coerced her into marrying yet another man she deemed "a stranger" to her (Passet, *Sex Radicals* 114). After leaving her second marriage, she was forced to place her children in other homes, though she maintained contact and seemed to preserve a close relationship with them (Passet, "Power through Print" 232). Waisbrooker then threw herself into writing and lecturing, a career she would continue until her death, despite financial, physical, and legal obstacles. She resided in the West most of her adult life, briefly joining the anarchist community of Home, Washington. Frequent legal trouble with the Comstock law increased her financial difficulties. One of her arrests for obscenity, in 1894, dragged on in the courts for two years, and the statement from the attorneys in the case noted her advanced age and ill health ("Mrs. Waisbrooker's Case"). She died penniless in the home of her son in Antioch, California.[22]

Waisbrooker was a prolific writer, producing pamphlets as early as 1868 and penning her last article for the *American Journal of Eugenics* in 1907. She also published didactic fiction in the 1870s featuring women deserted by the fathers of their children, depicting their survival despite being branded "fallen women." She dedicated her popular novel *Helen Harlow's Vow* to "woman everywhere, and to wronged and outcast women especially." Her most prominent work of fiction, one recovered by second-wave feminists, was her 1893 feminist utopian novel, *A Sex Revolution*, depicting women striking, not to prevent war, but to demand equality by fighting alongside men. The men in the novel agree to the women's terms for a complete revolution of the social system, and the book details many of Waisbrooker's philosophies on sex, equality, war, and temperance. Waisbrooker also produced nonfiction pamphlets and books on the power of sexuality. A frequent contributor to *Lucifer*, she became editor of the paper in the early 1890s during one of Moses Harman's imprisonments, coediting at one point with Lillie D. White, and began two short-lived periodicals on her own to spread her distinctive philosophies: *Foundation Principles* and *Clothed with the Sun*.

Waisbrooker's rhetoric often seems less radical in her aim to find the "purest" use of sex (*Fountain of Life* 14), but she believed that sex provided the key to higher spiritual evolution, or regeneration, in spiritualist terms. Sex, to Waisbrooker, was the most important force in humanity but too often seen as merely a tool for propagation (*From Generation* 53).

Instead, she urged, "Our sex-forces are life's motor power. They may be used physically, intellectually, or spiritually" (*Tree of Life* 109). She often criticized men who focused purely on the physical side of sex in works like the sarcastically titled *Anything More, My Lord?*, her 1895 treatise detailing her views on birth control. Her free-love feminism incorporated critiques of economics, which also appeared in her work on other social issues. For example, in her criticism of temperance workers, *The Temperance Folly; or, Who's the Worst*, she berated the temperance workers for ignoring the economic inequalities that produced drunkards. She also explored the effects of economics on sexuality in her speeches, but her solution for these inequalities, which led women to prostitute themselves, legally or illegally, was women's sexual emancipation and equality: she offered free love as an all-encompassing panacea. Her arguments intertwining economics and sex became controversial among free-love feminists, especially when she suggested the idea that a man should provide for his female sexual partner not as an exchange but because he should be so enlightened as to realize that she needed financial support (Waisbrooker, "Woman and Economics"). Readers of *Lucifer*, including Lillian Harman and Lillie D. White, protested Waisbrooker's assertion and equated it to the very sex slavery she was proposing to end. It would not be the first time that Waisbrooker would earn wrath from the pens of other free-love feminists. Waisbrooker's voice of dissent on these issues provided a notable addition to free-love feminism, and she remained an important voice, bringing the debate back to the lived experiences of women on the margins of society. Called "the female Abraham Lincoln" by lawyer Edward W. Chamberlain (qtd. in McAllister 4), Waisbrooker never renounced or converted from her free-love views, despite the trouble she received because of them. She published articles, journals, and novels until her death.

Lillian Harman: Victim or Revolutionary?

Another voice important to free-love feminism, Lillian Harman (1869–1929), also receives less critical attention, overshadowed by her radical father. The daughter of anarchist Moses Harman and Susan Scheuk Harman, Lillian did not escape the influence of her father, though some in the free-love community saw her as a victim of her father's radical ideologies. Born in Missouri, Lillian Harman lost her mother at the age of seven, after which she moved with her father and brother to Valley Falls, Kansas, the first site of Moses Harman's publications. She began helping him with publishing at the age of thirteen and later became a publisher of her own paper, with Edwin C. Walker, *Fair Play*. She spent much of the late nineteenth century residing in Kansas and Chicago, moving to Los Angeles in the early 1900s. Her "free union" with Walker, entered into when she was sixteen, caused an uproar, not only in the courts but also in the free-love community. While some, such as Juliet Severance, championed Lillian Harman's "moral heroism in refusing to pay a criminal's fine" ("From Dr. Severance"), others condemned her actions, believing her under the influence of much older men, including Walker himself. For example, Angela Heywood supported Lillian's right to enter the union but wondered at the free will involved in the joining of a sixteen-year-old girl to a man in his thirties (Passet, *Sex Radicals* 137). Lillian defended her actions but still found herself overshadowed by the voices of her father and Walker. While she did not live with Walker during much of their "marriage," they did have a child together in 1893, a daughter named Virna Winifred Walker (138). After the end of her relationship with Walker, she legally married George O'Brien and retreated from the public eye (Sears 268).

During her career as a radical revolutionary, she contributed articles to *Lucifer* and other American free-love periodicals, as well as to the *Adult*, a British periodical. She was elected the president of the British Legitimation League and was also active in several American free-thought and labor reform groups. She lectured, mainly to free-love, free-thought, and anarchist societies, in both the United States and Britain and published many of her lectures as pamphlets. She took strong stands against the institution of marriage, the economic inequality of women, and age-of-consent legislation, which she opposed since she believed it masked the real problems facing women who married. As editor of *Lucifer* in the late 1890s, Lillian extended its sphere of topics to cover anti-lynching campaigns, corresponding with and supporting Ida Wells-Barnett in the pages of *Lucifer*. She included black women in her calls for women's self-ownership, whereas other free-love feminists did not specify race and presumably limited their calls to white women. Instead, Harman criticized the mobs that lynched black men to "protect Southern womanhood" and noted their hypocrisy in the face of the rapes of black women during slavery ("Race Question"). She earned praise from Wells-Barnett for her courage in taking these views ("Various Voices," June 1899), though this focus incited criticism from some of *Lucifer*'s loyal followers. From these criticisms, we can see that Lillian clearly pushed her own agenda as editor, veering from the course of her father and becoming a radical rhetor in her own right.

Harman's free-love feminism offered the same critiques of married women's enslavement as Severance's, but she also concentrated on the economic and moral issues tied to marriage. One of her definitions of marriage relied on economic terms: "Marriage is an insurance concern which does not meet its liabilities. It guarantees support to the wife and children in return for the submission and loss of liberty of choice of the wife. But in case of non-support on the part of the husband, or in the event of his disability through disease or death, what becomes of the boasted 'protection?'" ("Some Common Objections"). Harman often offered free love as a solution for the problems plaguing women but thought that social freedom should be the solution under the law, since she believed choice the vital necessity in sexual relations. In an 1898 speech, she clarified that while free love was her choice, she would not advocate it for everyone: "I consider uniformity in mode of sexual relations as undesirable and impracticeable as enforced uniformity in anything else. For myself, I want the right to profit by my mistakes" ("Some Problems" 123). Harman's caveat, that she supported free love but championed social freedom as the best method of reform, fit with her views on liberty in choice for all.

Harman also rejected definitions of morality that relied on traditional values. In a speech titled *Marriage and Morality*, delivered to the Ohio Liberal Society in Cincinnati on November 19, 1899, and published the following year, Harman transformed definitions of morality based in religion and pronounced marriage "the foe to true morality. Morality often exists in spite of, or regardless of, marriage, but I do not believe morality ever came into being because of marriage" (17). She also took aim at the sexual double standard, another rhetorical move popular with free-love feminists: "I do not believe in a 'double standard' of morality for men and women. Neither do I believe in a double standard of morals—one inside, the other outside—marriage. I believe that right conduct and wrong conduct do not change their natures merely because of the words of priest or magistrate" (21–22). Harman's rhetoric of redefinition all came back to her definition of liberty. No reform of marriage would be acceptable to Harman unless it restored that liberty.

Harman's ideals matched those of many in the free-love movement, though she faced criticism for some of her more controversial views and actions. Whether or not her union with Edwin C. Walker was influenced by her father, Lillian's defense of it began a long writing and speaking career that defined the values of free-love feminism. Her reign as editor of *Lucifer* helped sustain its feminist ideas at a time when the men of the movement moved away from them. Her arguments also proved influential to the rhetoric of the "new woman" of the twentieth century, though she retreated from the public sphere after the death of her father. It seems that her career as a radical rhetor needed his support, though she shunned some of his ideas. Coming out of the shadow of her father, Lillian Harman asserted a free-love feminism based less in ideals and more in practical reform.

The Crossover Appeal of Free-Love Feminism

These brief biographies of some of the more prominent free-love feminists reveal many similarities in how women came to support free love and in the arguments they used to defend it. To examine the rhetorics of free-love feminism, we should also look at how they crossed over into other social movements of the time, most notably suffrage, social purity, and anarchism. Suffragists who espoused "voluntary motherhood" found their arguments supported and extended by free-love feminists; they also agreed with many of the free-love feminists' critiques of the coverture laws. Some suffragists, such as Elizabeth Cady Stanton, added divorce to their discourse of women's rights, but not all suffragists embraced their more radical sisters. Some, in fact, went out of their way to distance themselves from free love and in the 1870s found themselves split over the new voice in their midst, Victoria Woodhull. The fact that histories of the women's suffrage movements written during the nineteenth century often ignored the voices of Woodhull and Waisbrooker, despite their contributions to the suffrage cause, testifies to the suffragists' fear of "free love."

Social purity was another misunderstood social movement that shared many similarities with free love. Historians have often grouped social purity advocates together as the prudish, "vice" watchdogs, epitomized by characters like Anthony Comstock. In doing so, they neglect the feminist side of social purity, often as radical as the free lovers. The social purity movement had much in common with the free-love movement in how advocates addressed sexuality, but their final aims were quite different. While rhetors in both movements critiqued the institution of marriage, social purity advocates did not urge its abolition but rather its reform. The arguments for social purity also succeeded since their proposals were actually implemented, such as reforms in divorce laws and age of consent. Thus, their rhetorical techniques ultimately proved more persuasive. Key figures advocating social purity include physician Elizabeth Blackwell and Frances Willard. Social purity advocates urged the elimination of the double standard that repressed women's sexuality but encouraged male sexual license. While they recommended chaste relationships, they did not negate the importance of women's sexuality. They, too, refuted the "passionless" ideology but did so for different aims. In contrast to free-love advocates who often encouraged sexual relationships outside of marriage, social purity advocates wanted men to be held to the same standard as women, with both in chaste relationships before and after marriage. As a result, some historians tend to group social purity advocates with their more prudish constituents, but others have acknowledged their more feminist goals. Estelle Freedman, for example, recognizes that criticizing men's sexual indulgences did not necessarily equate to enforcing prudery (209), since many social purity advocates conceded the sexual desires of both men and women. Historian Lesley Hall has also reframed the goals of social purity advocates, noting their feminist adherents and applications as well as their later influence on the scientific study of sex, sexology (36). Social purity advocates occupied a central place in the connection between science and reform discourse since both male and female physicians often subscribed to social purity ideals and many reform societies aligned with social purity goals included both physicians and lay reformers. (The medical community contained its own adherents of free love, such as Dr. Edward Foote and his son.)[23] Finally, historians of free love have enumerated the marked similarities between the two seemingly antithetical movements and pointed out, "Free love, in fact, may be viewed as a version of Social Purity, one that sought amelioration through rationalist, libertarian means rather than through restriction" (Sears 26). Some free lovers supported social purity goals but thought such goals should be self-imposed rather than government-imposed (Blatt 112). Several free-love feminists, such as Woodhull and Claflin, went on to critique sexuality from a social purity framework after turning their backs on the solution of free love. The key distinction between free love and social purity was often not beliefs about sex but about ultimate goals.

Some women espousing the values of free-love feminism are often grouped with the social purity cause rather than as adherents of free love. Lucinda Chandler and Elmina Slenker, for example, adopted relatively moderate ideas on sexuality more popular with social purity activists. Yet their ideas and places of publication locate them as more conservative participants, but participants nevertheless, in free-love feminism. Lucinda Chandler (1828–1911), born Lucinda Banister, espoused several reform causes throughout her life, including dress reform, labor reform, spiritualism, and suffrage.[24] In her writings on sex and marriage, she hoped for a "higher standard of marriage" (qtd. in Frisken, *Victoria Woodhull's Sexual Revolution* 53), equating her with social purity advocates, among whom she counted herself. But her central tenet, woman's ownership of her own body, matched free-love ideals. Like Severance and Woodhull, Chandler critiqued women's status as sex slaves within the bonds of marriage and equated marriage to legalized prostitution. In an 1895 article, "Woman Is Irresponsible by Her Legal Status," she defined herself as a supporter of free love by referring to the calls for more liberal divorce laws as patriarchal solutions to the problems of patriarchy (2). Instead, she urged freedom from marriage as women's emancipation. Her views on sexuality, though, were more conservative, as she seemed to view males as hypersexed impositions on women's purity. She did not reject women's sexuality but said that women's true sexual desires could not be determined so long as they remained chained to the legal bondage of marriage (2). Thus, Chandler blended the more radical factions of social purity with the more conservative side of free love and ended up straddling the slim divide between the two philosophies.

Elmina Slenker's views were similar to Chandler's in advocating a higher moral standard in sexual relations but proved more controversial. A Quaker and then a spiritualist, Elmina Drake Slenker, born Elizabeth Drake (1827–1908), supported and wrote about many causes, including suffrage, temperance, abolition, and free love.[25] When Slenker sought marriage, she advertised for a husband in the *Water-Cure Journal* and thought she found a like-minded individual in her husband. Her arrests for obscenity tested their relationship, and he became increasingly wary of his wife's radicalism, even refusing to pay the costs of her bail. Her views also alienated the couple from their community in Snowville, Virginia (Sears 206). Slenker, who often signed her articles as "Aunt Elmina," called herself a "Dianist free lover," referring to the practice of Dianism. She initially supported continence as an ideal sexual practice but shifted to support Dianism, where couples would refrain from sexual intercourse except for procreation. Such a view of sexuality made her unpopular with other free lovers, and she increased these reactions with her advertisements for correspondents in the pages of *Lucifer* and other free-love publications. She received many letters from men looking for "like-minded individuals" to correspond with but fewer letters from women (Slenker, "Woman Who Does"). Other free-love feminists, such as Waisbrooker and de Cleyre, viewed her solicitations for correspondents as inviting trouble from men who had different ideas about what women involved with free love might view as acceptable (Sears 220). Slenker, on the other hand, viewed these correspondences as "talks on paper" ("Letters") and equated her correspondents and comrades at *Lucifer* to a membership in a church ("Listen!"). Though she counted them as "like-minded" individuals, she also found herself in frequent debates with other readers, including one with Celia Whitehead on birth control that led to the arrest of *Lucifer*'s editors. In 1898, she debated the definition of free love with Lillian Harman in the pages of *Lucifer* because Slenker had rejected the definition of free love as variety ("Free Love"), not based on any moral standards but on the basis that "a multiplication of duplicates despoils many a thing of much of its value" ("Old and the New Ideal"). To Slenker, free love represented a way for women and men to forsake the "debauchery" of the marriage institution and indulge a more chaste existence. Her ideas on sexuality seem to group her with social purity advocates, but she identified herself as a free lover, with her own interpretation of "free" sexual practices.

Social purity represents the more conservative crossover of the free-love movement, just as anarchism represents its more radical crossover. Anarchists were drawn to free love since they rejected government involvement in personal relationships. Anarchism matched well with free-love philosophy in its denunciation of government control and focus on individualism. Many free-love feminists identified as anarchists, such as Waisbrooker, Lizzie Holmes, and Voltairine de Cleyre. Holmes, in particular, earned accolades from other free lovers for her radical views, including Francis Barry, a male free lover and leader of the Berlin Heights community, who saw her as one of the pioneers of the movement (Barry, "Who Were the Pioneers" 355). Lizzie May Hunt Swank Holmes (1850–1926) was the daughter of radical Hannah J. Hunt and lived with her parents in the Berlin Heights free-love commune.[26] Following the death of her first husband, she began her reform career in the 1870s as a labor activist in Chicago. She organized women in labor reform societies and attempted to unionize women workers while frequently contributing articles to the *Alarm*, a prominent anarchist periodical, and to *Lucifer*. In 1885, she married her second husband, William Holmes, who shared her reformist sympathies. A close friend of Albert and Lucy Parsons, she was also personally affected by the one of the most prominent anarchist scandals, the Haymarket massacre.[27] Holmes's personal philosophy included an endorsement of free love as a way to emancipate women from sexual and economic bondage, elaborated in *Hagar Lyndon, or A Woman's Rebellion*, a free-love feminist novel serialized in *Lucifer* in 1893, which she published under the name May Huntley.[28] Holmes's contributions to free-love feminism often highlighted the link between women's sexual and economic oppression, and while she initially advocated free love, she made waves by protesting its use as a "universal panacea" ("More of the Problem"). She questioned whether free love would be successful in solving the problems of women ("Revising Our Opinions"). Insisting that "woman's freedom is human freedom," in an 1899 article of the same name, she actually decried the focus on sexuality in *Lucifer* and urged a more complex view of women's oppression. Holmes's protests illustrate the status of free-love feminism at the turn of the century and indicate the factors in its eventual death as a feminist movement.

Fellow anarchist Voltairine de Cleyre also espoused free-love feminist philosophies and became increasingly dismayed at the direction of free-love arguments at the turn of the century. De Cleyre (1866–1912) became one of the most prominent feminist anarchists of the time period, second to Emma Goldman. Born in Leslie, Michigan, as Voltairine de Claire, she was named after Enlightenment thinker Voltaire, whom her parents idealized. She was well educated and turned to writing early in her life, producing both poetry and nonfiction. De Cleyre not only proclaimed the values of free love and anarchism but also lived them. For example, she never cohabited with any of her lovers and bore a son that she left to his father's care. In this way, she was more of a practical free lover than a theoretical one.

A troubled student of hers and fellow anarchist shot her in the back in 1902, and the bullets were never removed. De Cleyre suffered ill health for the rest of her life as a result, and she too knew the burdens of depression and made several attempts at suicide. Instead of pressing charges against her assailant, de Cleyre solidified her pacifist goals by urging treatment for the young man rather than punishment, practicing what she preached.

She was also an active and in some cases formative member of several liberal leagues and social science clubs, particularly in Philadelphia, where she resided for several years.[29] In her speeches, she rejected the "permanent dependent relationship" bestowed by marriage and endorsed the free-love tenet that unions should be held together by love rather than by law ("They Who Marry Do Ill" 13). But she also expressed doubt that free-love unions would work, because they too would reinforce dependent bonds (19). She therefore argued that "moments of union should be rare and of no binding nature" (20), a philosophy she also lived. Thus, while she agreed with the main tenets of free-love feminism, she also offered an objection to their solution, much like Lizzie Holmes did. De Cleyre's protests against sex slavery and marriage encapsulated the appeal of free-love feminism to anarchists but also showed a distinct difference. To de Cleyre, marriage represented all that was wrong with ideals about property: "Marriage and Family are the social expression of Property, they come with it and go with it. . . . What remains for us to do is to realize independence of life for the individual, to study the sources and effects of sexual passion, to acquire and disseminate a knowledge of contracepts,—above all to battle ceaselessly with the *propertarian spirit of marriage* which is within" ("Love in Freedom"). Thus, the anarchist protests of marriage focused not on the abuses of marriage but on its very definition: no one could be free within an institution with a "propertarian spirit."

Holmes's sister Lillie D. White was also a pivotal figure in the movement, a voice of protest who showed the differences between free love and free-love feminism. The daughter of radical feminist Hannah J. Hunt, her family lived in the free-love community at Berlin Heights at midcentury. Her sister Lizzie Holmes and brother C. F. Hunt also contributed to *Lucifer* and other periodicals, depicting a family steeped in nineteenth-century radicalism. Details of White's marriage (or marriages) and children are unknown, though she had a least one son living in Louisiana at the turn of the century. She resided mostly in the Midwest and was active in the Kansas Freethinkers Association.[30] She served as editor of *Lucifer* in 1892 and 1893, first as coeditor with Waisbrooker, then as chief editor. One historian commends White's stint as editor, noting that "during her six months' tenure as editor, *Lucifer* demonstrated a level of intellectual engagement with the question of women's rights which it never achieved under Moses Harman's sloppy and martyristic style of editing" (Sears 148) and that "perhaps if White had stayed on after Harman returned from prison, *Lucifer* could have become a journal of direct, national importance to more than a few. As it was, the journal lapsed into the free-lovers free-for-all that it had always been under Harman" (250). Clearly, White's editorship changed the face of *Lucifer*, as illustrated in the change of banner (depicting a woman), more attention to women's rights and to economic issues affecting women, and one particular issue during her tenure hailed as "A Woman's Number."

White's rhetoric revealed her as one of the more radical feminists of the movement, often in conflict with other participants. She shared with them, however, the desire to attack the status quo. In articles such as

"Woman's Dangerous Friends," she attacked the institutions that fostered inequality, such as the church, woman's "greatest enemy" (3), separate spheres ideology, and the system of education that denied women equal opportunity. "Woman's Dangerous Friends" did not stop there. She also criticized those who professed to be women's rights advocates but did not recognize women's self-sovereignty. For example, she denounced J. A. Houser's book *Is Marriage a Failure?* despite its praise in free-love circles because his arguments for women's education reinforced separate spheres ideology. White attacked Republican motherhood arguments, even if they often led to feminist goals. Her ideals, incorporated into her free-love feminism, placed her in contrast to free-love feminists such as Woodhull and Waisbrooker, since she viewed free love as a means to bring about women's complete equality and self-ownership rather than as the end in itself. She cautioned against advocating free love at the expense of individual rights and assailed the hypocrisy of free lovers who scorned others for their choices, comparing them to religious fanatics who would require every person to adhere to their philosophies ("Progress"). For White, free lovers' insistence that their plan was the right one violated the individual choice they stood for ("Old and the New"). These views garnered White criticism from fellow *Lucifer* writers, mostly male, who charged her with condoning "sex slavery" by not insisting on free love for all (Barry, "Crudities Criticized—No. 9") and not supporting complete revolution (Studebaker).

White also believed that free love might replace a corrupt system with one equally devoid of women's rights. She pointed out that male free-love philosophies still relied on false ideals of women and would not dismantle the system that idealized "womanly perfection" but created new standards that women must conform to ("Woman's Dangerous Friends"). In fact, White's arguments often revealed the idealism of many free-love arguments. She expressed skepticism at this idealism, saying, "I am not sure the destruction of the marriage institution if it could be accomplished at one stroke would help the race into happiness or wisdom or freedom" ("Old and the New"). White insisted that even destroying the marriage system would not bring about the utopia that so many envisioned and poked fun at their ideals, saying, "Some of my comrades who write for *Lucifer* seem to be looking forward to a heaven, or a condition of perfection on earth, when men and women will be absolutely consistent, unselfish and wholly free. I am not looking for such a time or place" ("Progress"). These "comrades" might have included women like Waisbrooker, who believed free love would instigate a spiritual awakening and evolution. White's free-love philosophy relied on practicality, a defining feature of her rhetoric. White stood her ground on these issues, despite condemnation from her "comrades." Charged with inconsistency by others, White would respond, "I refuse even to be consistent when consistency stands in the way of my happiness" ("Old and the New"). In focusing on individual happiness manifested in material conditions and rejecting idealism, White created a more practical version of free-love feminism, focused on the material conditions of women rather than on the often abstract and idealistic philosophies of other free lovers. In a provocative 1899 piece titled "Does Liberty Slay Love?," she reversed cherished ideals and belittled idealism. When she later concluded, "Love is dead—crucified between the sweet deceitful flattery of the past and the honest—brutally honest philosophy of today. Peace to his ashes" ("Playing at Love" 234), she provoked an uproar among free lovers who defined love as one of their central tenets (Walker). Unique to free-love feminism, White also attacked the idealization of motherhood in free-love rhetoric, since she viewed it as another conformist ideal that prevented women from achieving true freedom. White's emphasis on true equal rights and on free love as a means rather than an end and her attention to the practical characterized her rhetoric, as did her statement, "Remedies are always impractical and utopian" ("Woman's Work").

White became an important voice in this movement, always questioning the practicality of the solution of free love but also revealing how free-love feminists fought against the male free-love philosophy that could, in their view, replace one infringement on women's sexual rights with another. In particular, anarchist free-love feminists such as White, Holmes, and de Cleyre critiqued how many writers conceived of free love because it would allow male privilege in sexual relationships to persist. Thus, free-love feminists wanted their sexuality not to be defined by male standards but struggled with how to define their ideal practice.

The Values of Free-Love Feminism

The men and women advocating free love often disagreed on applications of free-love theory and the primary emphasis of it, but they found themselves united in one goal in particular: protecting "free speech," which in their specific case meant speech about sex, from those who would silence it. They faced their biggest challenge in the machinations of "social vice" watchdog Anthony Comstock, who in 1873 successfully lobbied for laws barring obscenity from the US mail. Comstock also secured a special position in the government that allowed him to enforce the law, and he targeted many of the rhetors discussed in this project for their "obscene" sex speech. However, the laws did not specify a definition for obscenity, leaving Comstock to define it in his own terms. One of his first arrests, of the Claflin sisters, was dismissed because the definition and mode of transmission went unspecified; the sisters were released on a technicality since the original law did not include periodicals. Comstock remedied this oversight and thus had the power to pursue the editors of free-love periodicals.

Comstock targeted both free-love advocates and medical practitioners who wrote about the body. In fact, sometimes free-love advocates were arrested for distributing medical manuals rather than their own writings. One of Ezra Heywood's arrests, for example, included his actions in mailing Russell Trall's *Sexual Physiology*, a text one historian has included as a "prudery" text of the nineteenth century (Walters, *Primers for Prudery* 82). Comstock frequently took aim at the editors of *Lucifer*, but not always for their more radical views. One of their first arrests was a result of "the Markland Letter," which discussed the issue of marital rape, but another resulted from a more conservative letter by Celia B. Whitehead, criticizing Elmina Slenker's support of birth control. Although Whitehead denounced birth control in the letter, it was deemed "obscene" for even mentioning birth control. Whitehead was not arrested. The male editors of *Lucifer* were. In fact, one scholar has noted that when Comstock had a chance to arrest either a man or a woman, he usually chose the man (Blatt 147). Comstock did arrest women, though he never arrested one of the most "obscene," Angela Heywood, preferring to incarcerate Ezra instead, though it was often for something Angela had written. Other women who fell under Comstock's attack included Waisbrooker, Slenker, and Ida Craddock. Comstock's cause lost much sympathy because of his persecution of Craddock, which led to her suicide. He also resorted to entrapment, writing letters to the periodicals posing as someone asking for advice and requesting literature on birth control that the editors were circulating, then arresting them for doing so. His laws remained on the books for many years into the twentieth century, and he helped define an era of battle between censorship and free speech.[31]

Free-love advocates fought back, and free and open speech about sex and sexuality became one of the central tenets of free-love advocacy and also one of its central debates. A unifying feature of these different rhetors was their insistence on "plain speaking" on sexual matters and rejection of euphemisms. They blamed silence, ignorance, and what they termed "mock modesty" for many of the abuses women suffered within the marriage system. They made it their mission to reveal hypocrisy both in the system that denied sexual knowledge to women and in the men who condemned "promiscuous" women and free love, yet who by their actions showed that they did not revere the institution of marriage. The need for a language to express sexuality occupied many free-love feminists. In her 1874 speech, Woodhull noted that direct terms were essential; they were "not to be explained . . . in terms of glittering generalities, or of poetic fancy, or in gingerly words that may leave any in doubt as to what is intended, but plainly, honestly and earnestly, so that no one can misunderstand" (*Tried* 1). The sexual education she endorsed required "plain speech," though many of the terms she employed would not be considered very radical in our day. The same cannot be said for the editors of *The Word*, who printed a story about a young girl asking her mother the meaning of "fuck" and the mother responding with "plain speech" and visual aids (Battan, "'Word Made Flesh'" 101). As Jesse Battan has noted, Angela Heywood, writing for *The Word*, denounced the hypocrisy of "cultured men," whose speech to working-class women she characterized as insulting and degrading (112). She celebrated the language deemed "vulgar," believing it contained more truths than prudish euphemisms. Free-love advocates took language deemed "private" into the "public," foreshadowing late-twentieth-century feminism. Other free-love feminists rejected "vulgarity," instead endorsing "scientific terms" to discuss sexuality. Waisbrooker, for instance, criticized Heywood's language but found herself in the same situation, pursued by Comstock for the scientific terms she preferred when she reprinted a report issued by the Department of Agriculture on horse anatomy in an incident Sears refers to as "The Horse Penis Affair" (229).

Free-love advocates, then, rallied together to combat "Comstockism" and "Grundyism," a term they often employed as an insult that had its root in the prudish and nosy character of Mrs. Grundy in *Speed the Plough*, the 1800 play by Thomas Morton. But their unification on free speech did not extend to all matters that became hot-button topics to Comstock. Their divergence on issues like birth control and abortion caused several heated debates. Though many of them vacillated on their opinions about birth control, most deemed it a necessary evil: since women lacked the freedoms they should have, birth control practices and devices were necessities. They believed that no unwanted children would be born to free-love couples, but until others came to embrace their philosophies, women had to rely on birth control methods. They disagreed, however, on the best methods, with some advocating contraceptive devices and others, like Waisbrooker, denouncing such methods as unnatural. Most free-love feminists also condemned abortion, viewing it as a symptom of the problems inherent in the sexual system, and their condemnations survived even if their reasoning did not. For example, a Google search on Tennessee Claflin will reveal many antiabortion quotes and individuals using Claflin as an example of a radical feminist against abortion. Such uses of Claflin's writing are incorrect and incomplete. While she did condemn abortion as "one of the evils of society," she acknowledged its necessity in a world where women were not free to choose when to have children. In fact, her essay seen as an antiabortion text actually critiques the practice because of the dangers it posed to women's health; at the time, it was certainly a risky procedure. To Claflin, "abortion is only a symptom of a more deep-seated disorder of the social state" ("One of the Evils" 125), and only sexual freedom would prevent abortions (126). Angela Heywood remained the only free-love feminist to openly assert abortion rights without qualification.

The Decline of Free-Love Feminism

The central tenets of free love were not without disagreement, but all who asserted this radical form of feminism preached the evils of marriage and the benefits of women's sexual self-ownership and sex education. Free-love feminism eventually waned, with some adherents espousing more anarchist ideals and others turning to the emerging appeal of eugenics. By 1907, the date I place as the end of a free-love feminist movement, the message of the free lovers had become more mainstream: sex education, birth control, and women's rights were no longer considered unspeakable ideas from radical people (D'Emilio and Freedman 166). Historian Taylor Stoehr also encapsulates their successes: "Broadly speaking then, free love may be said to have won out, under a series of other banners" (7). He also, however, provides a key point about their rhetorical failures, noting that their central mistake was proposing free love as "a single solution to multiple problems" (7). The end of free-love feminism, though, can also be attributed to feminists' persecution by Comstock, the advancing age of many of its adherents, and, in my view, their shift from free love to eugenics. The feminism seemed to drop out of their arguments. Looking at the lives and rhetoric of some of the individual free-love feminists helps one to gain a sense of the origins, evolution, and eventual death of free-love feminism.

It is through looking at their discourse alongside scientific discoveries that we can begin to understand the logic and eventual waning of this social movement. Going back to the letter quoted at the beginning of this chapter, we see the influence of science in the writers' references to the "higher civilization," which read alongside evolutionary theory means a more evolved civilization, and in the insistence on plain "physiological" terms, which gains new meaning when we look at this call alongside the discipline of physiology. These feminists championed science over religion, seeing it as a "handmaid" to their radical goals. But their collusion with science did not end well, and free-love feminists found themselves immersed in yet another battle, between social reform and eugenics, elaborated in the subsequent chapters.

When Darwin said, "The season of love is that of battle" (*Descent of Man* 48), he referred to the battle among males to compete for females, a key component of his theory of sexual selection. From the critiques of marriage by Mary Gove Nichols to the more radical critiques of free love by Lillie D. White, free-love feminists showed that the private sphere contained a battle between the sexes for the right of women to "own and control" their sexuality. They revealed the battle between social values and the actual lived experiences of women. They positioned marriage as a battleground where the scientific and the personal met. Their speech created a battle over what was sexual knowledge and what was obscenity. Free-love feminists fought for changes that would free women from the constraints and repression of the marriage system, and the discoveries of science were their weapons in that battle.

2

Evolutionary Theory: (R)Evolutionary Rhetorics in the Free-Love Movement

> There is no such thing as standing still in nature. Either change and growth must go on, or death and decay take place. Every healthy, intelligent woman capable of growth in mind and body, desires the change, the chance to grow. The dishes, the pretty things, satisfying the wants of the husband and baby, no longer make her life complete. She demands a change, and if it does not come freely and wisely, then she becomes the rebel, the "unwomanly woman," the "Woman who dares"; or worse, the hopeless, submissive and patient automaton; or worse still, more deplorable than all, is the woman who never feels an aspiration to get beyond the lines prescribed for her. For her there is no hope.
>
> —Lillie D. White, "Woman's Work," 1893

In *The Coming Woman*, originally a lecture delivered to the International Congress of Freethinkers in Chicago in 1893, Lillie D. White insisted, "There is not so much difference between men and women as we have been led to believe. There is a vast amount of humbug in marking out the characteristics that are feminine and those that are masculine. The apparent differences are mostly artificial, the result of ages of one-sided education and wrong conditions" (9). White, a unique free-love feminist, rejected all ideologies that emphasized difference between men and women and idealized women as angels of the home. In fact, most of her philosophies seem more in line with second-wave feminism than with nineteenth-century feminism. She attributed the differences between men and women not to nature but to the systems of inequality that had perpetuated these differences. White envisioned "the Coming Woman" as one who had demanded change and evolved beyond the spheres that had defined her. It would seem that Darwin's work, often used to reinforce sex differences and confine women, would not be compatible with White's radical aims. On the contrary, Darwin's work provided the warrant for White's and many other free-love feminists' claims for women's sexual self-ownership.

Free-love feminists did not base their women's rights arguments on natural rights or even on their perceived higher morality but argued for rights as a natural evolution. Women could not remain stagnant; like the species, they needed to grow and change. White's ideal woman would recognize this need and evolve to claim her own rights in public and in private. Thus, women's rights discourse grew out of the same discourse often used to justify sexism in the late nineteenth century. This chapter demonstrates how the logic of free-love feminism was based in adherents' surprising applications of Darwin's theories of evolution, natural selection, and sexual selection.

Darwin and Sexuality

The publication of *The Origin of Species* in 1859 ranks as one of the nineteenth century's scientific milestones, and its effects on popular discourses of the time were matched only by the later discovery of the germ. Written in an accessible style, Darwin addressed both scientific and nonscientific readers, spreading his book's appeal and offering a new discourse to lay audiences. Using metaphor and other figures, Darwin's language not only proved accessible but told a story that resonated among lay readers.[1] Once his work was disseminated, however, Darwinian discourse took on a life of its own, transforming in many ways.

One of the many images and arguments that resonated with nineteenth-century readers, particularly in the free-love movement, was Darwin's idealization of the natural world, where progress could be observed. Darwin privileged the actions of nature, as when he said, "Can we wonder, then, that Nature's production should be far 'truer' in character than man's productions; that they should be infinitely better adapted to the most complex conditions of life, and should plainly bear the stamp of far higher workmanship?" (*Origin* 70). This juxtaposition of "true" nature with "man's productions" lent an important line of argument to free-love writers, one that became central to free-love feminism. The hierarchies Darwin established also played a central role in feminist arguments. Darwin's focus on variability and progressive evolution provided a model of increasingly complicated hierarchies. Evolution went in an upward scale of progress, and social reformist discourses exploited that directed hierarchy. That the population was in danger of outgrowing its resources had already been established by Thomas Malthus, but natural selection explained who would survive to enjoy the remaining resources. Darwin claimed that "the vigorous, the healthy, and the happy survive and multiply" (*Origin* 66), a claim that would resonate for free-love feminists attempting to use women's sexual health and contentedness to justify the practice of free love. Several of Darwin's metaphors also became popular. His comparison to the breeder, his description of the struggle for resources, and the imagery of the tree of life not only helped to make his theories more accessible to the public but also offered a new language to discuss sexuality.

Most surprising of all was free-love feminist uses of Darwin's theory of sexual selection, mentioned in *The Origin of Species* and elaborated in 1871's *The Descent of Man*. Although it was often challenged by other scientists, especially in the late nineteenth century, and was later discredited,[2] many male and female reformers found support for their arguments in this theory. Sexual selection explains that males compete for females and the females then choose from among the most superior males, making female choice the rule in the animal kingdom. Sexual selection refers to the process that occurs when male secondary sex characteristics, or characteristics that do not deal with reproduction, evolve to make males more desirable to females. Darwin's example of sexual selection centered on the plumage of the bird: the bird's plumage attracts the female, who then exercises her choice. While female choice is the rule, the onus of change and competition is on the male: "The result [of sexual selection] is not death to the unsuccessful competitor, but few or no offspring. Sexual selection is, therefore, less rigorous than natural selection. Generally, the most vigorous males, those which are best fitted for their places in nature, will leave the most progeny" (Darwin, *Origin* 73). To free-love feminists, the interpretation that males must make themselves worthy of females warranted the logic of women's rights in sexual relationships.

One key distinction Darwin made in elaborating sexual selection concerned the reversal of the process in human beings, with the males given the agency of choice. Additionally, free-love feminists would agree with Darwin's interpretation of this choice: "As far as sexual selection is concerned, all that is required is that choice should be exerted before the parents unite, and it signifies little whether the unions last for life or only for a season" (Darwin, *Descent* 360). Darwin's claims, then, instigated arguments concerning the practices of human sexuality and its regulation in the marriage system. Free-love writers appropriated such logic: if the length of time of such couplings, or relationships, between males and females did not matter in the animal kingdom, they should not matter among humans. Furthermore, the emphasis on choice before the parents united lent a valuable warrant to free-love feminists who argued against the social strictures that led female choice to disappear.

Darwin spent little time discussing human sexuality, but his theories encouraged others to apply them to human practices. Historian of science Vern Bullough explains that Darwin's focus on sexual selection as central to the evolution of the species prompted a greater emphasis on the study of sex by later sexologists (5). He also notes that some of these scientists, based on Darwin's emphasis on sexual selection, "went so far as to hold that sex existed for the good of the species" (5). The twentieth-century sexologists whom Bullough discusses were not the first to assume this purpose for sex—free lovers had done so throughout the nineteenth century. Historian Helen Lefkowitz Horowitz identifies several frameworks for nineteenth-century discussions of sexuality, one of which she calls "sex at the 'core of being.'" She notes of the free lovers, "Believing that sex lay at the core of being, adherents held that sexual expression in heterosexual intercourse was the most vital facet of life, as important for women as for men. They asserted that because sex was so valuable to the self, it must be freely expressed, that any diversion or repression of sexual urges from their 'natural expression' in coition was harmful" (*Rereading Sex* 9). My analysis of free-love feminist texts shows how they came to this argument through Darwinian warrants. The new emphasis on sex sparked by Darwin's writings granted women rhetors the language to discuss the once-taboo topic of women's sexuality and to do so in a scientific register.

Antifeminist Darwin

As Darwinian language infiltrated spheres beyond the scientific, the antifeminist uses of Darwin's work often overshadowed the feminist applications. Twentieth-century feminist historians and critics have documented how Darwin's work often justified gender bias and antifeminist views of women's inferiority. Cynthia Eagle Russett, for example, analyzes how Darwin's views on the differences between the sexes reinforced female inferiority and set the stage for later psychologists who would elaborate these views (40). Fiona Erskine also considers the negative connection between Darwin's work and feminism. Even though *The Origin of Species* does not explicitly address gender, Erskine sees in it an implicit view of female subordination (101) because "patriarchy and the subordination of women were for him unchallenged assumptions" (100). Many find Darwin's theory of sexual selection the most blatant culprit for

"Darwinian sexism" because of its explanation of the differences between the sexes. Angelique Richardson notes that while the *Origin* implied a reinterpretation of women's roles, the *Descent* reinforced traditional gender roles, especially in its emphasis on sexual selection (78). Erskine agrees that sexual selection as discussed in the *Descent* is "intrinsically anti-feminist" since it posits that males become more powerful through it (99–100). Clearly, traditional views of women affected the way Darwin wrote about them, particularly in the *Descent*. But he also revised several of his theories from the *Origin* to the *Descent* (for example, he took Lamarckian views on acquired characteristics in the *Descent* and espoused social Darwinism).[3] Nevertheless, free-love feminists found the warrant of female choice vital to their arguments.

Of the many nineteenth-century popular writers expanding and applying evolutionary theory, Herbert Spencer (1820–1903) often draws the most ire from feminist historians. For example, Jill Conway finds that Spencer's view of sex differences exemplifies the sexist uses of evolutionary theory since he asserted views on women as less developed than men, positing an "earlier arrest of individual evolution in women than in men" (Spencer, *Study of Sociology* 373; qtd. in Conway 140–41).[4] Yet, free-love feminists found Spencer's theories of evolution and population useful, and he was enormously influential to their rhetoric, particularly in his applications of evolutionary theory to the social realm. Free-love feminists seem to have taken what they liked out of Spencer's work and ignored what they didn't.

It would seem evolutionary theory lent more fuel to antifeminists than to feminists. Granted, Darwin's theories opened the door for further reinforcement of female inferiority. I do not refute these views, but there were also ways in which Darwin's work reinforced feminist values, particularly in free-love feminist rhetorics. Free-love feminists seldom focused on Darwin's discussions of sex differences (as found in 1871's *Descent of Man*) or defended their intellectual capabilities against charges they were less evolved than men. Instead, they appropriated several Darwinian metaphors and lines of argument to argue for radical reforms. Many free-love feminists became social Darwinists in the worst sense of the term, as subsequent chapters will discuss, but this chapter focuses on particular lines of argument promoting the practice of free love that took their warrants from Darwinian arguments. Thus, we will see how the evolutionary discourse of free-love feminism was itself evolutionary: it evolved into a different kind of discourse by the end of the century, and these initial lines of argument provided the foreshadowing to the eventual death of free-love feminism.

Marriage as an Unnatural State: Darwinian Support for Free Love

The pages of free-love periodicals such as *Lucifer, the Light Bearer* often contained references to a "natural" morality and juxtaposed the "natural" with the government-imposed. For example, an 1886 *Lucifer* editorial (most likely composed by Edwin C. Walker) differentiated between the two: "The individual . . . man and woman is a natural product, does not owe his or her existence to the state—can have and enjoy life to the fullest extent without the existence or assistance of the state. On the contrary, the state is an artificial product, does not exist in nature, is made and unmade by man at his pleasure" ("Autonomy"). The juxtaposition of the natural versus the man-made, socially imposed, "artificial" state of marriage became a common thread in these texts. Similarly, in urging society to accept "illegitimate" children, free-love feminist Lucinda Chandler argued:

> The first step practiceable for removal of what is termed "Social Evil," is to make maternity legitimate under any and all circumstances, and to make motherhood in or out of legal form, the supreme controller of itself. Motherhood is the agency of "the requirements of natural morality" to promote an ascending grade of life. Man-made laws have reversed the operation of the laws of natural morality. ("Requirements")

Chandler's call for a "natural morality" may seem to evoke the "natural rights" discourse of the Enlightenment, or even a more feminist-essentialist standpoint, but post-Darwinian free-love reformers employed the term "natural" in a specific framework. For example, Chandler's references to "an ascending grade of life" and the contrast of "man-made laws" with natural laws evoke the discourse of evolution, especially if we read her references alongside other free-love feminist texts. Darwin's work produced a more urgent call for free-love feminists to examine what was "natural" versus socially imposed. Free-love feminists also extended Darwinian logic, particularly the female choice argument, to cover female choice in all matters pertaining to sex, rather than just choice in mate. Finally, free-love feminism gained an ultimate goal from Darwinian discourse: that free love both represented and produced progress.

Sexual Instincts under Attack: Contrasting "Natural" and "Unnatural"

Victoria Woodhull, already notorious for declaring herself a free lover and denouncing marriage as sexual slavery in her 1871 Steinway Hall speech, branched out in both her speaking engagements and lines of argument with *Tried as by Fire*, originally an 1874 speech on free love given in numerous cities on a for-profit lecture tour. The subtle and explicit ways she wove evolutionary discourse into her critiques of traditional marriage reveals how Darwinian lines of argument had infiltrated the public discourse on a number of subjects. Woodhull's specific uses of Darwin set the stage for later free-love feminists who extended her logic. Her speech took as its premise that marriage is an unnatural state. For example, she argued that marriage had "outlived its day of usefulness" (*Tried* 5) and "stands directly in the way of any improvement in the race" (7). The warrant that social customs inhibit nature shaped her definition of marriage as "an assumption by the community that it can regulate the sexual instincts of individuals" (7). Her logic that the limits set by society on individuals' choice in sexual relations stand in the way of natural evolutionary progression was warranted by the emphasis on "nature" in Darwin's text. Woodhull elaborated this premise when she announced, "When a limit is placed upon anything that by nature is free, its actions become perverted" (23). That is, the sexual relations have become "perverted" because of the limits set upon them by social and legal codes—not by "nature." Woodhull also presented marriage as "at variance with everything in nature"; everywhere but among humans "the female has supreme authority in domain of sex" (39). Woodhull's claim used the evolutionary hierarchy as its warrant: if other species give the female this "supreme authority," then why don't humans? She used Darwin to idealize the "natural world" as the place where progress was unhindered.

Her references to the female's "supreme authority" also engaged Darwin's theory of sexual selection. While some of these arguments merely alluded to sexual selection theory in their focus on female choice, she also explicitly addressed it: "Sexual selection has very little scope in our conventional system" since women often marry for the wrong reasons, such as economic necessity or social pressure (Woodhull Martin, *Rapid Multiplication* 20). Therefore, she argued, women do not exercise their "natural" choices but are forced to make choices in mates by social mores. Using this line of argument, free-love feminists relied on the authority of sexual selection: if females in the animal kingdom can choose from among the most appealing males, women should certainly be given a similar choice rather than be pressured into relationships based on social class, the need for a provider, or the desire to be married, regardless of love. Sexual selection theory, to them, proved the "right of woman to rule in the domain of affections" (Woodhull, *Elixir* 22).

Elaborating the importance of nature, Woodhull saw female choice as a part of nature's endowments when she urged, "To woman, by nature, belongs the right of sexual determination. When the instinct is aroused in her, then and then only should commerce follow. When woman rises from sexual slavery into freedom, into the ownership and control of her sexual organs, and man is obliged to respect this freedom, then will this instinct become pure and holy" (*Tried* 40). Referring to sexual relations as an "instinct," one that all women possess but must choose when and with whom to exercise that instinct, appropriated language often used for antifeminist purposes. Here, though, "instincts" are natural but unnaturally restricted by social mores. Woodhull's argument received additional backing from medical authority: John M. Scudder, a physician who insisted, "The wife should not lose control of her person in marriage. It is hers to rule supreme in this regard. This is a law of life, and is violated in no species except in man" (Scudder 62; qtd. in Woodhull, *Tried* 43). Woodhull contended that the lack of analogies in nature to the marriage system proved the unnatural condition of marriage (*"And the Truth Shall Make You Free"* 14). Thus, a Darwinian warrant became "a law of life" in this discourse.

Woodhull's sister, Tennessee Claflin, espoused similar definitions of marriage as unnatural in her 1871 book, *Constitutional Equality, a Right of Women*, where she advocated suffrage as "undoubtedly . . . a step in the right direction" (6) but also viewed the denial of suffrage as a symptom, rather than the cause, of inequality for women. Instead of focusing on suffrage as the panacea, Claflin contended, the economic and sexual inequalities of women were the roots of oppression. Making an argument similar to Charlotte Perkins Gilman's later, more famous statement on women and economics based on a Darwinian framework, Claflin insisted that women could never attain true equality unless they became independent of men and supported themselves financially (*Constitutional Equality* 6–7). She later advocated for the professionalization of housework (32–33), also similar to Gilman's later argument. Like Woodhull, Claflin noted that women often marry for economic support or societal strictures; they thus perpetuate their unequal positions. Like Gilman's, Claflin's argument was warranted by evolutionary theory—holding back women holds back evolution.

The connections to Darwinian discourse become more apparent in Claflin's exploration of what marriage is:

> What is marriage? Is it a legal union between av male and female of the race of animals known as man; or does it have a wider and deeper significance? Are the "unions" between the males and females of the types of animals below man, marriages, or are they something else? Are the

"unions" between the male and female species of plants, by which they reproduce and increase, marriages, or should they be designated by some other term? If these are marriages, who is there that will prepare some marriage law not in harmony with natural law, that shall compel each of these to forever remain mated, whether they would or no, and, by so being compelled, be enabled to ever remain respectable (?) members of their "society?" (*Constitutional Equality* 114)

Her inquiry follows along the same lines as Woodhull's definition of marriage: if marriage is a natural state, other species would have similar unions. Since they do not, marriage is an unnatural state. For Claflin and Woodhull, "natural law" differed from the "natural law" professed by Enlightenment thinkers and earlier, male, free lovers. "Natural law" in free-love feminist discourse became identified with nature: it was dictated by the occurrences in nature. Darwinian discourse thus gave them a frame of reference to redefine what was considered "natural." Claflin's rhetoric privileged the actions of "Nature": "Nature is our best and only authoritative teacher. If we look to or accept other than her laws, we shall be under the necessity, sooner or later, of revolting, to free ourselves from the voluntary bondage we place ourselves under" (75). She defined marriage as "voluntary bondage" that could not be a natural state.

In an 1872 speech delivered at New York City's Academy of Music, *The Ethics of Sexual Equality*, Claflin premised her argument with the statement, "Human life is not different in absolute existence from the other forms of life. The same general laws govern its manifestations, though in a higher stage of development. And when we seek to discover the laws which govern it we must proceed by the same rules of analysis and deduction as when we discover laws in other forms of life" (5). This premise evoked hierarchy by comparing higher and lower forms of life to reveal how women's lack of status violated nature. Claflin also evoked sex as the mechanism for evolution and alluded to the goal of marriage reform as creating progress:

> The union of the sexes is the natural condition, and man and woman should enter it from an equal dignity of position and equally voluntarily. Society should be so that no woman should feel obliged to marry or connect herself with man for the object of support, and she should be in such condition that she should never enter upon the new relation, from any other reasons than natural law, and from the fact that there exists a mutual attraction. (*Constitutional Equality* 42–43)

EVOLUTIONARY THEORY • 65

For Claflin, "natural" was not defined as inherent or god-given; it was defined as the endowments of "Nature," which could evolve to conform to environment. Thus, she argued, giving women rights and amending her status in marriage would not only conform to "Nature" but would create a new environment where "progress" could occur. Contrasting the present system to "savage life," she looked ahead to a time when education would allow women to ensure progress in evolution ("Mothers and Their Duties" 49). Claflin insisted that women who were to become mothers required extensive education because "so long as she is true to Nature, Nature is kind to her and hers. But the universal mother avenges herself on all who disregard her laws—first by pain, and afterwards by extinction" (49). Her logic relied on the primacy of "Nature," which must be aided by humans. Her evidence also depended on a hierarchal perspective, such as when she said, "In savage life instinct will supply almost all a mother requires, but in a high state of civilization like ours instinct must be supplemented by careful training" (49). Thus, "instincts" guide human behavior, but humans have power to amend them.

Claflin also evoked sexual selection theory, though she did not engage it as explicitly as Woodhull did in her arguments for female choice. Instead, Claflin used the female choice premise to assert the right of women to reject tradition and propose to the man she chooses ("Who Should Propose?"). Like Woodhull, she highlighted the restrictions perpetrated by marriage, since economic and gender inequalities often led women to make choices based on economic support (Claflin, "Short History of Marriage" 35). She critiqued traditional courtship rituals where "the role of the man was to win, and of the woman to be won" ("Who Should Propose?" 49). She then refuted this ideal by claiming that we have evolved past this standard routine:

> These methods may have been suitable for a barbarous age when men wooed like the birds and beasts of the field . . . but at this period of human evolution we require more rational processes of mating—processes which will promote truth and honesty between the sexes prior to marriage, and thus prevent unpleasant developments. And in order to accomplish this we must first sweep away the cobwebs of superstition, particularly those which render it immodest for a woman to make the first advances in affection. Women are far shrewder than men in the matter of sexual choice, and are less governed by blind passion. If they had the same freedom to propose as men have, there would be fewer unhappy marriages. ("Who Should Propose?" 49–50)

Claflin's reference to "the birds and beasts of the field" implies knowledge of the examples Darwin used in elaborating sexual selection theory. Claflin saw these acts in nature as "barbarous" and forecasted a new age where women would shrug off societal strictures to be the pursuer, rather than the pursued, a subtle critique of the gender ideologies implied in sexual selection theory. In a sense, she redefined the conditions in which female choice should occur. In the new era she envisioned, women would "have the same right to propose to men as men have to women. And every woman should be allowed to choose the father of her child if he be willing" ("Maternity" 35). Such choice would produce more "natural" children since "her instincts are true, and she would select the bravest and best" for the father of her child (35). Therefore, while she critiqued sexual selection theory, she also exploited its emphasis on instincts and female selection of mates. For Claflin, humans would never advance so long as they stuck to outdated concepts of marriage and sexual relations. Instead of letting religion or social custom dictate the rituals of marriage, "it remains for us to bring [marriage laws] into harmony with the scientific" ("Short History of Marriage" 8). She thus called on feminists to adhere to science, imagining that science would free women.

Physician and free-love feminist Juliet Severance also insisted that legal marriage stood in the way of proper evolution because of the "unnatural" sanctions placed upon women's sexuality, and she added to applications of Darwin by focusing on women's health. In *A Lecture on Life and Health, or How to Live a Century*, published in 1881, she did not confine her discussion to ways women could maintain a healthy lifestyle; she found that women's lack of status in sexual relations affected their health, and evolutionary theory became part of her discourse on health. Severance envisioned evolving past marriage, where both partners would be free to exercise choice, since, she argued, it was time to evolve past old customs:

> Legal marriage has been a necessary step in the evolution of society; but not a final one. Evidences are not wanting to show that it has done its work; and that it may, nay that it will, be succeeded in the near future by the next step in social evolution in which woman will have her natural rights restored and be protected in their possession and exercise beyond the power of usurpation. (8)

For Severance, women needed their "natural rights" and choice in sexual partners to be truly healthy. Since the bearing of children has consequences on women's health, Severance had to show how sexual selection theory supported a voluntary motherhood argument. Using the analogy to the natural world, Severance observed how legal marriage violates the rule of female choice, "usurping" that natural choice: "Let them acknowledge that man alone, of all the animals, takes from the female the control of her person and compels her to maternity, and that he has invented and maintains laws to perpetuate this usurpation. Woman wants the control of her person and right to exercise her maternal instincts under her own direction. These our present marriage system takes away" (7). While Darwin invoked the rule of female choice to cover choice in mate, which leads to the occurrence of sexual selection, Severance expanded this rule of female choice to cover both choice in partners and choice in when sexual relations occur. Consequently, the voluntary motherhood argument urged by many nineteenth-century feminists received scientific backing through an interpretation of sexual selection theory. To Severance, this choice was innate; it was given "by virtue of her functions": "Woman should exercise the right entrusted to her by virtue of her functions, to determine when, and under what circumstances she will, and under what she will not become a mother, and it is her right and sacred duty to do this inexorably" (6). "Female choice," a key term in Darwin's theory, became gospel in free-love feminist arguments, extended to cover all choices made in sexual relations, not only the choice of mate. It became a stricture against marital rape and a justification for birth control.

Envisioning a more evolved future for women, in an 1892 article titled "Sex Hypnotics" Severance compared the ideal "natural" relationship between men and women to the present perverted one. Severance predicted, "In the 'to-come' a man will scorn to accept any expression which was called out by his desire in the stead of her demand, and she will grow to know the difference between her natural demand for magnetic exchange and her desire to please some man and minister to his wants in that direction" (1). Both men and women needed to reject "false teachings" that allowed religion or social codes of morality to dictate their sexual relationships to enter this ideal future. In doing so, women must recognize their own sexual desires and not confuse them with the desire to please men. Severance evoked spiritualist discourse by characterizing sex as a "magnetic exchange." Therefore, when the man does not recognize the woman's right to determine when to heed her own sexual desires, he commits what Severance called a "psychic rape": "This is a psychic rape, and as the spiritual is above and superior to the physical, so is this crime the more heinous and destructive, as it relates to the higher conditions of life" (1). Similar to Lois Waisbrooker, Severance defined a higher purpose to sex than the physical; for her, it was also a spiritual union, and thus usurping the natural authority of women over their bodies was also a kind of spiritual rape. What exactly Severance and Waisbrooker advocated when they celebrated the virtues of a higher purpose to sex seems unclear, but Severance said that the higher purpose could not be known until social freedom and free love were more commonly practiced (1). Then, she argued, free love would both represent progress by shrugging off social customs and would produce progress by ensuring "the best results in any direction in the conjugal relation" (qtd. in M. Harman, "Marriage Problem"). The idea that evolution represented progress warranted the following logic: giving women sexual freedom will allow evolutionary progression. Free-love feminists knew that critiquing the status of women was not sufficient to gain their ideal conditions; they had to focus on the results of this depraved condition: the children that resulted from such unions. As subsequent chapters will illustrate, these women believed that children born from legal unions would be inferior to those born from "free" women. Thus, elevating women's status would enable them to produce superior children. As Severance explained, "The basis for all improvement in the race, is the best beginning of life" ("Farmers' Wives" 277). Since women's sexual instincts would lead to the "best beginning of life," the basis for improvement lay in valuing women's sexual instincts.

Radical Angela Heywood also stressed the perversion of the legal status of women and its harmful results. In her article "Woman's Love," published in *The Word* in July 1876, she pointed to the woman's body as the place where progress would occur: "The most genial and natural garden is woman's womb; men realize its existence, but do not appreciate its value. It is the planting-ground of all human society, wherein Nature readjusts herself, in her most subtle deficiencies, unless coerced by the physical-force plan of men" (1). Heywood thus redefined the place of nature. Women's bodies were the places where evolution physically occurred. Heywood also noted the false customs created by men when she argued, "We hear of 'the man of the house,' as though the woman was one of the children, the daughter of her husband. . . . How can men think straight, when they take things as they have arranged them to be the real facts of Nature?" ("Woman's Love"). For Heywood, men have ruled over women because of their "great selfishness which grows out of his unnatural ascendancy over woman through property usurpations and the subtle relations of physical force to her as his mate in primitive stages of growth, as from the animal to the human animal" (1). She continued, "Having arrived at a human identity, we wish to be recognized as a part of the collective identity, and, once escaping animalism, we do not wish

EVOLUTIONARY THEORY · 69

to become the victims of manism" (1). Heywood's evolutionary discourse was less explicit than the arguments discussed above, but reading them together shows the influence on her ideas. Heywood pointed out the "unnatural ascendancy" provided by unnatural customs created by men. She also alluded to the evolutionary hierarchy in her statements on the "primitive stages of growth" and thus showed that the rule of men over women reversed the progress of evolution. Thus, women's inferiority in marriage and sexual relationships were the "primitive stages." Rejecting marriage and embracing free love would lead to the "higher" stages. Defining marriage as an unnatural invasion of "personal liberty" ("Men's Laws"), Heywood reveals how free-love feminism was combining the values of the free-love perfectionists of the 1850s with the new science of the era: her references to "personal liberty" engaged writers like Stephen Pearl Andrews, who focused on individual self-sovereignty in his theories of free love; her characterization of marriage as man-made evoked the new scientific framework for free love that many would exploit.

Sex as the Mode to Evolution

Lois Waisbrooker's arguments followed these important tenets of free love, but she also covered a spiritual side of both evolution and sexuality. Like other free-love feminists, she insisted, "The evils under which we suffer are rooted in the unbalanced conditions of creative life as manifested in the relative position of man and woman—in the subjection of woman to man," and added, "Does Nature—does evolutionary law so change its methods on its upward course?" (*Eugenics* 4). Since humans were considered higher than animals both intellectually and spiritually (*Fountain of Life* 83), human females should not be subject to suppression. Waisbrooker also used the warrant of "female choice" to argue, "Nature has given to every woman the inherent right to decide when she will bear a child and who shall be its father" (*Eugenics* 5). She extended this popular logic, however, to explore the spiritualist concerns with conquering death and ascension to higher forms of life. Her 1879 spiritualist tract, *From Generation to Regeneration; or, The Plain Guide to Naturalism*, began with a focus on spiritualist issues until Waisbrooker laid out the logic of her argument, which placed sex as the central mechanism for spiritual evolution. She proclaimed, "Love (sex-love) is the bottom subject of civilization. . . . There is no subject so important and none so little understood. . . . There can be no true progress toward general happiness till the true natural relation between the sexes is settled by . . . a *full discussion* and not a skirmish into one department and then into action" (7).

With this declaration on the importance of sex and need for "full discussion," Waisbrooker brought the conversation on spiritual life back to her own core principles: that there cannot be reform until the roles of sex and of women's sexuality receive attention. Though her language and focus in this tract seem more spiritual than scientific, science influenced her investigation into the spiritual side of sexual relations; in particular, she incorporated evolutionary discourse to show how sex would bring humanity to the higher forms of existence desired by spiritualists.

Waisbrooker's analogies to the natural world differ from those previously discussed. She did not employ analogies to prove the unnaturalness of women's status in this particular text; she used them to show how humanity could reach a higher state of existence through embracing the power of sexuality. In one instance, she elaborated:

> The growing belief in the possibility of overcoming Death is also an indication that the time for the commencement of the consummation is close at hand; in illustration of which assertion let us go again to the vegetable kingdom for corroborative evidence. We find that when a tree commences active life in the germ it goes on for a time developing roots, leaves, branches, till finally, when all is ready, it puts forth its blossoms as the promise of fruitage. The blossom is its first thought, so to speak, that fruit is a possibility, and immediately it goes to work to embody that thought—to perfect itself by bearing fruit. (*From Generation* 13–14)

With this analogy, she not only established sexuality as the mechanism to perfection but also asserted that some form of perfection must come before sex commences. In doing so, she related back to the spiritualist goal of overcoming death. Going beyond the procreative function, she clarified a higher purpose of sex as a standard of perfection that would allow humanity to evolve:

> [T]here are those who have caught glimpses of a higher use [of sex] therein than the propagative, and they will not, they cannot, rest till the mystery of this higher use is solved. Going back to the time when organized forms first existed upon this planet we find that the highest in the scale of development were crude compared with the lowest of to-day; not so much, perhaps, in form as in substance, while the distance between them and the highest now upon the earth is so great that we are astonished and naturally ask for the law through which this advance has been made. And upon investigation we learn that sex lies at the base of it all—that the masculine and feminine forces are the factors and sex union the steps in the spiral stairway which Progress has continued to

climb . . . and it is hardly supposable that the greatest blessing which can come to the race through the joint action of these factors has yet been reached. (15–16)

By intertwining the Darwinian goal of progress with the ideal of love, free-love feminists could also allude to spiritual evolution, seeing progress in the species not as the last step but as one more step to an even higher goal. Waisbrooker's language revealed the influence of evolutionary science. She evoked the hierarchy of species and then noted that there may still be a goal above humanity, spiritual growth. Furthermore, it is important that she said, "Sex lies at the base of it all," since she illustrates Horowitz's sex at the "core of being" framework for discussions of sexuality (*Rereading Sex* 9). For Waisbrooker, change could occur only through sex: "It seems, then, that change, improvement . . . can become organic—and thus the base for still greater improvement—only through the law of sex. There is no other way possible" (*From Generation* 21–22). That human beings have focused only on the propagative side of sexuality was one of the most fundamental tenets of Waisbrooker's free-love feminism. She believed, "Sex, then, in its uses is, first, propagative; second, refining; and, lastly, regenerative" (53). On the second use, she contended that sex "can be made a purifier, a refiner to the body" (35), but she did not elaborate on this claim specifically. Nor did she provide specifics on the spiritual side beyond her argument that a spiritual side to sex exists that can lead to the spiritualist goal of regeneration in the afterlife. She acknowledged the lack of details in her argument because it was not about the specifics but about the goal itself. Like Severance, she envisioned a higher evolution but explained that she could not conceive what that higher evolutionary state might be until present customs were reformed. For Waisbrooker, the agitation for free love was the "germ" and just the act of thinking about the higher uses of sex was the "blossom"; but the fruit would not be born until sexual freedom became the rule (13–14).

Lillian Harman also explored "regeneration" in an 1898 speech delivered to the Manhattan Liberal Club. However, her idea of "regeneration" seems different from Waisbrooker's. While Waisbrooker envisioned regeneration in a spiritualist sense, Harman applied the term to what society could do to regenerate itself. In doing so, she recalled the arguments of Herbert Spencer and other devoted followers of social Darwinism. Harman criticized current sexual practices by noting that the church and the law had usurped the power of women by dictating the conditions under which procreation—and therefore progress in the species— took place ("Regeneration," May 20, 145). From this premise, she argued how progress should occur, and her logic recalls earlier free-love feminist texts on the unnatural state of marriage:

> The state has barred the way of evolution, has rendered natural selection of the best human characteristics impossible, by holding together the mismated and preventing those who are adapted to each other from claiming their right to reproductive association. The Church has ever given the lie to the edict, "Whom God hath joined together, let no man put asunder." It has given lip service to the letter, but in spirit it has said, "Whom *Grundy* hath joined together, let no God, let no natural attraction, put asunder." (146)

Harman's evocation of the popular "Grundy" trope solidified her claim: the state and social mores prevented natural evolution when they allowed man-made conceptions of morality to dictate the sexual relations between individuals. When marriage laws forced two "mismated" partners to stay together, they lost the chance of allowing nature to produce the best results. She therefore blamed the state code of morality, particularly idealizations of "virtuous" women reinforced by medical "experts," for the abundance of neglected children in the world. Her logic anticipated the eugenic turn of this particular strand of evolutionary discourse.

Harman also pointed out an important prerequisite to progress in the species: sex education. Attacking the "conspiracy of silence" on sexual matters, she insisted that since the "salvation of our race must rest in the hands of our descendants," the "proper instruction in the sacredness of the sexual functions" became a necessity ("Regeneration," May 27, 154). She thus asserted a unique argument (though common among free-love feminists) in the history of sex education. For Harman, attitudes on sex education that assumed "that the functions of our beings which called our loved ones into existence are so vile, so despicable, that the children born thereof will lose respect for us if we frankly tell them the truth" restrained progress in the race (154). She then returned to free love as the solution with, "It must not be forgotten that only through unobstructed development can evolution do its perfect work, and through growth in freedom only, can come the true regeneration of society. Our work should be to clear the way, to help to remove the debris, the gods and ghosts, the superstitions and prejudices of the past" (155). Therefore, a combination of sex education, female choice, and free love would ensure the regeneration she envisioned. Finally, Harman used evolutionary theory to redefine the roles of women:

People waste a great deal of time in arguing for and against theories of what is "natural" for women. It may be of interest to look back over the pages of history to see the various stages through which they have reached their present development. . . . But because an emotion may be "natural" at one stage of development is no reason why women should feel or simulate it under changed conditions. The tail is "natural" to the tadpole in the pond; but will anyone maintain that therefore the frog must drag a tail around after him as he hops on dry land? ("From My Point of View," March 1900)

In the new era, the woman must shrug off the "tail" of her infancy to become the new sexually emancipated woman. In this evolution, the old mores and ideas of what is natural for women will become adapted to new conditions.

The Tree in the Forest: The "Natural" State for Women

Two free-love feminist texts around the turn of the century illustrate how the focus on free love as a form of social evolution became *the* most important line of argument to support women's sexual freedom. Hulda Potter-Loomis's work *Social Freedom: The Most Important Factor in Human Evolution*, published by Moses Harman around 1890, encapsulated the arguments other free-love feminists explored.[5] A treatise for the abolition of institutional marriage and the establishment of sex education, it contained lines of argument by then common to free-love feminist texts: that marriage was outdated and unsuited to further evolution and that the husband controlled "the sex organs" of the wife. But it also brought a slight shift to the discussion of women's sexuality in an evolutionary framework: Potter-Loomis discussed progress not as producing a more evolved race but as a result of the power of women's sexuality.

Potter-Loomis began with the premise that human beings have advanced past the stifling institution of marriage and that choosing partners and sexual conditions in freedom, without the standards set by human society, would help them advance further, both morally and intellectually. She named happiness as the "chief end and aim of human existence" and showed how marriage hinders this particular aim. Employing the analogy to the natural world as her warrant, Potter-Loomis objected, "No one can be happy while chafing under the restrictions which society now enforces upon the strongest and, without doubt, the best instincts of our nature, namely, that which manifests itself through the affections" (7). Under her logic, embracing this natural sexual "instinct" would forsake the limits set upon choice of partners and conform to natural laws.

Her critique also alluded to how the medical establishment restrained women's sexuality by denouncing women who embraced it as "unnatural." For women to acknowledge their sexuality and act on their feelings would be the "natural" state for Potter-Loomis, since, as Darwin's analogy warranted, females in the animal kingdom were not thus restrained.

Potter-Loomis elaborated that man has controlled nature and hindered progress: "Thus, unconsciously does man overreach himself when he presumes to set up limitations to nature, for nature knows no limitation and will not be restrained without causing much havoc and destruction" (8). Her argument is illustrated through a comparison with a tree growing free on its own but restrained and fighting for light while in the forest: "There the tree is forced to conform to its environment and the limitations placed upon it by its surrounding companions" (13). The tree is "forced to modify its natural habit" because of its surroundings. She concluded, "The tree, however, has less power to choose or reject its own environment than we have" (13). This metaphor linking sexual freedom with freedom in growth illustrates how the natural instincts of humans are restricted by community standards, like marriage. Extending the metaphor, Potter-Loomis noted that "unnecessary laws" and public opinion restrain the tree: "We grow to be much like the trees in the forest, differing from each other only according to the light we can get which struggles through intermingling of the heavy foliage of traditions, creeds and dogmas" (13). Laws and public opinion covered women's sexuality, allowing her to grow only so much. But women have power that the tree does not: the power to choose. Moreover, Potter-Loomis's claims demonstrate how feminists could adapt the writings of antifeminists, such as Herbert Spencer, to their aims. Consider, for example, Spencer's evolutionary narrative in his essay "Social Statistics":

> The modifications mankind have undergone, and are still undergoing, result from a law underlying the whole organic creation; and provided the human race continues, and the constitution of things remains the same, those modifications must end in completeness. As surely as the tree becomes bulky when it stands alone, and slender if one of a group; as surely as the same creature assumes the different forms of a carthorse and a race-horse, according as its habits demand strength or speed . . . as surely as a passion grows by indulgence and diminishes when restrained . . . so surely must the human faculties be moulded into complete fitness for the social state; so surely must the things we call evil and immorality disappear; so surely must man become perfect. (Spencer, *Herbert Spencer* 13)

His theory on humanity's ability to aid evolution became a founding principle of later feminist arguments. Potter-Loomis rewrote the tree metaphor popular with both Darwin and Spencer to show that humans have more agency than the tree. Human beings have the power to change their environment and become agents to aid evolution. Her extended metaphor of sexuality as the tree, which carried throughout her work, exemplified her claim that social freedom remains the most important factor in human evolution; women are restrained unless they can express their sexuality in a healthy way. Those who survive will be the ones who express their natural sexual instincts. Her comment that "the tree . . . has less power to choose or reject its own environment than we have" also evokes the questions on agency that loom throughout Darwin's work (Beer xxiv). Like Spencer, she made humanity the agent but specified the agency of women.

Furthermore, Potter-Loomis emphasized how social freedom allows "desire" to be "the sole guide" (14), not marriage. She indicated that outdated ideas of the sexual appetites of women restrain progress (15), shifting the argument to make women's sexual appetite the focus. Women need to act on their desires in a natural way and thus allow progress. While she alluded to "progress" being healthy children, she concentrated more on demonstrating that women's sexuality is a power for good, and she separated sexual desire from the desire to have children. Therefore, her argument differs from that of other free-love feminists who viewed the outcome of sexuality as progress, often defined as better, healthier children. Instead, acting on sexual desires was the progress Potter-Loomis sought, and the children question was incidental. Moses Harman, however, published her pamphlet with an appendix titled "The Right to be Born Well" (22), bringing the discourse back to better children as the desired goal.

Like Potter-Loomis's pamphlet, Dora Forster's 1905 pamphlet, *Sex Radicalism as seen by an Emancipated Woman of the New Time*, illustrates how Darwinian discourse had changed the rhetorical situation for speaking about sex. For Potter-Loomis and Forster, the exigence was Darwin's work. Other free-love feminists had used Darwinian warrants to respond to other exigencies, but these two rhetors responded to the situation of a conversation about Darwin to insert a women's rights argument into that conversation.[6] Forster's case used evolution as a premise for arguing the more enlightened view of sexuality. She took as her premise that "most of our sex problems begin in false custom" (46). Forster's arguments were similar to Potter-Loomis's in looking more specifically at sexual "instincts" and viewing sexual desire as separate from maternal desire. Like Potter-Loomis, Forster viewed sex as vital to happiness, which was the key in the evolution of the race: "We think, perhaps, that the falling in love of human beings is a mean trick of Nature's, to ensure the reproduction of the race: not so: children are the product, no doubt, but the byproduct is yet more important—the efficiency of the race stimulated by the love passion. And efficiency means happiness" (14–15). Her logic blended scientific language with the ideals of love and companionate marriages characterizing the utopian free lovers at mid-century. The new free-love feminism relied on newer values—those of science—and differentiated the free-love feminism of the late nineteenth century from earlier, perfectionist incarnations. Under Forster's logic, sexual partnerships do not revolve around an instinct to propagate, and this absence is a "true sign of high development and success" (15). The value of love, for Forster, demonstrated that progress had occurred. She employed Darwin's language of struggle to point out how humans have evolved over animals in claiming a purpose to sex other than procreation:

> The puritans have concerned themselves chiefly with the propagative function. This, to borrow one of their own expressions, is the *animal* side of sex. Plenty of children is the plan of the lower animals, and of early man, to hold their own against outsiders. "Happy is the man who hath his quiver full of them." But we have now found other things better than our children to hurl at our enemies; and military skill first, and general scientific ability later, are more valuable than prolificness in the competition of races. Not children in quantity, but quality in children. (40–41)

Forster's argument becomes eugenic here with the idea that progress can be measured through "quality in children," an argument popular by 1905.

Most startling about Forster's rhetorical strategies are the ways she used evolutionary theory to justify her unique—even among free-love feminists—arguments for variety in sexual relations. While other free-love feminists rejected the ideals of variety produced by men and instead advocated monogamy, Forster supported variety and turned it into a free-love feminist ideal. To do so, she defined variety as a step in the evolution of sexual relationships. Beginning with the premise that monogamy, or what she called "exclusive love," was an outdated concept, she provided justification for moving from the "passing ideal" to the "coming ideal": a more evolved state where exclusive love is a relic of "puritan" ideals and variety becomes the more sensible, and natural, way of organizing sexual relations. A series of articles printed in *Lucifer* in 1903 elaborated her arguments for variety and depended on Darwinian discourse.

For example, naming "exclusive love" as a "puritan" ideal, she showed how humanity should have evolved past it: "Exclusive sex possession in marriage is a marked characteristic of the most primitive races of men, and also of the man-like apes. . . . If the course of evolution were towards exclusivism away from varietism, we should find promiscuity flourishing in the lowest races and in the primitive ages of human history" ("Passing Ideal"). She thus reversed the logic of earlier free-love feminists: since "exclusive" love was found in "primitive" races, it demonstrates not that humanity should have it as well but that humanity should evolve past it. Thus, exclusivity should not be an ideal of an evolved species.

In "Jealousy and Violent Theorizing," Forster looked at Darwin's arguments on sexual selection to support variety as a more evolved state, since, she argued, Darwin was never refuted on the statement that "the males who were willing and able to fight and overcome their rivals, that is, the jealously pugnacious, were most successful in leaving numerous offspring; and thus through countless generations in each successive type, from fishes and even lower animals up to anthropoid apes, the heredity of jealousy has been handed on" (57). She also pointed out, "Of course we all must admit with Darwin that 'the manner of development of the marriage tie is an obscure subject'; but it is certainly no violent assumption that marriage is fundamentally connected with jealousy" (57). Forster's reading of *The Descent of Man* provided her main evidence, but unlike the feminists discussed above, she focused not on the female choice issue but on its more problematic—from a feminist standpoint—aspects. Her use of such logic confirmed how such antifeminist views could still be used in more radical feminist arguments.

Finally, Forster's support for variety relied on the premise that one person cannot provide everything a partner needs or desires: "We must face the fact that in highly developed races, character and temperament are so various that bodily and mental adaptation to another can often not be found in the same individual" (10). Using language that recalled evolutionary theory, such as references to "highly developed races" and "adaptation," Forster made her unpopular arguments more acceptable to an audience of *Lucifer* readers who favored the scientific over the superstitious. What Forster's specific use of Darwin demonstrated was how the use of evolutionary discourse in free-love feminism shifted. Her repeated references to "savage" cultures and the practices of more evolved people reflected the more problematic elements of Darwinian discourse at the turn of the century. Thus, we begin to see the evolution of free-love feminist rhetoric.

Evolutionary Rhetorics

In all of their specific "Darwinesque" lines of argument, the question of agency arises, whether it is the agency of nature over humanity, the agency of females, or the agency that causes progress to occur. The question of agency, left ambiguous or unanswered in some of Darwin's writings, receives an answer in social Darwinist discourse. Free-love feminist arguments divided agency between nature and those who could steer it in the right direction. For example, echoing social Darwinism, Woodhull argued that it was humanity's job to aid evolution (Woodhull Martin, *Rapid Multiplication* 19), and she decreed the superiority of the laws of nature to the laws of government (*"And the Truth Shall Make You Free"* 19). Similarly, Waisbrooker maintained that nature must be aided by the external conditions of freedom (*Eugenics* 8–9). Thus, free-love feminist logic seemed to appropriate what some viewed as the problematic agent in Darwin's theory (Beer xxiv); it made humans, specifically women, the agents to aid evolution. Their arguments supposed that only when humanity shrugged off its false customs and limits would natural evolutionary progress occur. For them, free love represented progress over false customs and led to progress in the race through creating "quality" children.

According to free-love feminists, for women to evolve from the "sex slaves" of men under unjust and unnatural laws to emancipated new women with complete autonomy, they needed to recognize the unnatural limitations placed on them since, as one *Lucifer* editorial claimed, "All progress must begin in dissatisfaction. The moner, the protozoan, the first forms of animal or vegetable life must have been dissatisfied with their state of development else they would have remained . . . simple cells, and all their generations after them" ("Dissatisfaction"). For free-love feminists such as Lille D. White, women would have to recognize and overcome their "dissatisfaction" in order to evolve. In her 1893 article "Women's Work," White entreated the women of the nineteenth century to evolve beyond the epithets that might be thrown at them if they struggled to end their dissatisfaction; they could not evolve into the emancipated woman by standing still. Thus, White specifically noted the agency of women to aid their own evolution. However, this (r)evolutionary discourse of free-love feminism evolved into something quite different by the end of the century, replacing the goals of free-love feminism with something more sinister. However, to understand that shift, we need to look at how other scientific disciplines aided their (r)evolutionary rhetoric.

3

Physiology: Rewriting the Body and Sexual Desire

To sum up the best conditions for health and long life which all can now attain: First: prospective fathers and mothers should be in perfect health from right living, not only as regards diet, exercise, rest, personal cleanliness, cheerfulness and all hygienic conditions, but also in regard to their relations with the other. The mother should maintain the control of her own person under an intelligent comprehension of sexual science.

—Juliet Severance, *A Lecture on Life and Health, or How to Live a Century*, 1881

When early-twenty-first century women need their "embarrassing questions" answered, they go to daytime talk shows like *The Oprah Winfrey Show* and *The Dr. Oz Show* to hear doctors explain the inner workings of the body using computer-generated visual aids, give advice on personal hygiene and diet, and answer questions regarding how much sun-tanning is harmful, what constitutes a healthy bowel movement, and how often women should douche. When such topics are raised, Oprah will sympathize with male guests in the audience who probably feel uncomfortable listening to such intimate discussions. When early-nineteenth-century women wanted to know more about the body, they went to lectures hosted by ladies' physiological societies to hear Dr. Mary Gove explain the inner workings of the body using her own unique visual aids, such as mannequins and a corset placed over her clothes to demonstrate the harms of tight lacing (Passet, *Sex Radicals* 22), give advice on personal hygiene and diet, and address issues of how much exercise women should get, whether masturbation is harmful, and how to maintain the health of the sexual and reproductive organs. When topics particular to women were raised, there was no uncomfortable male presence—these lectures were led by women and for women only.

PHYSIOLOGY

Ladies' physiological societies did not need a male Dr. Oz to answer their questions; they had Dr. Mary Gove with her medical knowledge and appropriate gender.

Physician Sylvester Graham and reformer William Alcott felt inappropriate lecturing about physiology to female audiences, so they invited Gove to speak instead, beginning a prolific lecturing career for this female physician and reformer in the 1830s that stretched into the 1850s (Passet, *Sex Radicals* 22). Her lectures sponsored by the Ladies' Physiological Society of Boston and the Ladies' Physiological Society of New York, among others, drew large crowds from 400 to 500 listeners per lecture (Silver-Isenstadt 35–40, 38).[1] The numbers of women gathering to hear Gove's lectures on anatomy, physiology, and hygiene attest to the intense public interest in these topics. Throughout the nineteenth century, physiology lectures drew crowds, and popular health manuals explaining the body became best sellers. Physiology became the central discipline of the medical schools, as well as a prominent discipline in many women's colleges.

The term "physiology" itself came to have multiple meanings throughout the nineteenth century, most of them associated with discussions of gender and sexuality. The term was often placed side by side with "anatomy," particularly in medical uses, as the study of the body and how it works. But writers and lecturers also used "physiology" synonymously with "hygiene," and the discipline of physiology entered women's colleges as "hygiene" and health reform, which encompassed both knowledge of the human body's organs and functions and how these functions produced health (Appel 307). Significantly, the most popular topics in these physiology and hygiene classes were sex and reproduction (307), showing how the study of physiology and hygiene seemed primarily concerned with sexual matters. The conflation of these two terms, "physiology" and "hygiene," shows that many believed that the discipline of physiology went hand-in-hand with prescriptive rules for living, and there was little distinction between the study of the body and the study of "rules" for hygienic living (307). Often, evoking the term "physiology" meant offering advice on specific sexual behaviors, as evidenced in the title of reformer Robert Dale Owen's 1859 book *Moral Physiology*, a Malthusian text that advised on both sexual behavior and birth control. Employing the term "physiology" often created a specific reform ideology, though not all reformers agreed on what constituted "physiological" behavior. The term "physiology" was also associated with a specific genre of writing popular at midcentury, that of "reform physiology."[2] Here the term seemed to mean knowledge of sexual matters itself (Horowitz, *Reread-ing Sex* 86).

In popular discourses, physiology became integral to arguments for women's rights. Explanations of physiology often became opportunities to support women's rights as a natural extension of the topic. For Mary Gove, explaining the parts of the body was not enough; she also had to explain how these body parts could be harmed, not only by restrictions on women, such as sedentary lifestyles and tight lacing, but also by the inequalities in the marriage system. Similar to Gove's message with its reformist agenda, Lillian Welch's physiology lectures at Goucher College urged the need for suffrage "as a tool for securing conditions in the community favorable to health" (qtd. in Appel 312). Marriage re-forms advocated by free-love feminists became connected with women's health through these discourses on physiology. As physician and free-love feminist Juliet Severance illustrated in *A Lecture on Life and Health*, diet, exercise, and "control of her own person" all became interconnected with and central to securing and maintaining women's health (29). This chapter shows how reading the claims of free-love feminists against the larger conversations on physiology among physicians reveals the logic of arguments grounding sexual freedom in women's health.

The Science of Nineteenth-Century Physiology

Unlike other scientific disciplines discussed in this project, nineteenth-century physiology did not offer new knowledge or groundbreaking dis-coveries. The discipline known as physiology in the nineteenth century often seems unrecognizable from a contemporary perspective, since we are looking back at the exact moment when science and medicine began to branch off into different specializations. For much of the nineteenth century, physiology combined different studies of the body. The modern discipline of physiology, which views the body as a series of chemical processes, developed in the late nineteenth century as a result of new experimental methods focused on laboratory findings.[3] The relevance of physiology to women's rights, though, did not come out of a laboratory but out of a rethinking of the body that began in the eighteenth century, which played a large role in nineteenth-century conceptions of sexuality, particularly the construction of a gendered, female sexuality.

One prominent debate during the Enlightenment that spilled over into nineteenth-century physiology concerned the views of the mechanists, also known as materialists, versus the vitalists. Mechanists viewed the body as a machine, with each part working to aid the body's processes.

For vitalists, the body's inner workings were affected by a "life" force (Mayr, *Growth* 114). Proponents of both mechanism and vitalism focused on classifying the body's organs and their functions (Bowler and Morus 170). However, they differed in their conceptions of the "laws" that produced bodily processes. For vitalists, such as Swiss biologist Albrecht von Haller writing in 1747 and Juliet Severance writing in 1876, disease was defined as an absence of "vital action" or "abnormal vital action" (Severance, *Lecture on the Philosophy of Disease* 4). By the end of the nineteenth century, the discovery of bacteria would refute some of these beliefs. Even before this discovery, however, vitalism lost popularity, as many physicians turned toward mechanist views and to physics and chemistry to explain the body's processes (Bowler and Morus 181). However, as we will see through analysis of the texts discussed in this chapter, both mechanist and vitalist philosophies played a role in nineteenth-century medical and popular debates over the physiology of women's sexuality.

Another important influence on nineteenth-century physiology came from competing conceptions of the relationship of mind and body. Under Enlightenment materialist views, there was little distinction between the psychological and the physiological: the body "became the seat of sensation and so the source of consciousness. . . . Touch was the prime sense" (Porter and Hall 20). This idea of "sensibility" would play a large role in discussions of sexuality. Others discussing the body sought to distinguish among its sensations. In 1747, von Haller published *First Lines in Physiology*, which promoted a new view of the distinction between the "parts of the body that are irritable (contract when touched) and those that are sensible (transmit sensations through the nerves to the brain)" (Bowler and Morus 174–75). As this view combined with Marie-Francois-Xavier Bichat's views of the systems of tissues, published in *Anatomie Generale* in 1801, wherein different tissues had specific "vital functions," sexuality became associated primarily with the nervous system (Bowler and Morus 175). That is, nineteenth-century thinkers concluded that sexuality came from an organism's sensibility that was a product of its nervous system, ruled in turn by the mind. Therefore, they emphasized the mind's power in producing sexual feelings in the body (Porter and Hall 108), an emphasis that became integral to nineteenth-century arguments that refuted the "passionless" ideology, such as Elizabeth Blackwell's refutation, discussed below. The idea of sexuality as a function of the nervous system also led to antifeminist arguments regarding "nervous" and "hysteric" women. But, by situating sexuality within the nervous system, sexuality also became associated with the system that enabled the body to perform as an organized whole (Jordanova 171). Later free-love feminists accentuated the role of sexuality in the individual, exploiting this association.

Connected to these debates was the law of conservation of energy, which emerged in the late eighteenth century. Applications of this law to sexuality during the nineteenth century produced some popular misconceptions: fears of men losing energy through ejaculation and fears of excessive sexual activity causing "nervous disorders" resulted from a combination of the law of conservation of energy, vitalist views, and the association of sexuality with the nervous system. These fears were famously extended to cover women's menstrual cycles, notably by physician Edward Clarke. Under his logic, women's menstruation was a loss of energy. Clarke used this notion as support for limiting the education of females in his bestselling 1873 book, *Sex in Education: A Fair Chance for Girls*.[4] He argued that educating females in the same manner as males would harm their reproductive organs, since energy would be drawn from the activity of menstruation to intellectual activity in the brain. These ideas persisted throughout the late nineteenth century, but they were also contested.[5]

Another question vexing nineteenth-century medical science was the nature of female pleasure and orgasm. Earlier thinkers maintained that female orgasm was required for conception, an idea that dates back to classical sources and persisted in sex manuals from the 1600s. In the 1820s, one physician cited females who conceived from rape as clear evidence that orgasm was not required, requiring revision of the laws concerning rape that negated a rape charge if the victim conceived (Laqueur 161–62). Many nineteenth-century physicians accepted that female orgasm was not required for conception. However, since earlier theorists had defined female orgasm as, like men's, a discharge, questions over whether women could achieve orgasm became central to nineteenth-century debates. The rise of the "passionless" ideology was of course tied to social and economic factors in the nineteenth century, as has been well documented. But there was no unified consensus concerning women's sexuality in the medical community.[6]

The Scientific and the Social in Medical Discourse on Women's Bodies

The immense interest in anatomy and physiology during the nineteenth century spurred a wealth of resources responding to this interest that illustrates the multifaceted nature of debates on women's sexuality, including lectures to popular audiences and to women's societies, textbooks and marriage manuals, and pamphlets advocating "reform physiology." These texts, written by physicians, both informed their audiences about the body and exhorted audiences to advocate women's rights, creating a hybrid genre with specific rhetorical negotiations common to all of the texts, whether written by a male or female physician.

The medical advice book was not a new genre, but it did undergo a new incarnation during the nineteenth century. Older advice books dating back to the seventeenth century, such as *Aristotle's Master-piece* first published in 1684, and Nicolas Venette's *Tableau de L'amour Conjugal*, first published in 1686 and later translated as *Conjugal Love, or the Pleasures of the Marriage Bed* in the 1780s, were still widely circulated in the first half of the nineteenth century, though they were edited to reflect the values of the time. *Aristotle's Master-piece*, not written by Aristotle, of course, but by an anonymous compiler, was a sex manual; however, its format differed from the kind of advice popular in nineteenth-century sexual advice books since it had no advice about "proper" sexual behavior but rather treated sex as the means to procreation (Porter and Hall 39, 49). Venette's text, like *Aristotle's Master-piece*, was less concerned with the moral dimensions of sexuality than with the structure and functions of the sexual organs and the connection between sex and love (69). Venette's text also reflected the attitudes of his time period, such as a belief in the similarity in the sexual appetites of males and females (76), and it even advised women on how to fake virginity (80–81).[7] For the first few decades of the nineteenth century, *Aristotle's Master-piece* was widely held as the authoritative text on sexual matters (126). It and Venette's book also previewed the nineteenth-century genre produced by physicians, which added a new component: advice on sexual behavior, hygiene, and lifestyle choices, as well as birth control in some texts. In fact, this new hybrid genre incorporated reform arguments more so than its predecessors, and one of these reforms included women's rights. While most of these physiology texts claimed their "sole purpose is to instruct the masses of the people on those subjects which have hitherto been to them as a sealed book" (Trall iv), reform played a prominent role in the purpose of these texts; physicians writing on physiology for lay audiences expected not only to change perceptions of sexuality but also to change sexual behaviors.

Sexual physiology texts also participated in the growing debate over the existence and nature of women's sexuality. Although the dominant medical culture often denied the sexuality of women—such as physician

William Acton, whose statement that women do not have sexual feelings is often reprinted in contemporary criticism—the debate was complicated by many in the more reformist medical sects, such as those advocating water cure. These homeopathic movements worked to distinguish themselves from the "allopaths," who promoted harsher drugs and surgeries; the homeopaths offered more natural remedies and advice on prevention.[8] They also tended to "naturalize" women's bodies and functions, in contrast to the images of women as "diseased" and "defective."

These texts also illustrate the multiple meanings of "physiology" in the nineteenth-century and what writers may have meant when they used the term. In addition to the meanings of physiology as a scientific discipline and as hygiene, we see physicians employing the term as an adverb and adjective, such as when they implored their readers to live "physiologically." Often, "physiology" seems to be used as a synonym for "natural" in nineteenth-century texts, in order to reveal the social constructions that affected ideologies of sex and the body. For example, when Mary Gove railed against the fashion of tight lacing in 1846, she urged that fashions change "in accordance with the physiological laws of our nature" (*Lectures to Women* 70), emphasizing the unnaturalness of these fashions. In addition, Dr. John M. Scudder's *On the Reproductive Organs, and the Venereal*, published in 1873, asserted that physiology is a "better guide than religion" on sexual matters (20). These uses of the term echo those of the social reformers who juxtaposed "natural" with "unnatural" effects on sexuality imposed by laws and the church. To live "physiologically" in this context was to acknowledge the body's needs without interference from church guidelines that limited the body's needs or from constricting popular practices, such as fashion. Emphasizing "physiology" as the guide to a natural way of living then associated specific lifestyle choices with science.

Not all writers, however, necessarily had the same meaning when they advocated "physiological" behavior. Edward Clarke's famous argument in 1873 against educating women in the same manner as men employed the term "physiology" in several ways, using it as a noun, adjective, and adverb. When he introduced the problem of sex in education, he advocated consulting "physiology" rather than ethics (12), evoking the meanings of "physiology" as the science of the body and as a way of living. His uses of the term also suggest "natural," as when he protested against "un-physiological work" (103). "Physiology" is personified in his text, as when he insisted that "physiology protests against" coeducation (127) and in his conclusion when he wrote, "Physiology condemns the identical and pleads for the appropriate education of the sexes" (181). Clarke's uses of the term show that "physiology" could justify a specific way to live, which in his case meant conforming to specific gender roles. To Clarke, to live "physiologically" would also mean "natural behavior"—conforming to what the body needs—which he defined much differently than Gove and Trall did. Thus, different factions in the debate over physiology employed the term in similar ways but for different goals.

These new nineteenth-century texts also faced constraints that influenced the rhetorical negotiations of their authors, including the growing divisiveness in the medical profession caused by the increasing professionalization of the discipline, and pressures exerted by the government on the dissemination of sexual knowledge. As medicine became more professionalized, requiring licenses by the end of the century, many physicians in homeopathic sects and many female physicians were viewed with wariness by the new dominant medical culture. In particular, the "allopaths" criticized the increasing popularity of medical texts available to the public that not only provided information on physiology but also empowered patients by giving them medical knowledge and encouraging them to treat themselves. In his address to the Annual Meeting of the Association of Medical Editors on May 1, 1871, Dr. Horatio Storer, a pioneer in the field of gynecology, reacted against the increasing trends toward popularization, noting that "we would not advise every man to be his own physician" (357), as many water-cure practitioners did, and that "the present extreme tendency to popularize, upon the part of our more prominent professional writers, may bring dignity and permanence of standing into jeopardy" (356). Storer's backlash shows the threatening nature of these popularized medical theories as they gained cultural prominence. Water-cure physicians reacted to such criticism with a rhetoric of public rights, such as Dr. Juliet Severance's argument in "The Medical Monopoly," where she advocated the right of the public to choose their own physicians and methods of healing, in the face of new laws restricting certain medical practices (*Marriage* 36). Governments also put pressure on medical popularizers, as in the 1846 obscenity trial of physician Frederick Hollick and in the laws instituted by Anthony Comstock in 1873 that prohibited "obscene" materials from being sent through the mail. Physicians then defended their right to disseminate such knowledge in their works, leading to one common rhetorical device among these texts.[9] For example, Scudder, whose 1873 medical textbook was quoted by Victoria Woodhull, prefaced his advice by defending his goal to make medical information available to the public. A proponent

of the eclectic school of medicine that combined the methods of allopathic and homeopathic medicine (or the use of surgery and drugs with
the use of natural remedies), Scudder believed, like the homeopaths, in
the power of physicians as teachers of the public and disseminators of
physiological information. He advised his audience of medical students
to promote these aims and addressed the constraints against his purpose
in his first few lines:

> The author begs leave to introduce this work to the reader as a plain
> statement of facts which deserve careful consideration. It may shock the
> modesty of some, but it is to be hoped that the majority may see the ne-
> cessity and the great good which may grow out of this study. Physicians
> have manifested a degree of *mock* modesty with reference to diseases of
> the reproductive function, which has prevented their investigation, and
> turned the many sufferers over to the hands of advertising quacks and
> charlatans. There may be some excuse for this in the "innate" modesty
> of man, but the time has now come when an intelligent knowledge is
> demanded. (v; emphasis in original)

The call for the reader to shrug off his or her modesty appears to be a
trope in many of these texts, one that seems based more in the writers' interpretation of the reader than in the actual readers; "reform physiology"
texts were often best sellers. Scudder asserted a kind of Bitzerian "imper-
fection" exigence by claiming that many physicians were not equipped
to deal with sexual problems, and, thus, he stressed the timeliness of his
work, especially in the face of increasing numbers of persons suffering
from sexually transmitted diseases. This appeal evoked a kind of "public
good" exigence. In addition, recognizing some of the controversy over
publishing works about sex in his insistence that his book was a "plain
statement of facts," he constructed his audience as the intelligent factions
of the medical community who would not call his book "obscene" because
of false modesty. Scudder would have been aware of physicians who put
forth the kind of information contained in his text and went on trial
for obscenity, such as Frederick Hollick, who asserted more liberating
views of sexuality in his popular marriage guides and lectures.[10] Scudder, whom one historian notes as the "author of two of the most sexually
explicit books ever to go to press in the nineteenth century" (Leach 62),
provided vivid descriptions and pictures of the sexual organs that may
have raised the ire of the obscenity watchdogs, so he constructed his
audience as intelligent in contrast to those like Comstock who would
call his work obscene. Comstock, however, seemed to most frequently

attack works that were too specific in their descriptions of birth control methods, so it may not have been the sexual material itself that led him to label a book "obscene."

Thus, these advice books and lectures held constraints even for men who authored them. With women physicians as authors, these constraints increased (Skinner, "'Purity of Truth'" 105). The genre of the physiology lecture or advice book provided an opportunity for physicians to recruit the public in their campaign for health and to change attitudes about sexuality and sexual practices. The following analyses show these medical writers responding to these constraints, offering specific definitions of women's physiology that revised the notion of women as "hysteric" and/ or "passionless," which also warranted the claims of free-love feminists.

Mary Gove (Nichols): Advice to Ladies

Mary Gove, later Mary Gove Nichols, intertwined advice on healthy lifestyles with a women's rights agenda and urged women to take control of their own health and well-being. Her *Lectures to Women on Anatomy and Physiology*, published in 1846 and based on lectures she delivered to women's physiological societies in the 1830s and 1840s, argued for causes such as dress reform, healthy diet, education for girls (particularly physical education), and exercise. Each lecture was divided by parts of the body: she taught on the formation of the bones, on muscles, and on the nervous system, where she placed her discussion of sexuality. Within each section of the lectures, Gove explained parts of the body and how they work, but each section also had a reform purpose buried within it. Thus, her arguments may seem less explicit than later physiology texts that devote specific sections to arguments for women's rights. For example, in the section on bones, she tells stories of quacks who could injure broken bones even more. However, she noted that women who were educated on the bones of the arm, for instance, would be able to tell when a person was setting them incorrectly. She then moved from an argument that women should know how the bones work to an argument for women's rights:

> Let woman use her energies, let her attain that moral and intellectual elevation which is her right. Let her attain that height where men cannot look down upon her, if they would. . . . Let her nobly resolve that she will have science, that she will be no longer a plaything. . . . When woman thus arises in the greatness of her intellectual strength, then there will be a new era in the history of our world. (49–50)

Gove accommodated the genre of the physiology lecture or advice book to the constraints she faced as a woman physician addressing these issues.

Gove often downplayed her ethos as an expert and invited audience participation in her argument, which conformed to her agenda to have women take responsibility for their own health. Several times, she strategically underplayed her role in order to let the evidence speak for itself, suggesting, "I need not attempt to demonstrate to you the truth of this assertion; your own good sense will lead you to assent to its truth at once" (15). When she provided drawings of the natural female chest to compare with a compressed one in order to support an argument for dress reform, she said that she would allow the drawings to speak for themselves (88). These gaps in the argument that she left the audience to fill show that she empowered her audience and thus strengthened her ethos in positioning herself as a collaborator with her audience.

Gove's rhetorical negotiations empowered the audience to take responsibility for their own health. She condemned the "authority" of the mainstream medical establishment with her mantra, "The end at which physiologists aim is prevention. We should live in such a manner as not to need medicine of any kind" (22), reflecting her homeopathic ideals. Her main premise—that good habits lead to good health (31)—is clearly accepted medical knowledge today. Gove's redefinitions of health and disease, and definition of the water-cure system itself, stressed the power of nature over "medicine." However, she did not turn away from science in her redefinition of what medicine is, but redefined science itself. In her book *A Woman's Work in Water Cure and Sanitary Education*, she exclaimed, "The water-cure treatment is a scientific application of the principles of nature in the cure of disease. It changes conditions, removes or promotes the removal of . . . matters laid up in the system, cleanses, and invigorates. It is the handmaid of nature and the minister of health" (17). Thus, her redefinition of the field of medicine made it not an interventionist strategy but a "handmaid" of nature. In emphasizing the role of nature, she gave the audience the power to govern their own health through adherence to what she called the "laws of health." She stressed that practicing water cure did not just embrace the treatments of the physician (which included cold-water sheets and the like). The patient had to be involved in the process of restoring and maintaining health. As she explained, water cure worked only when diet and regimen were "also in accordance with the laws of health" (235).

Countering perceptions of women as naturally weak, Gove attributed female illnesses to habits and atmosphere, arguing that women should have fresh air, exercise, and stimulation. This connection between environment and physiology was particularly emphasized during the Enlightenment, when the environment's impact on the body was intensely studied (Jordanova 162). Gove, like other nineteenth-century physicians, saw poor habits and environment as factors in ill health. She wrote, "Females are more particularly victims [of disease] than males, as the customs of society deny them out-door exercise and make them, in many instances, mere dolls and pretty things" (*Lectures to Women* 26). Here, Gove refuted arguments that women are naturally weaker, attributing illness to "customs of society" rather than to nature. Thus, for Gove, ill health was something women could control and prevent, a line of argument that empowered her female audiences. Using the same logic employed by physicians writing more antifeminist arguments about physiology, Gove attempted to define the "natural" condition as a "healthy" one in order to make women view their bodies' functions as natural rather than "sick" or "weak." She asserted:

> The science of health is based upon a sound physiology—a study of nature and the laws of life . . . but the conditions of health and the causes of disease are simple and easily understood: health is a natural condition; disease unnatural. Health is simple; disease complex and difficult. Health is the result of the regular and orderly performance of the functions of life, and gives vigor and enjoyment; disease is disorder, exhaustion, and the effort of nature to overcome evil. (Gove Nichols, *Woman's Work* 14)

Defining health as the natural state and juxtaposing it with disease as the unnatural state, Gove redefined women's physiology and refuted arguments that women should be restricted from certain activities because of their physiology. She positioned disease as an outside force rather than an innate state, joining together a more "vitalist" philosophy with the increasing focus on environment in medical texts. In contrasting the terms "disease" and "health," Gove reversed the dichotomy attempted by some physicians, a tactic also used in free-love feminist arguments. Gove also defined the state of health as incorporating "vigor" to counter medical advice that encouraged women to stay within their sphere to avoid damage to their "delicate" conditions.

Water-cure physicians also refuted ideas that women's sexual and reproductive functions kept them sickly and redefined these processes as natural. As Gove explained in 1850, "Gestation and parturition are as natural functions as those of digestion" (qtd. in Cayleff 56). Menstruation and pregnancy are not "pathological conditions" but natural ones that should not cause women to be ill or delicate. Gove, in fact, stressed the importance of physical activity during these times (Gove Nichols, *Woman's Work* 14–15). But, Gove's discussions of sexuality within explanations of the nervous system also reflected, rather than contested, the scientific discourse of the time. For example, she was concerned about masturbation leading to ill health and other nervous conditions, ideas based on interpretations of the law of conservation of energy.[11] However, contrary to the views that only abnormal women had sexual feelings, she stressed that it was abnormal for women to be without these passions. She even noted the importance of sexual activity and sexual pleasure to women's health, saying that sex "exercised according to the dictates of nature, or of reason, and of virtue" has "a beneficial influence upon the health and longevity of the system" (*Lectures to Women* 172). Other physicians, such as Russell Trall, also took up this line of argument, exclaiming that "the sexual orgasm on the part of the female is just as normal as on the part of the male" (Trall 69). Gove extended these lines of argument in her writings on free love, and later free-love feminists relied on her important redefinitions of women's physiology and sexual health.

Russell Trall: Emphasizing the Natural

Russell Trall (1812–77), an adversary of Gove Nichols since they operated competing medical schools, also practiced water cure and espoused similar arguments. Born in Vernon, Connecticut, Trall earned his medical degree at Albany Medical College and practiced medicine in New York City. He promoted temperance, vegetarianism, dress reform, and the education of women as physicians, as did Gove and Sylvester Graham. Trall opened the second water-cure establishment in the United States in 1844, and he also founded several water-cure medical schools that gave degrees to women. Trall's water-cure philosophy emphasized the naturalness of women's bodies, and he became a mentor of free-love feminist Juliet Severance in her water-cure medical practice (Passet, *Sex Radicals* 126), though not in her free-love ideologies—Trall condemned free love and used Mary Gove Nichols's advocacy of it against her. In his best-selling advice book, *Sexual Physiology: A Scientific and Popular Exposition of the Fundamental Problems in Sociology*, first published in 1866, Trall endorsed a view of women's physiology as natural rather than "diseased" or "hysteric." Trall's appeals to ethos placed him as a mediator between the scientific medical community and the public. He presented his work as filling a void in the public's knowledge of sexual physiology and claimed that his book was, to his knowledge, the "first attempt to popularize, in a scientific work, the subject of Sexual Physiology" (iv), which discounted Gove's earlier work.

As many historians have noted, the nineteenth century saw a rise in diagnoses of "hysteria," often associated with sexuality, with some physicians viewing women as naturally weak and prone to diseases and defining them by their physiology, particularly their reproductive organs.[12] Trall rejected such a definition, repeatedly emphasizing the naturalness of women's health, such as when he clarified that pregnancy was not a "pathological condition" (133). He also espoused more liberating views in his discussion of women's orgasm. He recognized that orgasm was not necessary for conception but added that orgasm, while not necessary, benefited women's health. If women could not achieve orgasm or did not have sexual desires, it was a sign of ill health. His views contrasted those that positioned sexual desires and orgasms in women as abnormal. He specified, "The normal condition and exercise of the sexual organs, for far from diminishing sexual pleasure or gratification, would actually augment it" (Trall xiii). He also said, "It is true that sexual orgasm on the part of the female is just as normal as on the part of the male" (69). Both quotations refute views of the "passionless" woman. Thus, Trall's premise was the naturalization of women's bodies, which extended to their sexual organs and sexual feelings.

Trall's manual illustrates how these physiology texts advocated specific reforms as they informed the public about sexuality. Trall's insistence that the female should have "supreme control of her own person" aligns him with the arguments of the free-love movement (xi), which used the same phrasing to show that women held the power of deciding when and how sexual acts should occur. He also provided advice on birth control, though he specified that he was against "unnatural" or "unphysiological" methods of birth control, meaning contraceptive devices, and instead advocated what we know now as the rhythm method. His women's rights agenda once again shines through, since he, like Woodhull and Tennessee Claflin, viewed birth control as an unfortunate necessity since woman had yet to achieve "supreme control of her own person."

Trall's text demonstrates the status of physiological knowledge and discourses of "reform physiology" at the time. He did not know the exact timing of the menstrual cycle, leading to misleading advice on birth control, and he did not know about hormones—this knowledge would not come until the twentieth century. It is also unclear how he differentiated between sex and reproduction, other than his comment that sex was not only for procreation but also a "love act" (206). His advice on sexual behavior also reflected the time: sex should be a temperate indulgence, since like other behaviors, overindulgence could lead to poor health. In his social views, he acknowledged that women suffered under institutional marriage, but he did not believe radical philosophies like free love would ease their suffering. His text responded, then, to several rhetorical situations: the public's need to know more about the sexual organs and their functions, the mistaken view of women's bodies as "diseased" and "hysteric," the prevalence of "nervous disorders," and the public awareness of more radical philosophies, like free love. While he did not endorse their views on the solution, Trall did acknowledge that free-love advocates were right in their identification of the problem with institutional marriage—the inequality of women. To Trall, true equality for women would enable them to live more "physiologically."[13]

Elizabeth Blackwell: Refuting Passionlessness

Elizabeth Blackwell (1821–1910) has always interested modern critics as the first woman to achieve prominence as a physician. As a member of the social purity movement, she has often been read by critics as anti-sexuality.[14] However, not all critics share this reading of Blackwell's views on women's sexuality. Margaret Jackson's 1994 study confirms my own reading of Blackwell's rhetoric: Jackson credits Blackwell with creating a feminist model of sexuality (61). Blackwell's 1894 book *The Human Element in Sex* elaborated this model and added another important refutation to the discussion of sexual women as unnatural, or in some cases even pathological. Written from "the standpoint of the Christian physiologist" (Blackwell, *Human Element* 3), her essay took as its main premise that women are sexual beings. The reason that they do not outwardly appear as sexual as men, she maintained, results from their more evolved morality concerning sexuality, a key feature of the arguments of social purity reformers who believed in the moralizing power of women's sexuality, and one that also overlaps with some free-love feminist texts. Like Gove Nichols and Trall, Blackwell attempted to reverse popular associations of what was natural and unnatural in terms of women's sexual feelings.

Blackwell and others enumerated possible causes for why women may feel diminished sexual desire or pleasure and, in doing so, reiterated that sexual feeling in women is not unnatural. Excessive childbearing and demanding husbands were two such causes asserted by Blackwell, Trall, and Gove, a refutation argument picked up by the free-love feminists to validate their critiques of marriage. Blackwell also pointed out the role of the mental condition in the experience of sexual pleasure: "Pleasure in sexual congress is an incident depending largely on mental constitution" (*Human Element* 18). Thus, if women did not feel sexual pleasure, it must be because the environment of the marriage system had made them mentally unable to achieve sexual pleasure. Finally, Blackwell highlighted venereal disease as a factor potentially reducing the sexual desires of women (*Essays* 90–91).

Blackwell's refutation of the idea of the "passionless" woman did not rely on knowledge of anatomy, because she did not need to—her audience understood the functions of the sexual organs. It was, however, premised on other ideas incorporated under the rubric of physiology: the relationship of mind and body, the positioning of sexuality within the nervous system, and the role of the mind in feelings of sexual desire and pleasure. Her refutation came in three parts: first, that women are as sexual as men, just more evolved to control their sexual feelings; second, that women can actually be perceived as more sexual than men since social conditions have forced them to place more weight on romantic feelings (*Human Element* 49); and third, that if women do not have sexual feelings, it is a result of excessive childbearing, the oppression of the double standard, and venereal diseases. Though she admitted that sexual feelings in both men and women vary, making any comparison impossible (48), she pointed out that because of social factors, "physical sex is a larger factor in the life of the woman, unmarried or married, than in the man" (49–50). The underlying logic here supposes that since men have more options open to them in terms of what occupies their daily lives, women think about sex more, and their experiences of sex shape their experiences of life more fully. Blackwell's text differs from Gove's and Trall's in that the idea that disease comes from bad habits and "nervous conditions" is not present—Blackwell wrote after the discovery of the role of bacteria in disease. Consequently, she gave less attention to the argument that humans should observe "temperance" in sexual indulgence because of diseased nerves; instead, she argued, temperance is a natural condition, a result of the higher evolution of humanity. Her text then combined ideas on sexual physiology with evolution and other concerns of her era.

Physicians' Advice on Sex

When they read physiological works like Gove's, Trall's, Blackwell's, and Scudder's, nineteenth-century free-love feminists saw their experiences as valid to the scientific study of sex and used the language of this physiology discourse rather than moral guidelines. However, it is important to note that their participation in this discourse was not unidirectional. For example, many physicians also responded to the ideas raised by free lovers; Trall saw free love as a theory "agitating the public mind"

(x) and used it as an exigence to discuss physiology. Furthermore, historians have noted that more liberating ideas of female sexuality emerged at midcentury (Kern 95), the same time that free-love ideology gained prominence. Thus, nineteenth-century discourses on physiology confirm that scientific values influenced social ideologies just as much as social values influenced scientific ideologies. Reading popularizations of physiology and free-love feminist arguments alongside each other shows the multifaceted nature of the conversations over sexuality and offers insight into the scientific logic behind free-love feminist arguments for sexual choice and pleasure as vital to women's health.

Free Love as the Answer: The Argument for Women's Sexuality and Women's Health

Like many medical reformers, free-love feminists participated in the conversation over women's physiology and emphasized women's sexuality as "natural" rather than as a product of a "diseased" or "pathological" nature. What is interesting about their arguments, though, is that while they did not accept the argument that normal women lacked sexual feelings, they did accept the premise that women's sexual organs controlled their physiology. However, instead of using this premise to support arguments for "hysteric" women, they used it to promote the argument that women need stimulating sex in order to maintain their health. Thus, free love became their solution for maintaining women's health.

The Abnormal Lack of Sexual Desire

As both a physician and a free-love feminist, Mary Gove Nichols asserted a strong ethos to speak about sexual matters, which she did in several genres: medical lectures, articles in water-cure journals, novels, and free-love treatises. While my previous analysis focused on her arguments in the medical genre, this section will focus on her writings on marriage and free love. As a novelist, Gove Nichols critiqued the institution of marriage and its effects on the health of women in a fictionalized yet highly autobiographical 1855 novel, *Mary Lyndon*.[15] This novel traces the life of a heroine who suffers under the constraints of the marriage system and whose ill health results not from her "weaker" physiology but from a system that keeps her confined to the home in a sedentary lifestyle and views her body as her husband's property. Gove Nichols espoused similar ideas in her 1854 treatise on marriage written in collaboration with Thomas L. Nichols, where she often used narratives from her medical practice to illustrate the harms done to married women. The solution, she argued, was a more active lifestyle, sex education, and woman's "ownership" of her own body through free love rather than marriage.

Gove Nichols blamed the institution of marriage for the "obliteration of the maternal and sexual instincts in woman" ("Murders of Marriage" 304). She invoked the image of "diseased nerves" in a woman brought on by the "enslaved and unhealthy condition in which she lives" (304). For Gove Nichols, the "slavery" of the marriage system led to depravities, one of which was masturbation. This connection aligned her with many in the medical profession who posited masturbation as a cause of "diseased nerves," an idea coming out of the link between the nervous system and sexuality. However, she argued that healthy nerves would lead to a healthy sexual life and overall healthy body: "The truth is that healthy nerves give pleasure in the ultimates of love with no respect to sex; and the same exhausted and diseased nerves, that deny to woman the pleasures of love, give her the dreadful pangs of childbirth" (304). She was careful to emphasize here that "diseased nerves" could affect either sex and that both sexes had the capacity to experience pleasure if they had "healthy nerves." Thus, she participated in the growing dialogue on the capacity for pleasure in women, showing that healthy women could achieve such pleasure. In addition, Gove Nichols attacked the standard of "purity" that would have women believe that sexual desires and pleasures were abnormal. She attributed such falsity to clergy and physicians who perpetuated the stereotype, relating the story of a woman with a "nervous" condition caused by "solitary vice," or masturbation: "Her standard of purity was that unconsciously adopted by the Church and the world, that a woman should be 'chaste as ice'; that there should be no attraction felt by her, or, at least, manifested for the masculine principle; that all such attraction derogates from feminine purity and propriety. This lady, as hundreds of others have done, brought her disease and false virtue to me" (305). This redefinition of what was "virtuous" and critique of the moralists and physicians who withheld sexual knowledge from women while insisting upon chastity became key features of free-love feminist rhetoric, which redefined "purity" and "virtue" and labeled the lack of sexual feelings and pleasure as "disease."

Gove Nichols also countered some of the ideas of the dominant medical culture, such as William Acton's, that women's desire for sex sprang out of maternal desire rather than a desire for pleasure. She thus differentiated between sexuality and reproduction in her refutation:

> There is an idea prevalent, that the ultimation [sic] of love in the sexual union, is intended solely for the production of offspring. There is no

physiological foundation for this belief. The desire for the sexual union, is not adapted to, or governed by, this result in man or in woman. . . . In woman the maternal function ceases at the age of forty-five or fifty, but the desire to love, and the faculty of enjoying the sexual embrace continues to a much later period. (Nichols and Gove Nichols, *Marriage* 365)

Gove Nichols used simple logic, showing that women who could no longer have children still desired sex. Her argument on the importance of love to sexuality in women, a result of the nineteenth-century focus on companionate marriage, previews Blackwell's later logic. By placing love as the basis for sexual union between men and women, Gove Nichols supported an argument for free love. Without this love between partners, in addition to knowledge of sex and ownership of her own body, marriage would continue to have ill effects on women's health.

Rachel Campbell also offered a response to the claim that women lacked sexual desires, similar to Gove Nichols's response: that institutional marriage has expelled sexual desire from women. In her 1888 pamphlet *The Prodigal Daughter*, Campbell wrote that most men seem to have more sexual desire than most women but emphasized that this difference is not innate but rather caused by external factors. She referred to the "strange disparity," asking whether it is a "normal condition": "Nearly every case of marital discord has its root in the strange disparity that exists in the sexual needs and desires of husbands and wives, and we ask, is this a normal condition? Are husbands excessive in their demands, or wives morbid in their apathy; or, are they each equally divergent from a natural condition?" (27). Campbell's inquiry about the normality of the difference in sexual desire between men and women matches the language and logic used by medical writers of the time: Trall and Gove Nichols had both questioned such a state.

Campbell would seem to be feeding the opposition, those who subscribed to the ideology of women as inherently passionless. She did, after all, admit that she found herself in the position of having less sexual desire than her husband and painted him as a lustful brute. In a letter to Mary Florence Johnson, she described the unequal sexual relationship between herself and her husband: "He was twenty-two, strong, healthy and with large sexual demands; while I was young, with my passional nature undeveloped; and from this one cause sprang all the trouble. I thought him exacting and selfish, and he thought me unaccommodating and capricious" (qtd. in M. Johnson 33). This experience obviously influenced her later stances on the sexual relationship between men and women, but while she admitted to having less desire for sex, she did not attribute it to a natural tendency but to her youth. Nevertheless, Campbell might have seemed to be buying into the idea of women as passionless, but she did not think this condition normal for women. Instead, she highlighted the inequalities in marriage as producing weaker sexual drives in women:

> Is not this disparity the result of the slavish position held by woman in the sexual partnership? In a condition of perfect equality would not woman develop to a sexual status more nearly approaching that of man? Would not association with a healthy, womanly woman be so much more satisfactory and beneficial to a man, that all abnormal desire would subside, and his treatment of woman be more manly and just? Would not a larger endowment of sexual power on the part of women, fit them to become better wives and happier mothers of healthier children? (27–28)

Campbell's strategy matches Gove Nichols's rhetoric: marriage "murders" the sexual desires of women. If women were free to own themselves and their own bodies and achieved full equality with men, their sexual desires would also approach equality. She also claimed that such an unequal relationship caused men to be more sexual than "normal" (27).

Furthermore, Campbell posited that current unequal conditions would breed a race of "passionless" women. Using natural selection as her warrant, she explained her logic. Since society condemned women with "passion," it was "weeding out the ardent, passionate girls, and selecting for motherhood only the cold and passive ones" (*Prodigal Daughter* 13). Thus, the practices of white upper-class society "has produced its legitimate effect, in giving us a race of passionless women as poorly endowed sexually that their husbands feel justified in seeking pleasanter relations elsewhere" (13). Campbell found a basis in science, evolutionary theory in particular, for the lack of sexual feelings among many women. Unlike Gove Nichols, she did not move to then discussing how women's sexual pleasure would aid their health. She did, however, have harsh words for men who ignored their wives' antipathy to sex:

> When men understand that all passionless, mechanical service is essentially masturbation; and when women learn that a willing or even loving giving of one's self, without desire, but for the sake of pleasing a dear companion has nothing meritorious in it, but is doing him, as well as herself, a positive injury, both will be willing to wait for the still, sweet voice of mutual attraction to lead them in the way of love and equity. (Campbell, "Criticism" 87)

Like Gove Nichols, Campbell was wary of sexual "abuses" and urged "mutuality" as the general rule. We can read her references to "mutuality" as about the desire for sex, or we can read them as about the mutual pleasure in sex. I think she is referring to the latter, especially since her language is similar to the language employed by Woodhull on the topic of women's sexual pleasure, though Woodhull was more explicit in endorsing "mutual desire" and "reciprocal benefit" in *Tried as by Fire*.

Both Gove Nichols and Campbell rejected the claim that women desired sex only out of a desire for maternity, and they provided clear evidence. Another free-love feminist writer, Elsie Cole-Wilcox writing in 1897, employed these same lines of argument to discuss birth control. She contended that opponents to birth control assumed a lack of sexual desire among women, except when they desired offspring. Cole-Wilcox refuted them but also acknowledged that there were women for whom their statements might be true. Like Gove Nichols and Campbell, she attributed the lack not to women's innate nature but to "ages of repression on the part of women, in obedience to religious and 'grundious' teaching" (114). She said that moral standards on women have "weakened woman sexually until she is no longer man's equal in that respect. But if free to consult her own needs and desires she would soon recover much of her lost vigor" (114). Thus, Cole-Wilcox offered free love as the solution to correcting the unequal desires between men and women. If they practiced free love, women could recover their lost sexual desires, as both Gove Nichols and Campbell attested. Woodhull would take such arguments even further, accepting the premise that a healthy woman would have strong sexual desires and extending the logic to show that healthy women needed *pleasurable* sex to remain healthy women.

Sexual Pleasure = Healthy Women

Victoria Woodhull was more specific both in enumerating the values of increased sex education and in using the benefits to women's health as an argument for free love. Both her 1873 and 1874 speeches elaborated her free-love feminist philosophy and conversed with "reform physiologists." She advocated sex education starting in childhood, ensuring that children would be knowledgeable about sex before their sexuality awakened (*Tried* 16). She would have had this education extend into adulthood, as she blamed ignorance of their bodies for many of the trials women suffered in the institution of marriage. Listing the tragedies that result from such ignorance, her argument focused on the consequences of this lack of knowledge to child-bearing, and she recounted the increasing number of deaths of infants and infertility caused by sexual diseases (32–33). She also linked sexual knowledge to sexual pleasure, explaining that women who know more about their bodies will achieve increased sexual pleasure (15, 43). Both Woodhull and Gove Nichols used similar strategies in positioning lack of sexual knowledge as dangerous, not the knowledge itself. Their arguments not only reflected the exigence for their discussion of sexual matters but also picked up on a recurring trope in many "reform physiology" texts. Both "reform physiology" texts and free-love feminist texts envisioned a public unaware of sexual physiology, an ignorance resulting from "false modesty," which resulted in propensity for disease, and thus conceived their purpose as a civic duty.

Woodhull shamed the "newspapers" and "preachers, teachers, and doctors" for the ignorance of sexuality that many women had (*Elixir* and *Tried*), but she did not repudiate all doctors. She singled out Scudder as a "large-hearted man and widely-experienced physician" (*Tried* 43). Her strategy was similar to that of other sex radicals who attempted to chastise physicians for certain ignorant practices but also tried to build a bridge to them. For Woodhull, sex education should have been under the provenance of doctors, but doctors' inability to move beyond "false modesty" necessitated reformers' discourses on the topic. Indeed, speeches on free love often overlapped in phrasing and strategies with "reform physiology" texts.

Tried as by Fire presents the most apparent use of medical discourse, as she quoted Scudder directly and even endorsed his book as one that every woman should read. The influence of medical discourses in general can be seen in some of the phrases she used, such as "mock modesty," but also in her argument that marriage restricts the sexual instincts of individuals. Whether or not Scudder himself explicitly engaged in conversation with her and other free lovers is unknown, but his book does invoke rhetoric often used by free lovers before the time of its publication. In *Tried as by Fire*, Woodhull used a quotation from Scudder's medical text to tie together her three main arguments toward the end of the speech: that relationships between men and women should be based on mutual love and desire rather than on economic security, should involve women who are knowledgeable about their own bodies and sexuality, and should allow women "ownership and control" of their "sexual organs." Woodhull argued free love would remedy the problems women experienced under the control of their husbands. She quoted Scudder, saying, "The wife should not lose control of her person in marriage. It is hers to rule supreme in this regard. This is a law of life, and is violated in no species except in man" (Scudder 62; qtd. in Woodhull, *Tried* 43), giving scientific authority to her argument that the woman should have "ownership and control of her sexual organs." She embraced sexuality as virtuous and lack of sexuality as vulgar, inverting cherished beliefs:

> Others again seem to glory over the fact that they never had any sexual desire, and to think that this desire is vulgar. What! Vulgar! The instinct that creates immortal souls vulgar! Who dare stand up amid Nature, all prolific and beautiful, whose pulses are ever bounding with the creative desire, and utter such sacrilege! Vulgar, indeed! Vulgar, rather, must be the mind that can conceive such blasphemy. No sexual passion, say you? Say, rather, a sexual idiot, and confess that your life is a failure, your body an abortion, and no longer bind your shame upon your brow or herald it as purity. Call such stuff purity. Bah! Be honest, rather, and say it is depravity. (*Tried* 24–25)

Woodhull's arguments for sex education and for free love also owed much to the debates over women's physiology—even the antifeminist views in that discourse. Woodhull took the logic of women's "diseased" and "nervous" conditions perpetuated by antifeminist medical practitioners to support an argument for the importance of sexual pleasure and free love to women's health.

In her 1873 *The Elixir of Life; or, Why Do We Die?*, a speech given to an audience of spiritualists, Woodhull employed a rhetorical tactic similar to the medical community's in positioning sexuality as a natural sign of health: "It is an axiom in the medical profession that the patient who experiences sexual desire is not dangerously ill; and also that the patient who has been dangerously ill is convalescent when sexual desire returns. Thus it is held that the presence of the sexual appetite is a symptom of health" (5–6). She emphasized that sexual desire was normal and natural in women and echoed the logic of Trall, Blackwell, and Gove Nichols in showing that those without sexual desires must be suffering from ill health. Tennessee Claflin, Woodhull's sister, made a similar statement in her 1872 speech when she discussed how marriage affects the health of women and attributed health in women to happy and fulfilling marriages (*Ethics* 11). Both women endorsed the premise that women's health is controlled by their sexual organs but used it to justify the sexual emancipation of women from the bondage of marriage.

Woodhull also appropriated some of the logic of the physicians who found a correlation between sexuality and "hysteria" or other nervous conditions when she said, "If health depends upon proper sexuality, it follows that disease follows from improper sexuality" (*Elixir* 6). She, however, took this logic even further, attributing all disease to sexual conditions (6). Such logic had its start in the medical profession but then changed to support more radical feminist arguments. For example, free-love texts used the logic from the medical community that women's health was based in their sexual and reproductive organs as the warrant for why women should have pleasurable sex. If their sexual and reproductive organs ruled women's physiology, free-love feminists like Woodhull contended that more attention should be paid to exercising and stimulating those organs in order to prevent negative consequences to health.

Furthermore, Woodhull extended John Scudder's logic, such as when he argued,

> If the act is complete, so that both body and mind are satisfied, no disease arises, though there be frequent repetitions; but if the act be incomplete, the organs being irritated merely, and the mind not satisfied, then disease will surely follow. There is no doubt that the proper gratification of the function is conducive to health and longevity; or that its abuse leads to disease and shortens life. (42–43)

Woodhull quoted this passage as support for free love in *Tried as by Fire*. Thus, while Woodhull's arguments that unsatisfying sex leads to disease may seem unusual, they actually repeated arguments made in medical writing of the time. Woodhull claimed a firm scientific basis for her contention that women were entitled to sexual pleasure, because the lack of such pleasure would lead to ill health. For example, she reprimanded husbands who ignored their wives' pleasure and connected their indifference with the poor health of women:

> I need not explain to any woman the effects of unconsummated intercourse though she may attempt to deceive herself about it; but every man needs to have it thundered in his ears until he wakes to the fact that he is not the only party to the act, and that the other party demands a return for all that he receives; demands that shall not be enriched at her expense; demands that he shall not, either from ignorance or selfish desire, carry her impulse forward on its mission only to cast it backward with the mission unfulfilled, to prostrate the impelling power to breed nervous disorder or irritability and sexual demoralization, and to sow the seeds of disease broadcast among humanity. (*Elixir* 7)

Woodhull began this diatribe with a kind of legal language and ended by evoking arguments that unsatisfied sexuality breeds nervous disabilities. She seemed to be entering the gap found in the contradictions that ran rampant in the medical community over women and "nervous" disorders to fulfill her own agenda: that men need to pay attention to women's pleasure in the sex act. In the same speech, she spoke of her conversation with a member of the New York College of Physicians, who agreed on the harmful effects for women who did not experience pleasure during sex. She thus transformed the discourse, going from claims that unhealthy women lacked sexual desires to the claim that unfulfilled sexual desires would produce unhealthy women.

Woodhull's often flamboyant rhetoric has clear connections with the discourses on "reform physiology": she exploited the focus on informing the public of sexual physiology to argue for her own brand of sex education; she relied on the connection between sexuality and the nervous system in positioning sex as integral to women's health; she quoted specific doctors who saw women's health as a women's rights issue; and she turned sexual pleasure into a right of women. Thus, she offered free love, where women were free to choose partners and sexual conditions, as the answer to many of the problems befalling women in the marriage system and to much of the ill health of women.

Women's "Evolved Sexuality"

Other free-love feminists, instead of drawing on the doctrine of health, used evolutionary theory to posit that women's sexuality differed from men's because it was more evolved. Their premise, the superiority of the female, especially in morality, seems to lend credence to antifeminist ideas of women's sexuality and found its basis in more of an essentialist feminism. However, as the writings of Elmina Drake Slenker and Lois Waisbrooker show, accepting the premise of women's evolved morality, and thus more evolved and "pure" sexuality, did not mean negating women's sexual desires. Their logic had its root in the same warrants that Gove Nichols, Campbell, and Woodhull used, producing the following argument: marriage has produced deleterious effects on women's sexuality, and until a more equal free-love ideal is reached, women should be able to exert a moralizing influence in the realm of sexuality.

Elmina Slenker's career as a writer on sexual matters shows an evolution of thought similar to the evolved sexuality she posited in her arguments. She began by supporting continence, with males refraining from orgasm, but turned to Dianism as a more effective strategy. Under Dianism, both partners refrain from sexual intercourse. Slenker, however, did not negate sexuality when she advocated Dianism. She believed that men and women had found equal depravity by being slaves to their sexual passion and that limiting sexual intercourse only to times when reproduction was desired represented a more evolved sexuality.

Slenker's logic found a warrant in the law of conservation of energy and thus in antifeminist medical discourse: that sex should be limited because excess causes a loss of energy, or vigor. Slenker applied such views to both men and women and contended that too many viewed sex as simply a pleasurable experience: "From Bible-times down to our own, the main teaching has been, that sexing was more a pleasurable act—one designed for the most exquisite joy of man and woman, than as a high and purposeful creative act" ("Dianism and Right"). Slenker's views reveal the multifaceted nature of the physiology debate, since she took as a warrant that sexuality and reproduction are separate and that both men and women are taught to indulge their pleasure, which seems like a shift from many of the popular, "prudish" ideologies of sex in the nineteenth century. That Slenker sanctioned sex only for reproduction would seem to support a "prudery" reading, but since she acknowledged sexuality as a driving force, she was not endorsing the view that lack of sexuality is innate. On the contrary, she thought humans should become more evolved by tempering their sexual drives.

Similar to other free-love feminists, Slenker also attributed what she saw as false views on sexuality to the false teaching and practices of nineteenth-century "middle-class" society: "Long habit, heredity, and wrong teaching have made many men and women more sensual and sexually intemperate than they should be" ("Dianism and Right"). While she differs from other free-love feminists in what she defined as false teaching, since others would attribute women's lack of sexual desire to false teaching and she attributed women's and men's heightened sexual desires to them, she is similar in critiquing the moral codes that dictated sexuality. She also offered free love as the solution, claiming that "every woman who cuts loose from her bonds helps to free the race" ("Dianism," October 1896). She thus viewed the sexual emancipation of women as a way to help both men and women reach the more evolved state of moderating their sexual appetites.

Drawing on the same lines of argument as Elizabeth Blackwell's, Slenker suggested the relationship between sex and the "will" and defined sex as more than just intercourse: "[Dianism] is simply love, affection-ateness, sympathy and comradeship, reserving the sex-act for parentage alone. It is being socially free to caress, embrace and fondle each other, with no expectation, and as little desire as possible for further association, unless children are wished for" (3). She also discussed nude contact as an alternative to sexual intercourse. For Slenker, "All forms of love, save the sex act itself are forms of Dianism" ("Dianism," June 1900). Such practices would lead to increased "health, happiness, purity, and ten thousand other blessings, instead of the one evil of needless sexing" and would "conserve the life forces and not needlessly waste them in mere momentary paroxysms of pleasure" ("Dianism," April 1897). Her writings reflect many of the medical writers' ideas of sex as a loss of "life force," but she added her own "Dianist free-love" rhetoric to the mix: sexual freedom would lead to this more evolved sexuality.

Lois Waisbrooker's rhetoric might also seem anti-sexuality, but, like Slenker, she asserted her own rhetoric of free love in the conversation. She differs from Slenker since she felt "sex-association [is] the natural right of the race" ("Last Word" 150). But she also cautioned against excess in sexuality and posited a more evolved sexuality, though her definition differs from Slenker's. Waisbrooker agreed with arguments like Gove Nichols's and Campbell's that marriage caused a lack of sexual desire in women. Like her friend Rachel Campbell, Waisbrooker blamed men for destroying women's sexual feelings:

> Some men throw off all delicacy and deference as soon as the nuptial knot is tied and rudely ravish the being who has trusted all in their keeping. Heaven pity the woman whose dream of happiness is thus rudely broken in upon. Such a course is sure to repel all but the grossest natures. Let the young husband make no claim, but wait patiently for the welcome indication of reciprocity. (*From Generation* 56)

Waisbrooker believed that such reciprocity of desire would come if women were free, under free love. Her argument also recalls the claims of Gove Nichols when she repudiated marriage:

> Women who are normal and who have been rightly treated, are not as a rule, so much less passional than men. It is this making of woman the property of man, this binding of her person to his use whether she desires him or not, I mean legal marriage, it is this that has taken the life out of woman and made her the irresponsive being she now, so often is. I say life, for normal sex desire is life if rightly used. ("Who Protects the Wife?")

Waisbrooker's logic is in line with the more progressive medical writers and free lovers of the time: normal women will desire sex if left free to do so.

Waisbrooker's logic recalls Blackwell's and was similarly influenced by Enlightenment ideas. Waisbrooker posited "the close connection existing between the brain and the sexual organs, and an excessive or perverted use thereof cannot fail to affect the brain to its injury. That there is a reactionary power between them there is too much proof to question, and this power, when rightly understood, can be used as a mutual good" (*From Generation* 21). Like Blackwell, she emphasized the power of the will and argued that sexuality for women was more evolved because of the stronger connection to the mind, a connection, for Waisbrooker, that could be a force for good, both in moral and spiritual evolution. Waisbrooker also agreed with interpretations of sexuality relying on the law of conservation of energy: she believed sexual pleasure had the potential to be a dangerous excess. Under the logic of the law of conservation of energy, sex brings a loss of energy. Waisbrooker reinterpreted such logic to show that it is not sex itself but lack of reciprocity, or mutual orgasm, that may cause an unequal balance in the "energies" of the male and female: "All sex-action on the man's part which is not reciprocated by the wife, so far from being a benefit to either, the magnetic sex-element is simply thrown away" (*Tree of Life* 116). Thus, the health of the woman would suffer. Waisbrooker's arguments here help to shed light on Woodhull's claims in *The Elixir of Life*: it would seem that both subscribed to philosophies of sex as a "magnetic" exchange and that such "magnetism" improved health. When sexual pleasure is not reciprocal, health will suffer. In fact, Waisbrooker contended that lack of reciprocity in sexual pleasure would also lead to poor health for men because of the "magnetic exchange": "Men, in their ignorance, and the idea of their right to the wife's person, have not sought to awaken a response to their desire but have claimed the right to satiate their passion, not knowing that an unresponsive woman can give them no compensation; not knowing that they are robbing themselves, wasting their own forces" (*Anything More, My Lord?* 20). It is difficult to read her claims without reading them through the lens of the development of nineteenth-century sexual thought since she combined older ideas of vitalism with her spiritualism and the evidence of the law of conservation of energy. Waisbrooker also alluded to the arguments of Slenker in cautioning against excess:

> In reciprocity the danger is in excess. That which is natural, spontaneous and mutual will be a blessing to both; but beyond this such high-wrought nerve action is injurious, exhaustive, and must, soon or late, destroy all power of enjoyment. Pleasure is as great a tax upon the system as is pain; and we are more in danger of being injured thereby, from the fact that we court its stay, while we rid ourselves of pain as soon as possible. We have a right to all the pleasure that comes from right action, but when we prolong

the act for the sake of the pleasure the injury is proportionally as great as when the act is excited prematurely—that is, before the body has so matured as to make sex commerce legitimate—an evil into which thousands of our youth are falling because not properly taught. (*From Generation* 57)

The fear of the loss of vigor and of "high-wrought nerve action" characterizes much of the earlier nineteenth-century rhetorics of sexuality. For example, we could go back to Gove Nichols and her fears of sexuality and masturbation leading to nervousness. Waisbrooker extended this logic to show why a more evolved sexuality was needed and why the free-love feminist goal of sex education was vital in producing this evolved sexuality.

Waisbrooker's idea of an evolved sexuality seems similar to Slenker's, especially in statements like "A woman wants more than passion; she wants to caress and be caressed without having the demands of passion thrust upon her" (*Anything More, My Lord?* 20–21). Both women seem to epitomize what historian Linda Gordon calls "sex-hating," though Gordon notes that such women did not express such ideas because of prudery but because of their own personal experiences (*Moral Property* 63).[16] They seemed to disdain sexual intercourse as something men forced women to do and that they would not do if they had the choice. They posited a more evolved sexuality, where women would be free to choose the form of intimacy. Reading the texts of Slenker and Waisbrooker in isolation may produce a reading of them as "sex-haters," but reading them alongside other free-love feminists shows how they were clearly in conversation with other rhetorics of sexuality of the time, and as unlikely as it seems, science influenced their logic. They were relying on older ideas of sexuality and combining them with the new focus on physiology to argue for free love as a necessity for women.

The Physician–Radical Reformer Alliance

These discussions of sexuality place these free-love feminists in conversation with the medical field. While they often constructed this relationship as a debate, such as when Woodhull "shamed" the doctors who withheld sexual knowledge, free-love feminists also sought alliances with like-minded physicians. Hulda Potter-Loomis and Dora Forster discussed this alliance and viewed science as a way to free women from outdated and repressive models of sexuality. Surprisingly, they were not looking to prove the ideas of science false, even though some nineteenth-century science produced the exact opposite of their aims. Instead, they posited an alliance among scientists, physicians, and reformers to find the "truth" about sexuality. Reaching this "truth" required more research, from a scientific rather than a moral perspective. They also insisted that the truth could not be reached until sexual emancipation for women and sex education were enacted. Thus, their arguments posited free love as a scientific necessity.

Potter-Loomis used her pamphlet *Social Freedom: The Most Important Factor in Human Evolution* to argue for free love as a means to higher evolution of the species and to urge scientific study of sexuality to denounce the "custom of institutional marriage with all of the false ideas connected with it" (4). Like physician John Scudder, she viewed medical science as the antidote to the "false" morality perpetuated by church and state. One impediment to correcting "false" ideas of sex, Potter-Loomis contended, was the ignorance many had about sex, which would continue unless sex was discussed openly and "scientifically." She supported discussion of sexuality from an early age to help society advance, "because each individual would be taught from childhood that the sex organs were not vile and unclean and that they were worthy of all respect and considerations" (17). She urged people to talk as freely about the sex organs as they did about the heart and the liver (17). This comparison between sexual organs and other, less "secret" parts of the body was popular within free-love feminist discourse, leading into arguments connecting sexual appetite with an appetite for food. For example, Potter-Loomis stated that human desire should govern choices in sex, just as appetite determines choices of food (14). Thus, both appetites were positioned as "natural" ones requiring gratification.

Potter-Loomis also owed the "reform physiologists" for promoting open discussion of sexuality and enabling an understanding of the body and its processes. Like Woodhull, Potter-Loomis exploited the connection between sexuality and overall health that were most often put to antifeminist uses by pointing out how physicians would find a correlation between insanity and "restrained or restricted" sexual desire (6). These arguments came from logic based on the connection of sexuality with the nervous system and also on the knowledge that healthy women did have strong sexual desires. She also made seemingly self-evident statements—that is, "the sex organs are wisely intended for use other than merely to propagate the species" (3)—that assumed that reproduction was an end but not necessarily the sole purpose of sexual unions (see Scudder 35). Potter-Loomis, like Forster, found a gap in the medical discourse—the question of women's lived experiences—and entered it with the solution of free love.

Forster's call for free-love reform in her 1905 treatise, *Sex Radicalism as seen by an Emancipated Woman of the New Time*, had a stronger bias toward science and called for an alliance between physicians and free-love thinkers. She began by critiquing some physicians in her chapter titled "Who Are Our Teachers?" but also tried not to blame physicians for their focus on disease rather than on health: "Sex radicals must study their subject for themselves. On the physiological side of the sex problem, I believe medical men can and will be our friends as soon as we encourage them to do so. The public will have health-doctors, instead of, or as well as, disease doctors, just as soon as it genuinely desires them; and those who want sex-science will get it" (9). Forster, like Gove Nichols and others before her, saw the radical free lovers as "students of the facts of sex" (13), with physiologists as their teachers. She pointed out that many questions had gone unanswered about sex and sexual feelings, and she hoped that women and medical scientists could work together to discover the "truth" about sexuality. In his *History of Sexuality*, Michel Foucault notes that in nineteenth-century discourses on sex, "sex was constituted as a problem of truth" (1.56). The way that some physicians and reformers discussed physiology as a problem of "nature" or of "truth" supports this view. Trall, for instance, contended that the various factions discussing sex proved that "the problem of the true sexual relations is not yet fully understood" (x). Similarly, Juliet Severance urged that discussions of sex should take a scientific approach in both method and viewpoint: "Then let this and all other subjects receive careful, thorough, and impartial discussion and analysis. In this way we will show ourselves scientific investigators instead of bigoted ignoramuses" (*Discussion* 11). By situating sex as a problem of scientific investigation, both medical and activist discourse communities aimed to bridge experience, or lifestyles, with science.

Forster called for such an alliance because women had the everyday experiences that could then be analyzed with "the highest reasoning and the most careful deductions of science" (*Sex Radicalism* 6). Like the free-love feminists before her, she urged training in science for lay people rather than training in religious morality in order to fully understand sexuality (8), because "thoughtful people are earnestly desiring a science of sex as a guide to conduct" (38). In terms of "what must we learn in health science," also the heading of her chapter after "Who Are Our Teachers?," she critiqued the "Puritan sex system" that had distorted the natural forms of sexual expression and influenced physicians writing on the topic (10–11). She mentioned the physiology books of Thomas Nichols and Alice Stockham,[17] saying that information had been made available to the public but was censored by social mores (10). Instead, she maintained, students of physiology needed to inquire more about the facts of sex, such as at what age sexual feelings are developed, and to cease calling the "natural" habit of masturbation the "solitary vice," which she deemed an "unscientific" term employed by many in the medical profession (11–12). Addressing the debate over women's sexual desires, she observed, "Whether the jealousy and tyranny of men have operated to suppress amativeness in women, by constantly sweeping strongly sexual women from the paths of life into infamy and sterility or death, we do not know" (40). She also employed the argument made by Gove Nichols when she refuted the notion that sexual desires were connected with maternal feelings, using the same logic: that the sex drive lasts longer than "procreative power" (41). Finally, Forster argued that science would show the public the "evils of celibacy" (23) and teach that both men and women should have freedom, choice, and pleasure in sexual relations.

Physiological Free Love

The medical community contained adherents of feminist and antifeminist views of women's physiology, but the rhetoric of free-love feminists shows that both the antifeminist and the feminist discourse of medical writers could be put to feminist ends. Instead of rejecting the arguments that women were controlled by their sexual organs as antifeminist, free-love feminists thought such rhetoric could aid them in their aims. To them, physiology dispelled the codes of morality repressing women, since they viewed science as "objective" and free of such moral tendencies. They entreated women to "study physiology more and prayer-books less" (White, *Coming Woman* 6) and made knowledge of physiology central to all of their goals for enlightened, sexually emancipated women. The focus on what women were capable of, and how their reproductive and sexual organs controlled their physiology, then became a reason why women should practice free love—for better health. These medical discourses provided the exigence and the logic for women to participate in the debate over their sexuality and to assert sexual rights for women. However, as texts like Forster's show, they recognized that even the discipline of physiology contained incomplete knowledge of sexuality and thus offered their own experiences as scientific evidence.

Foucault identifies the "confession" (or "case study" as we would now call it) as a scientific method in nineteenth-century medicine. Dr. Clelia Mosher attempted to let the female subjects of her sex study speak for themselves in her questionnaires. Such practices by physicians match what

Susan Wells has identified as a popular tactic employed by nineteenth-century female physicians: collecting the "heart history" of patients (28–34). Feminist reformers thought that they had something to offer to the discussion over physiology, and the medical profession's practice of patient observations and histories validated these tendencies. In the discourses of physiology, knowledge of the body was the first step to understanding women's sexuality in arguing for specific lifestyles; likewise, the discussion over lifestyles also added to the conversation over physiology. The relationship between the medical and lay writers on physiology proved reciprocal, but this relationship changed as scientific understandings of the body changed in other disciplines. While physiology was the site for questions about sexuality throughout the early and mid-nineteenth century, scientific discoveries would make these questions more specialized by the turn of the century. Thus, the "sex-science" called for by free-love feminists was eventually achieved, but was it the science they wanted?

4

Bacteriology: Marriage as a "Diseased" Institution

I have been "the thing called a wife," having no individuality, no
spontaneity. I have suffered a degradation that the Church and
the world call purity and virtue. I have borne children in torture
that the rack could no more than equal. I have had abortions and
miscarriages that were as truly murders as if my infants had been
strangled, or had had their brains beaten out, by a brutal father. I
have had my life drained away by uterine hemorrhage, and worse
than all, I have had the canker of utter loathing and abhorrence
forever eating in my heart, and for one who was, like the frogs
of Egypt, sharing my bedroom and spoiling my food. And yet
he too was a victim of a system, and a diseased brain and body.
He believed that a wife should obey her husband, and his morbid
impulses forced him to ask a deathly obedience.
                                    —Mary Gove Nichols, *Marriage*, 1854

When free-love feminist and physician Mary Gove Nichols critiqued
the institution of marriage in 1854, she invoked the metaphor of a
diseased institution and blamed marriage for many of the illnesses
befalling women (*Marriage* 265). By the late nineteenth century, many in
the medical and sexual reform movements would agree with her critique,
but their arguments would be refreshed, set in a new rhetorical situation
created by new warrants from science, which gave new meaning to the
characterization of marriage as a source of disease for women. Major
breakthroughs in the scientific community in the late nineteenth century reconfigured discussions of marriage and sexuality. One of these
breakthroughs was the discovery of bacteria and their relationship to
disease causation.

This new knowledge about disease produced new discourses and
images in the scientific, medical, political, and domestic spheres: soap

advertisements with militaristic metaphors to describe the act of washing, "A Course in Scientific Shopping" in the pages of *Good Housekeeping*, advertisements for household products and "home protection," the
rounding up of prostitutes to check disease, and the crowds of immi-
grants examined at Ellis Island. From the man of science bending over
his microscope in the laboratory, to the housewife making her kitchen
germ-free, to the reformer promoting sex education, discourses based
in bacteriology traveled through many different communities that produced arguments set in a new rhetorical situation with new warrants for
reform-based arguments.

The Warrant Established: Bacterial Agents of Venereal Disease

While most applications of the germ theory, such as widespread vaccina-
tions and pharmaceutical cures, would not be developed until the twentieth century, germ theory altered both health practices and the discourse
of disease in the late nineteenth century. Older ideas of disease posited
no single cause, and many physicians believed that people could catch
the same disease from different causes (Waller 3). Everything from hu-
moral theory, to heredity, to physiological weaknesses explained disease.
As the previous chapter showed, many nineteenth-century physicians
focused on diseases as a fault of the nervous system or a lack of "vital"
energy. By the late nineteenth century, however, not all diseases were
considered a fault of the body—germ theory provided an external agent
to fight. Venereal diseases, in particular, once conceived as punishment
for immorality, became linked to the germ theory of disease.

The Creation of a New Science

The history of bacteriology began earlier than the nineteenth century, as
far back as the seventeenth century, when Anthony van Leeuwenhoek
observed what he called "little animals" in his microscope. His work
was followed by Lazzaro Spallanzani's, which proved that these "little
animals" could not survive boiling water (de Kruif 35). Both men laid the
groundwork for nineteenth-century scientists aware of these microscopic
organisms but who had yet to connect them with diseases. Louis Pasteur's
work would be integral to producing a generation of "microbe hunters."

Pasteur (1822–95) is one of many scientists whose early life did not
forecast the valuable scientific contributions he would make. Not a strong
student but a good painter and orator, Pasteur had intended a career in
the fine arts but switched his focus to chemistry. His background helped
him to develop the rhetorical skills integral to the acceptance of his

scientific findings. During his tenure at Lille University in 1863, local merchants asked Pasteur to research the process of fermentation in order to solve their problems making wine and beer. Pasteur then discovered the importance of yeast to the process of fermentation and showed how specific wines required specific yeasts. He developed the process called "pasteurization," or the heating process used to kill organisms (Porter and Ogilvie 2.746–47). In noting the effects of microorganisms on substances, Pasteur then associated these microbes with disease causation. His 1859 paper theorizing germs as the cause of disease resonated with many in the scientific community, prompting them to try to isolate the germs responsible for certain diseases.[1]

Another request from the merchant community led Pasteur to his next important study. In the 1860s, the government asked him to investigate the disease that was killing silkworms, which was wreaking havoc on the silk industry (Porter and Ogilvie 2.747). In 1868, he announced his discovery of the parasite causing this disease in silkworms, which prompted him to pursue further investigations into disease-causing agents. Meanwhile, Pasteur's work was already beginning to produce reforms in the medical community. For example, surgeon Joseph Lister took note of Pasteur's findings and began using an antiseptic to prevent postoperative infections. Pasteur, though, did not stop his groundbreaking research with his proposal of the germ theory of disease and his identification of the specific microorganism attacking silkworms. In 1882, he began research on rabies, and in 1885, this research led him to use a vaccine on a young boy who had been bitten by a dog—and it worked. He was one of the leading figures attempting to link specific bacteria with specific diseases and trying to then create vaccines and cures for these diseases.

Robert Koch (1843–1910), also a pivotal "microbe hunter," had been an army surgeon for Prussia during the Franco-Prussian War after earning his medical degree in 1866. His positions as a district medical officer in Wollstein and as a town medical officer in Breslau lacked well-equipped facilities for research, but Koch's wife gave him a microscope that allowed him to begin his investigations into anthrax (Porter and Ogilvie 1.565). His wife would also be influential in his laboratory techniques—it was her fruit jelly recipe that he used to develop the plate culture technique that allowed him to isolate specific types of microorganisms (Otis 3). After developing techniques to stain bacteria to make them easier to observe under the microscope (Porter and Ogilvie 1.565), he successfully identified the anthrax microbe (*Bacillus anthracis*) in 1876, the first association of a specific microbe with a specific disease. In 1882, Koch also identified the microbe responsible for tuberculosis. He devoted the rest of his career to reforms in public health, leaving the legacy of his postulates and staining techniques for other researchers.[2]

The Shifting Knowledge of Venereal Diseases

New knowledge of venereal diseases also emerged in the early nineteenth century, even before scientists identified bacterial agents. Medical scientists at this time knew that venereal diseases affected the sexual organs and that the diseases spread through sexual contact. However, physicians tended to conflate these diseases, not recognizing, for example, the differences between gonorrhea and syphilis. French venereologist Phillipe Ricord remedied this misconception in 1837 through his study of syphilitic chancres, which enabled him to differentiate syphilis from gonorrhea. He also speculated about the stages of the infection (Brandt 9). These findings would be important to later scientists searching for causal agents.

While bacteria's role in infections had many scientists "converting" to the germ theory of disease, older ideas of venereal diseases still persisted. Unaware of the causal agent, physicians had theorized that excessive sexual contact led to these diseases (Brandt 10). Others posited that all women carried gonorrhea without exhibiting any symptoms, and thus all women were inherently diseased (Brandt 10; Spongberg). It wasn't until 1879, when a German dermatologist named Albert Neisser identified the gonococcus microbe, one of the first microbes to be linked to a specific disease, that the new science of bacteriology began to influence views of sexuality.

Like Pasteur, Neisser (1855–1916) did not show early aptitude for scientific discovery. In fact, he had to repeat the chemistry test before qualifying for his medical degree in 1877. During his studies, he learned staining techniques to observe bacteria and the smear test to identify them, both developed by Koch. He then came to the field of dermatology by accident; he had wanted to specialize in internal medicine but turned to dermatology because of a job opening (Gillispie 10.17). At this dermatology clinic, with the aid of a newer-model microscope, he successfully identified the gonococcus microbe in 1879, before his twenty-fifth birthday.

Neisser devoted the rest of his career to bacteriology, though it was not without controversy. He and Norwegian bacteriologist G. H. A. Hansen both identified the bacteria responsible for leprosy, and they clashed over who would receive credit. In the end, Hansen was credited for identifying the specific microbe, but Neisser was credited for discovering its significance as the cause of leprosy (Gillispie 10.18). Neisser would face an even greater scandal in his investigations of syphilis: he was accused of infecting innocent people with the disease in his search for an inoculation method (18). He spent his later career directing a prominent dermatology clinic, studying the causes of syphilis and lupus, and advocating sex education, prostitution regulations, and other public health measures (18). He also became the teacher of many later pioneers in the field.

Meanwhile, scientists were beginning to further understand the stages of infection in venereal diseases. Before Neisser's discovery, in 1872, American physician Emil Noeggerath proposed a "latency period" for gonorrhea to show that people could still be carriers and transmit the disease during intercourse, even without any visible symptoms. Later discoveries also tracked the progress of venereal diseases, showing how gonorrhea could result in arthritis, meningitis, and infections of the urinary tract, cervix, and fallopian tubes (Brandt 10). In tracking the progression of gonorrhea, physicians also showed how the disease affected the sexual organs of men and women differently and posited an effect on sterility. These scientific findings would be central to arguments for social reforms concerning venereal diseases.

Although physicians did not develop treatments until later, these discoveries changed discussions of venereal disease. The main findings in the scientific community—including germs as causal agents of disease, the existence of a latency period, the possibility of an unknowing transmitter, and the stages and later effects of venereal diseases—led to a new discourse that emphasized human agency in the body's protection from an outside force, the agent of the "germ,"[3] causing many prominent scientists to urge treating venereal diseases like other infectious diseases. Consequently, through alluding to the new discoveries, reformers gained an exigence to discuss sexuality and argue for social changes on the basis of disease prevention.

The Situation Exploited: Medical Writers and the Discourse of Disease

The popularity of the medical advice book escalated toward the end of the nineteenth century as these new advances in bacteriology occurred, and more physicians addressed audiences aware of these findings. Whether physicians endorsed or rejected the germ theory of disease, it influenced their arguments. In medical texts, bacteriology seems to have promoted a shift from emphasizing treatment to emphasizing prevention. Thus, physicians writing such texts noted the importance of lifestyle practices in preventing the spread of venereal disease, replacing older superstitions with practical information and shifting discourses of disease from questions of morality to questions of public health. According to historian Linda Gordon, physicians replaced the church as the authority on sexual practices, and a shift in language occurred that produced a "translation of ecclesiastical into medical language. What had been sin became physically injurious" (*Woman's Body* 171). Writing from 1873 to 1904, physicians John Scudder, Elizabeth Blackwell, and another key popularizer, Prince Albert Morrow, illustrate the shift in the discourse of disease, as the different stages of scientific knowledge regarding venereal disease became known, as well as the application of medical discourse to social reform.

John Scudder's Bridge Text

John M. Scudder (1829–94) participated in scientific, medical, and social conversations on disease.[4] Drawn to the eclectic practice of medicine because of the variety of choices it allowed for physicians, Scudder defined the eclectic practice as "the right to choose or select from all other systems of medicine whatever [physicians] may deem true and best adapted to the relief and cure of the sick" (qtd. in Garraty and Carnes 19.542).[5] Scudder wrote many textbooks for his students on the eclectic practice of medicine, as well as on the diseases of women and children. His medical textbook *On the Reproductive Organs, and the Venereal*, first published in 1873 and in its third edition by 1890, served as a bridge text between old and new discourses of venereal disease. Older theories focused on physiological causes and hygienic rules for prevention. Newer theories also stressed such hygienic rules but described bacteriological causes. Scudder wrote this textbook when this shift was just beginning to occur. Although the association of bacteria with venereal diseases does not feature prominently in his text, Scudder did take advantage of other vital discoveries.

One piece of new scientific knowledge Scudder applied was the differentiation between venereal diseases, established by Ricord in 1837. Scudder also hinted at germ theory with his statement that different diseases are produced by different "viruses": "Each of these has its peculiar virus, is propagated by direct contact, and produces its own specific poison. The gonorrhoeal virus always produces gonorrhoea, and never chancre or chancroid; chancroid produces chancroid and never gonorrhoea or true chancre; and true chancre reproduces itself, and never either of these diseases" (218). Since many people had blamed the spread of venereal disease on everything from heredity to "marked bodies," and may even have believed that they could catch different diseases from the same germ, Scudder's clarification eliminated these misconceptions. The language here is also significant, naming "viral" causes; the discovery of the microbe causing gonorrhea did not occur until 1879, after Scudder's text was published. Thus, his text incorporated the knowledge of the specific moment, when researchers had accepted germ theory but were still working toward identifying the causal agents of specific diseases. Scudder also spent considerable time enumerating the stages of venereal disease, which physicians had just begun to understand more fully, describing and providing visuals to aid physicians in diagnosis and treatment. His explanations also showed that people with the same disease could have varying symptoms, depending on its stage. These explanations became increasingly important when discussing the early stages of a venereal disease, since sufferers could unknowingly transmit it.

Historians of science Allan Brandt and Vern Bullough both propose that it was the discovery of the latency period that provoked action on the part of physicians. Latency was a new discovery at the time Scudder wrote his first edition. His discussion of the latency period foretold the kind of rhetoric that physicians would later employ: they emphasized the victim status of those who contracted a venereal disease unknowingly from someone in whom the disease was latent. In fact, discussions of the latency period evoked a new image—that of the unknowing transmitter. Scudder depicted this risk:

> A man will frequently disease his wife with gonorrhea before he has felt the first symptom of urethral infection, or feel it first or immediately after such intercourse. He may transmit a soft chancre from a sore not noticed, or that seems little more than an erosion; and true syphilis from the secretion of the diseased membrane before the chancre has formed. In woman, these unconscious sources of disease are far more common, for it may lurk in her genitalia, without producing sensible irritation, the secretion being but little if any changed. She may convey the contagion in this way for months, without being aware that there is anything wrong. (220–21)

The images of this unknowing transmitter with the disease "lurking" in the genitals correspond with many of the metaphors later produced by germ theory: germs as invaders, lurking in "unclean" crevices. The discovery of the latency period provoked urgency for physicians and reformers: they needed to understand the early symptoms to prevent unknowing transmission.

Scudder examined not only the scientific causes of disease but also the social causes. He devoted pages of his textbook to interrogating the practice of prostitution and critiquing how church and state dictated sexual practices, in passages that echo free-love feminism. Some of his theories expressed feminist principles, as he highlighted the double standard between men and women as a cause of prostitution. Like feminist reformers, he condemned the practices that led to the "vice" of prostitution. He also observed that not adhering to natural laws, such as Darwin's theory of sexual selection, specifically the role of female choice in the animal kingdom, caused prostitution (Scudder 62). He denounced the marginalization of women as a factor contributing to the spread of disease, such as when he noted that economic inequality also led to prostitution (67), an argument also made by free-love feminist Rachel Campbell. Thus, in equating the spread of venereal disease with these social problems and with women's inferior status, Scudder offered a link between scientific insights and social consequences requiring reform. Similar logic appears in free-love feminist arguments, as well as in those of physician Elizabeth Blackwell.

Elizabeth Blackwell's Healthy Skepticism

In speeches given in 1881 and 1897 to other medical professionals, Elizabeth Blackwell used her ethos as a physician and the new knowledge about disease transmission to promote sanitary reform. Blackwell's texts are particularly noteworthy since she opposed the germ theory of disease, but her texts still show its influence. She disagreed with those who revered germ theory as an explanation for all diseases, because she believed that both social and bacteriological causes should be attacked.[6] Having promoted sanitary education and advocated that physicians build relationships with their patients, Blackwell feared that the new science of bacteriology would encourage a shift away from these goals (Morantz-Sanchez, "Feminist Theory"). The latency period of gonorrhea, in particular, tended to discourage the belief in germ theory (because no symptoms were present) and fueled Blackwell's skepticism. Like other physicians, she expressed fear that men would infect their unwitting wives with venereal disease: "Sufferers are often a source of danger to innocent people" ("Medical Responsibility" 88). Thus, it was the scientific knowledge of the latency period of gonorrhea, rather than germ theory, that provided Blackwell the exigence to urge sex education reform.

Like other physicians, Blackwell targeted social ideologies that fostered the spread of venereal disease. For example, she refuted beliefs in the overpowering sexual appetites of men: "We must ourselves recognise the truth, and instruct parents, that it is a physiological untruth to suppose that sexual congress is indispensable to male health" ("Medical Responsibility" 103). Late-nineteenth-century physicians often tried, in treatises such as *Instead of Wild Oats* by physician Winfield Scott, to refute the idea that young men needed to "sow wild oats" and have their sexual urges satisfied to prevent ill health (Brandt 26). Similar to Scott, Blackwell endorsed eliminating the double standard in sexual practices for men and women and urged men to uphold the same standards to which they held women. However, Blackwell was not anti-sexuality. She clarified, "The fact of the powerful sexual attraction necessarily existent and dominating in woman, as mother of the race, seems to be quite overlooked . . . although it may exhibit itself in less spasmodic form than in men" ("Medical Responsibility" 92–93). It is important to note that she did not deny women's sexuality or portray them as asexual victims, especially in light of readings of social purity as anti-sexuality.[7]

Blackwell's "Medical Responsibility" speech also stressed the importance of prevention when she argued that physicians needed to look at the links between bacterial and social causes of venereal disease. She used comparison to emphasize her logic: "We may as well expect to cure typhoid fever whilst allowing sewer gas to permeate the house, or cholera whilst bad drinking-water is being taken, as try to cure venereal disease whilst its chief cause remains unchecked" (91–92). The idea that germs could be spread through sewer gas and drinking water seems like a combination of sanitary science with germ theory, and one that would appeal to audiences who would accept this comparison. Thus, her arguments for reform to check the spread of disease combined scientific and social causes of disease. In fact, the science gave new urgency to older social solutions.

Physicians often looked to governments to help check the spread of disease. The British government's response, however, reinforced gender inequalities and necessitated a new rhetorical response from physicians. The Contagious Disease Acts passed in Britain in 1864, 1866, and 1869, which arose in an effort to check the high rates of venereal disease among British soldiers, decreed that prostitutes could be quarantined if found to have venereal disease; women had to register with police and undergo forced medical exams, often without cause—just suspicion of prostitution could land a woman in hospitals undergoing tests and therapies that often resulted in brutal treatment (McElroy, "Contagious Disease Acts"). Blackwell and other social purity advocates, such as Josephine Butler, highlighted the inequities of targeting prostitutes but not the men who frequented them, rendering these acts ineffective in checking the spread of venereal disease. In "Rescue Work," Blackwell offered alternatives by emphasizing education as a means for combating vice and eliminating double standards:

> Inequality between the sexes in the law of divorce, tolerance of seduction of minors, the attempt to check sexual disease by the inspection of vicious women, whilst equally vicious men are untouched—all these striking examples of the unjust and immoral attitude of legislation will serve to show how law may become a powerful agent in producing prostitution through its direct attitude towards licentiousness. (121)

Like Scudder, Blackwell employed ethos as a physician to point out social and economic inequalities, and like the social purity advocates with whom she aligned herself, she focused on how the laws produced a double standard. Social purity advocates did not argue that women should be granted the sexual license that men had but that the laws should take away the license granted to men, which would ensure equal treatment of men and women. Their reform efforts often focused on changes in divorce laws, age of consent laws, and prostitution regulations, all noted by Blackwell. While Blackwell judged prostitutes with the phrase "vicious women," she pointed out that the men who frequented prostitutes should also be held accountable for their actions. Blackwell's argument also illustrates the shift toward human agency in preventing the spread of venereal disease. Based on the warrant that transmission of a germ could be prevented, she urged, "Whilst on the one hand you legislate, on the other hand you educate" (118). Responding to new rhetorical situations, she showed the trend among medical professionals toward both legislation and education to check the spread of venereal disease.

Prince Albert Morrow's Evidence for the "Diseased" Institution of Marriage

Another physician heavily involved in public health campaigns was Prince Albert Morrow (1846–1913). An American physician, born in Kentucky and educated at Princeton and in Europe, Morrow worked in dermatology and studied syphilis in New York City beginning in 1874 (Brandt 14). He was a great admirer of the French researcher Alfred Fournier, and in 1880 he published his translation of Fournier's important text *Syphilis and Marriage* for American audiences (Brandt 11). While practicing as a physician in New York City, Morrow became interested in the rates of venereal diseases among married couples, and after attending a conference on the topic in Brussels, Morrow returned to America, intent on creating public health campaigns to expose the danger of venereal disease to families (14). He formed the National Vigilant Committee in 1906 (which became the American Social Hygiene Association in 1913), a group that included physicians, academics, and hygiene reformers. These societies were instrumental in initiating sex education programs (Engs 145–46). But first, Morrow awakened the public to the prevalence of transmission of venereal diseases in marriage with his 1904 textbook *Social Diseases and Marriage*, illustrating the culmination of the findings of nineteenth-century bacteriology. It targeted a professional audience to accommodate the new knowledge of venereal disease transmission but also addressed a reformist audience, since he shared Blackwell's goals of education and preventative legislation. Morrow exploited the specific moment when more knowledge both of the science of venereal disease and of its prevalence in married couples clearly called for a response.

In the first few pages of his textbook, Morrow referenced Fournier's 1880 book on syphilis and Neisser's 1879 discovery of the gonococcus germ to celebrate how this new knowledge had led to more accurate tests and diagnoses. He also acknowledged new findings with his chapter titled "If Gonococci are Present, there is Danger of Infection; if Absent, there is None" (xi), showing awareness of Koch's postulates. After establishing these scientific axioms, he discussed suitability for marriage based on "risks of contagion" (38), which could now be more accurately diagnosed. The more accurate information on long-term effects of gonorrhea and syphilis leading to sterility and birth defects also helped him employ scientific arguments for reform. For example, he reported, "A percentage variously estimated at from 40 to 80 per cent. of endometritis, mesometritis, and perimetritis is of gonorrhoeal origin and a cause of sterility in women. Noeggerath found in 81 gonorrhoeal women 49 entirely sterile. In 80 sterile marriages, Kehrer found 45 caused by inflammatory and other changes—all of gonorrhoeal origin" (30). Morrow's figures created urgency for discussions of the effect of sexual diseases on women's health and also helped to refute charges of "race suicide" aimed at women, because he offered another explanation for the rates of sterility in marriage (Spongberg 165). Thus, he not only capitalized on the exigence created by scientific discoveries but also created a new exigence based on new knowledge about the prevalence and effects of venereal disease. Together, these exigencies created a new rhetorical situation of reform.

The implications of his work for feminists came from his finding that 30 percent of women infected with venereal disease had caught it from their husbands (Morrow 25). Morrow cited other statistics, as well, such as Noeggerath's finding that "of every thousand men married in New York eight hundred have or have had gonorrhea, from which the great majority of the wives have been infected" (26). He attributed this prevalence to the many sufferers who had been untreated and undiagnosed and added, "My own observations at the New York Hospital extending over a period of several years would indicate that fully 70 per cent. of all women who come there for treatment [of venereal diseases] were respectable married women who had been infected by their husbands" (26–27).[8] Thus, Morrow's statistics characterized the marriage system as a place that sheltered and transmitted disease, giving him a solid basis for a reform agenda. Like many physicians of the early twentieth century, he placed high value on education as a means of preventing disease, and his reform societies were eventually successful in instituting sex education curricula (Engs 145–46). In terms of legislation, Morrow pointed out that the more liberal divorce laws created as a result of the high rates of infection between married couples would not solve the problem, since the disease had already been transmitted (Morrow 35). He therefore supported laws that refused marriage licenses to men infected with a venereal disease.[9] Finally, advocating new sanitary measures to reduce the rates of infection, Morrow equated venereal diseases with other infectious diseases and suggested a similar strategy to that "adopted in the warfare against tuberculosis" (xxi, 385–87). Like other medical writers, Morrow noted the stigma attached to venereal diseases but showed how, by equating them with other infectious diseases caused by germs, the war against these germs could be won.

The Situation Transformed: Opportunities for Social Applications

Physicians were not alone in waging a war against germs. Many medical historians have noted that the popular reception for germ theory was often stronger than the reception it gained in the scientific and medical communities. An 1885 article in *Popular Science Monthly* summed up the American public's enthusiasm:

> The germ theory appeals to the average mind: it is something tangible; it may be hunted down, captured, colored, and looked at through a microscope, then in all its varieties, it can be held directly responsible for so much damage. There is scarcely a farmer in the country who has not read of the germ theory. A cowboy in Arizona was shot dead in the saddle recently by a comrade for the insult implied by calling him a "d——d microbe." (qtd. in Fellman and Fellman 49–50)

Other physicians likened the public's interest in germs to "bacteriomania" (qtd. in Warner and Tighe 234). In popular circles, the reception
of germ theory was almost akin to religious conversion, as historian
Nancy Tomes has examined in her work *The Gospel of Germs*. Scientists
promoting germ theory communicated their theories to the public in
understandable ways and even invited them to participate in this new
science. Tomes points out, "In a Glasgow address reprinted in *Popular
Science Monthly*, [Joseph] Tyndall urged his audience to 'observe how
these discoveries tally with the common practices of life' and offered
examples from his own household, such as his housekeeper's use of brief
applications of heat to keep pheasants and milk 'sweet'" (*Gospel* 40). He
also "asked listeners to think about the molds that grew on wet boots
or a piece of fruit left exposed to the air" (40). Consequently, the public
accepted the germ theory of disease even before many in the scientific
and medical communities did.

A rhetorical perspective further illuminates how the moment and
the audience for these discoveries affected the reception of germ theory.
Carolyn Miller has noted the importance of the concept of "kairos" to
scientific discourse. "Kairos," a term that connotes a specific situation
and exigence, shows us that a rhetor's success depends in part upon
making the right speech to the right audience at the right time. To audiences used to hearing the causes of disease as physiological or hereditary,
germ theory offered a new explanation; more important, this explanation
served to show that diseases could be prevented. Thus, the specific moment of the late nineteenth century, a time of increase in the prevalence
of venereal diseases, produced an exigence that allowed popular audiences
to be more receptive to the new science of bacteriology. In traveling from
the laboratory to the domestic space, the discourse on "germs" promoted
a shift in rhetorical situation. Instead of dealing with the questions of the
laboratory, where finding the bacteria associated with specific diseases
was paramount, the situation outside the laboratory dealt with destroying
the conditions that allowed germs to fester.

The metaphors used to describe germs and disease also contributed
to the popular understanding of germ theory and its use in social reforms. As historians Laura Otis and Tomes have noted, germs were often
portrayed as "invaders" that people had to guard their bodies against:
"William Marp told his audience that germs 'hunt in packs,' and another
physician referred to them as 'atmospheric vultures.' Microbes were often
described in martial terms as attacking, invading, and conquering their
human hosts" (Tomes, *Gospel* 43). These metaphors used to describe

the invisible "attackers" spurred a new rhetoric of responsibility. Tomes observes, "Hygienic infractions once regarded as merely disgusting or ill-bred, such as indiscriminate spitting or coughing, now became defined as serious threats to public health" ("Germ Theory" 257). The public now had a new scapegoat for disease, and the cleanliness of the person and the home gained a new emphasis.

Reforms caused by germ theory unfolded in the late nineteenth century as hospitals began to change their methods of disinfecting, plumbing and sewage treatment were upgraded, and household products, such as cleansers and disinfectants, were marketed as essential to ridding the home of unwanted invaders. The home became the setting for work in applied science with magazines advising "scientific shopping" as well as new appliances to fight germs (Tomes, *Gospel* 166). Such discourse positioned the home as needing protection from outside attackers— germs. Thus, women dominating these domestic spaces became soldiers in the fight against disease. In addition, some feminist reforms took on renewed importance as women's magazines in the 1890s urged "hygienic dress reform" such as shorter skirts because of the risk of trailing longer skirts in dirty water or dust (157). Altogether, germ theory provided the promise that sickness could be prevented through improved personal hygiene. With venereal disease, it was the cleanliness of the person that was emphasized: the metaphorical "unclean" body became the literalized "unclean body."

Once scientists understood sterility and birth defects as effects of venereal disease, reformers had a new line of argument to promote: protect women from venereal disease in order to protect future generations. Morrow and many other physicians emphasized the dangers of venereal diseases to future children, using a eugenic line of argument. For example, Morrow named venereal disease as "an actual cause of the degeneration of the race" (qtd. in Brandt 14). In a 1906 symposium of the American Medical Association, several physicians weighed in on the issue, with Dr. Abraham Wolbarst referring to women as "[t]he flower of our land, our young women, the mothers of our future citizenship" (qtd. in Brandt 15). These arguments emphasizing potential harm to motherhood prompted reform in divorce laws, allowing divorce when venereal disease had been transmitted. Several states also enacted laws in the late 1800s and early 1900s requiring men to get tested and present certification of health before being granted marriage licenses (Brandt 19–20). Other reforms included a higher age of consent as a result of the perceived threat "to the race" from venereal disease. More conservative marriage manuals also discussed venereal disease, such as conservative physician Emma Drake's 1901 manual *What a Young Wife Ought to Know*, which emphasized how syphilis could harm the children of a union, and urged young women and their parents to use their family physician as an ally in choosing their mate (62). Drake also applauded the law in Ohio that required premarital testing of men for venereal disease (62–63). However, as Morrow noted, changes in divorce laws would not solve the problem. It would be feminist reformers who would give presence to the inequality inherent in the marriage system that fostered the spread of disease.

Exploiting the Situation and Warrant in Feminist Rhetorics of Sexuality

Nineteenth-century discussions of women and venereal disease would seem to fall into two camps: blaming women for the spread of the diseases, "not merely as agents of transmission, but as inherently diseased, if not the disease itself" (Spongberg 6), or portraying them as "innocent, weak, and helpless" (Brandt 16), victims of men spreading venereal disease. Both characterizations focus on male-established binaries: women were either scapegoats or victims. Feminist arguments complicated this binary by blaming the spread of venereal disease on social codes restricting women from full sexual autonomy. Social purity feminists, for example, positioned women as the victims of male vice but also argued that the conditions of inequality between men and women needed to change in order to eliminate the conditions that allowed the spread of venereal disease. Frances Willard, the best-known social purist, would have increased exigence for her cause of "home protection" because of the new discourse of disease. In fact, her "home protection" motto implied a connection to the "gospel of germs" rhetoric that Tomes identifies. Germ theory promoted "home protection" from invisible invaders, including changes in plumbing, storing food, and cooking. Willard, however, showed that the home was under attack from within: "home protection" included the sexual practices of men and women, and men become the invaders capable of spreading disease in this discourse. Willard's 1890 speech, "A White Life for Two," argued for various reforms under the mantle of "home protection." Willard discussed both marital rape and age of consent laws, revealing the problems in the current institution of marriage. Unlike free-love feminists, though, Willard sought to reform the marriage system rather than to abolish it, thus making marriage more conducive to "home protection" and "social purity." Like Blackwell, Willard brought up the behavior of soldiers toward women as proof that men needed to be taught purity and also condemned the Contagious Disease Acts, since they punished only women (330). Instead, she emphasized the need for men to lead "pure" lives to become better husbands, rather than "sowing wild oats" (331). Bacteriology had revealed the dangers to women caused by the double standard and by men who led "impure" lives, creating new exigencies for women's rights in the home and accentuating the role of preventative measures in fighting disease and ensuring women's rights. Free-love feminists reacted to this rhetoric, but while they embraced the social purity critiques of sexual double standards, they did not accept the recommended conclusions. Instead, they saw the new rhetorical situation as increased urgency for their own radical reforms.

It would seem that the discourse of venereal disease would have damaged the goals of free-love feminists, since it called for more responsibility and oversight rather than for freedom in sexual relations. In contrast, the new discourse of venereal disease and its emphasis on personal responsibility validated free-love feminist critiques of the "diseased" institution of marriage and made sexual relations and sexual inequalities matters of public debate. Therefore, the kind of critiques spread by free-love feminists for decades became more widespread. They were able to prove that marriage was actually diseased, and, at the turn of the century, they had the statistics to prove it. The new rhetorics of disease also validated their arguments about prostitution; more people were looking at the conditions producing prostitution. However, rather than trying to "save" prostitutes to contain the spread of disease, free-love feminists renewed their claim for prevention: prevent the situations that produce prostitution by eliminating sexual double standards and inequalities in sexual relationships between men and women. Such an emphasis on prevention would have also seemed to weaken free-love feminist claims for women's control over their own bodies and their right to indulge their sexuality. While social purity advocates urged temperance as a result of the new discoveries on venereal disease, free-love feminists saw no reason why such discoveries should refute arguments for women's sexual self-ownership. They thus reacted to such rhetoric with increased calls for comprehensive sex education and women's sexual equality.

The "Diseased" Social Body

Rachel Campbell's 1888 free-love feminist treatise, *The Prodigal Daughter; Or, The Price of Virtue*, interrogated how the restrictions and double standards of female sexuality led to the conditions that spread disease. To make the argument that prostitution was the price for the "virtue" that marriage sought to protect in women, she examined the rhetoric of virtue and the social conditions leading to prostitution. Her treatise combined the old and new rhetoric of the "diseased" institution of marriage, looking at marriage as a figuratively diseased institution and moving into critique of the conditions that spread actual venereal diseases. Arguing that both wives and prostitutes suffered from the inequalities that produced sexual double standards, Campbell employed disease metaphors in her enumeration of the wrongs done to women in sexual slavery. She first turned her attention to the prostitute, deemed the "fallen woman" by a system that had driven her to prostitution because of economic and sexual inequalities, and put a new spin on "protect the women" lines of argument: "We are told society must protect itself, must shield its wives and daughters from all dangerous, contaminating contact with those who are fallen below the standard of sexual morality" (6). She showed, however, that such arguments made women "those who are fallen below the standard of sexual morality," not men. She questioned who actually needed the protection from "contamination," rhetoric that earns a double meaning when looked at alongside the new discourse of disease: the contamination was both the decreased sexual morality and increased instances of venereal disease.

Campbell then turned her attention to marriage, which she believed fostered the same conditions that spread disease among prostitutes. She enumerated the wrongs done to women whose marriage license protected their "virtue" but who, under the same license, could be raped, beaten, and infected with "unclean" diseases:

> Let me give one example to show the peculiar character of this expensive sham, bowed down to and worshiped as sexual virtue. The . . . filthiest and most sensual animal in human form may associate with a woman, so he be her husband, may treat her in the most shameful and brutal manner that woman was ever treated by man, may infect her with sexual disease until her whole system teems with rottenness without any damage to her virtue. The marriage certificate does double duty: it is at once his license and her shield of honor. Her health, her happiness, and even her life may be destroyed, but her virtue is safe. (10)

Campbell's own brutal experience with marriage influenced her attention to how the marriage license was supposed to protect "virtue" but did no such thing. Her logic showed how marriage instead reinforced double standards of morality and sexuality that also created the "fallen women" of prostitution. Thus, marriage was no protection for women but created the same conditions that fostered the spread of disease in prostitution. Campbell even postulated that the social purity goal of "protection" for women was a sham to disguise what men really wanted protected: their sexual power over women. She insisted, "[O]ur laws regulating marriage were not framed for the protection of the wife, the education of the children, nor the welfare of the home, but to protect each man from the encroachments of all other men and insure him the peaceable possession of the woman he claimed" (26–27). She presented an interesting twist on the nineteenth-century rhetoric of the "angel" of the home: the cult of domesticity existed to maintain men's sexual ownership of women. Why else, she asked, would men not ensure full equality for women? Why else would an institution that did not protect women be maintained under the mantra of her protection? She implored men to interrogate their own motives in keeping women from full economic equality, which would eliminate the need for them to turn to prostitution:

> O, men, fathers and brothers, how long will you deceive yourselves and try to deceive us? You claim to be generous towards the women, and yet you systematically deceive and defraud her. You affect great regard for her virtue, while your own is neglected and forgotten. You regulate the industry in a way that crushes her, excludes her altogether from many kinds of remunerative labor, gives her less pay than man receives for the same work, then you figure in the sex market as a buyer, and yet tell us you deplore prostitution. (30–31)

Campbell's argument exposing the sham of virtue also exposed the "diseased" institution of marriage. In addition to free love, economic equality would solve the problem of women's sex slavery in the diseased institution. Her logic, while not explicitly engaging the discourse of disease, reacted to the rhetoric arising from the new discourse about purity and virtue. While such rhetoric had existed prior to scientific investigations into venereal disease, the new scientific data refreshed such rhetoric and put it in a different light. Thus, free-love feminists responded to the new rhetoric of responsibility by pointing out that the problems would not be solved by curing disease or instituting new sanitary measures but by changing sexual inequality.

Campbell's friend and free-love feminist cohort Lois Waisbrooker also found a renewed urgency to critique "diseased" institutions and arrived at the same conclusions using similar logic. In *The Sex Question and the Money Power*, a speech she delivered in 1873 and published in pamphlet form with revisions in 1890, Waisbrooker attacked the economic system for causing sexual inequality and interrogated the connection between the power given to money and to sex. Based on the premise that the "whole social body" is "diseased all the way through" (77–78), Waisbrooker's conclusion matched Campbell's: metaphorical disease persisted because economic and sexual inequality led to literal disease.

Waisbrooker also critiqued attitudes toward prostitution, revealing their fallacy in condemning the "fallen woman" for having no other option while chaining the "virtuous" woman to legal prostitution—marriage. She insisted that the married woman could never be pure in an institution that degraded her. Similar to Campbell's claim that marriage was maintained to preserve men's sexual power, Waisbrooker called out the hypocrisy of an institution claiming to preserve the purity of women: "But when it is proposed to set woman entirely free from man's domination sexually, then the anxiety manifested for the preservation of purity is wonderful to behold. For the preservation of purity! We must first have [it] before we can preserve it; and true purity we never can have so long as we are under the rule of the present order of things" (*Sex Question* 80). She pointed out that opponents of free love often invoked the sanctity of an institution without sanctity, for how could an institution that never had purity claim to preserve it? Her logic aligned her with other reformers arguing that one could not cure actual diseases until metaphorical ones were cured.

Waisbrooker did allude to the actual diseases infiltrating "virtuous" institutions, but she mostly concentrated on the effects, particularly the effects of such diseases on offspring: "We know all this to be true; and know, also, that broken health and diseased, discordant children are the legitimate fruits of these legal prostitutions—evils fully as terrible as those that arise from illegal prostitution" (79). Her logic then elicited eugenic discourse: women needed freedom to keep themselves from disease and to prevent "discordant children." She evoked "woman's true position as the mother of the race" to remind those opposed to granting women's sexual freedom that they were consigning "the race" to disease when they failed to observe women's sexual rights. To Waisbrooker, the panacea for all diseases, both social and physical, was women's sexual freedom, her right to control her own body. However, like Campbell, she attributed the lack of freedom to a false economic system and contended that both men and women needed to be free of the disease that the "worship" of money spread over the population. Her more radical economic rhetoric then called for a labor revolution to solve the sexual problem, since the two were inextricably connected: "One is but the complement of the other, and the elements are at work which will bring both results" (91). The refreshed rhetorical situation arising from the new emphasis on disease prevention allowed radical reinterpretations of the true root of the problem.

Campbell and Waisbrooker seized the opportunity to drive the debate in a new direction, one that would attack the core of the metaphorical disease spread through false sexual teachings and sexual relations. Instead of insisting that the home, or the woman's body representing the safe home, be protected from disease, they urged prevention by curing "diseased" mentalities. Women did not need protection from disease but from diseased notions of virtue that then caused actual disease to spread. The "home protection" rhetoric spurred by the "gospel of germs" received new meanings in light of these radical rhetorics of sexuality. However, while Campbell and Waisbrooker rejected social purity values because they did not address the root of the problem, other free-love feminists embraced them.

"Home Protection"

One-time free-love feminist Tennessee Claflin devoted many of her later writings to critiquing the spread of venereal disease among women. Her earlier writings, when she still explicitly advocated free love, evoked these issues in critiquing the status of women under institutional marriage; her later writings, more in line with social purity aims, paid homage to free-love feminist rhetoric in her interrogation of venereal diseases. However, her solutions in later writings centered not on women's sexual emancipation, the free-love feminist panacea, but on government regulation, an anti-free-love tenet. Nevertheless, all her writings, whether advocating free love or social purity aims, critiqued women's status in sexual relations, given more urgency by the discourse of disease.

As early as her 1871 speech on constitutional equality, Claflin attacked the double standard that restricted women while condoning the same behavior in men. She interrogated the rhetoric of "purity" and "impurity," noting its uneven applications to men and to women. She clarified, however, that women perpetuated this double standard by accepting it, and they accepted it because of their unequal status in marriage (*Constitutional Equality* 29–30). Since women could not choose their own sexual conditions, they endured the unequal conditions, thus perpetuating the double standard. In further critiquing the double standard in *The Ethics of Sexual Equality*, she inquired why the male "reformed rake" was welcomed into homes and sought after for marriage, while the reformed female prostitute was not (15). Rachel Campbell also attacked such double standards, asking why the "boy sows his 'wild oats' as a matter of course, and then settles down into a sober industrious man, and becomes a good husband, a fond parent, and perhaps a distinguished citizen" (*Prodigal Daughter* 11). Such respectability was kept from "the girl [who] was his partner in the wild oat business," who could "become a good wife, a loving mother, and a valuable member of society. No good reason can be given why the door of reform is ever held invitingly open for a boy, and bolted and barred against a girl" (11). Such critiques of the double standard became common for free-love feminists and social purity reformers during this time period, the same time period where medical science revealed how diseases had infiltrated marriages. Earlier free-love feminists, such as Mary Gove Nichols, cataloged the wrongs done under marriage but did not have the same urgency to critique the double standards of sexual practices. The new discourse of disease provided that urgency. For Claflin, inequalities allowed marriages to become diseased, both literally and figuratively.

Claflin also attacked the conditions spreading such "diseased" notions of purity among men and women and took aim at doctors who, she said, would never cure diseases until they examined these inequalities: "True, our physicians with their vile stuffs profess to, and in some instances think they do cure disease. But I can assure them they never yet cured any diseases. They may have modified its symptoms, even have caused the effects to cease, but the causes are always left untouched, since next to nothing is known of causes" (*Ethics* 4). At the time of this particular speech, 1873, scientists had yet to discover the germs causing particular venereal diseases. Thus, she argued that doctors could not cure the problems of marriage until they looked to the chief cause of diseases in marriage: marriage itself. She exhorted:

> Were your vision outraged by an unsightly, poisonous tree, you would not attempt its destruction by first lopping off a few of its longest branches, and thus work from the circumference inward, but you would lay your axe to its very roots, and, by one grand felling, destroy it forever. Where, then, are the roots of the pernicious tree that has grown to such dimensions and extended its branches in such alarming directions? (6)

Claflin reacted to the calls for reform of marriage, rather than its destruction, by pointing out their fallacy. The "roots" that required the ax were both marriage and false ideas of women's virtue. She then shifted to rhetoric similar to Blackwell's, who wanted doctors to look more critically at the social causes spreading disease. While Claflin's discourse of disease is veiled here, since she invoked the metaphor of disease rather than the actual venereal diseases spreading among women, her later arguments shifted from the metaphorical to the literal discourse of disease.

Two essays in particular, "The Degradation of the Sexes, I" and "The Degradation of the Sexes, II," critiqued the new rhetoric of venereal disease and its applications to women. Her analysis aligned with Blackwell's as she attacked the Contagious Disease Acts for their uneven applications; she noted that the laws not only condoned but encouraged male sexual license, particularly among soldiers and sailors ("Degradation . . . I" 39). Of these acts, she wrote, "[They] would be admirable if [they] . . . applied impartially to both sexes, but . . . [are] grossly tyrannous when applied to only one" ("Maternity" 32). She also condemned those who blamed the prostitute for the spread of disease, since the same institutions that condemned her also led her into prostitution because of the sexual double standard ("Degradation . . . II" 52). The statistics she quoted on venereal disease led her to her sarcastic solution: "We require, therefore, a Male Rescue Society, and one on a huge scale. There is a vast number of philanthropic people of rank and influence in our midst, generous and sympathetic men who are willing to be presidents of Rescue Societies and Purity Societies for women. Are there no ladies of high position who will do as much for the men?" ("Degradation . . . I" 47). Though she often aligned herself with social purity aims in these later essays, her radicalism did not allow her to accept "Purity Societies" run by men to "save" prostitutes. Why not look at the social conditions and inequalities that produced prostitution? Such questions were common in the discourse of disease of the late nineteenth century. Germ theory did not solve all of the problems of interrogating the causes of venereal disease; therefore, feminists had renewed urgency for looking at inequalities in legal and illegal sexual relationships. New scientific discoveries produced more urgency for reform.

Claflin's writings also referred to the recent discoveries of venereal disease as a new exigence for sex education. In "The Degradation of the Sexes, II," Claflin praised both the medical profession's new methods and the latest sanitary measures instituted for decreasing the mortality from syphilis (49). She also noted the effects of syphilis on the body and its potential to affect fertility and cause "diseased" children (49). In her essay "A Short History of Marriage," she referenced new findings, such as the latency period of certain diseases, when she cautioned that people infected with venereal disease could transmit it without showing visible symptoms. Under Claflin's logic, such findings renewed the call for equality of the sexes. She lamented the "scourge called syphilis" and pointed out that "often men of rank and education are not ashamed to give their daughters to those who have suffered from it" (38); she thus renewed the call for these "daughters" to have more control. Viewing the transmission of disease as a new reason for advocating sex education, she enumerated its benefits in "The Degradation of the Sexes, II":

> Thousands of girls budding into womanhood would never have been seduced and driven to prostitution if their own mothers had only taught them what seduction meant; if they had only instructed them in all that relates to marriage and maternity; if they had properly guarded them against the practices of professional seducers. And thousands of boys would have been spared physical and mental life misery if their fathers had rightly warned them against secret practices, and how to "fell youthful lusts." (56)

The call for sex education, also made by social purity advocates, received new urgency: young women could protect themselves if provided such knowledge. Since she also attacked ideas that young men needed to "sow wild oats," Claflin was not advocating protection for women only. The sex education she promoted would also correct common social misconceptions about the sexual drives of men. Her type of sex education would not, however, make young people view their bodies as "unclean." In fact, she protested against such ideas, noting that ideologies that teach young people "to disregard [their] bodies, as things vile and unclean," actually increased the cases of venereal infection because of ignorance ("Advice to Parents" 136). Thus, while some of her "protect the young women" rhetoric seemed more conservative, her radical aims still persisted.

The portrayal of women as "pure" victims of licentious men found a place in Claflin's arguments. She lamented that "reformed" men were still deemed "fit to become a father or to ally himself with a pure and beautiful virgin" because traditional customs allowed it ("Regeneration" 63). However, Claflin blamed social customs for the emphasis on the "purity" of young women and noted that such customs also caused a young woman to "wither in her virginity" until a "suitable" man was found, who would often prove to be quite unsuitable since the same customs had allowed him to engage in behavior that led to venereal disease ("Maternity" 29). It seems that Claflin was not encouraging "purity" for women, though some of her rhetoric appears to stress it. Rather, she highlighted the hypocrisy in how customs forced women to remain virgins but then gave them over to diseased men.

Claflin's arguments also invoked the same kind of eugenic rhetoric used to support the new divorce laws. She emphasized the dangers of venereal disease "to the race" and diverged from other free-love feminists by insisting on testing for venereal diseases before marriage. Other, more anarchist free-love feminists would have disdained such mandatory testing but would not have objected to both partners examining their own "fitness" for marriage. Claflin's call for such testing was a matter of "fitness" as well: "But whether inspection ever be insisted on or not—and it will if parents demand it—the individual duty of testing one's own fitness remain the same. No man or woman has any moral right, whatever the law may be, to indulge in procreation at the cost of health and happiness of the offspring" ("Advice to Parents" 133). She thus advocated marriage only with "medical certificate of their fitness" ("Social Injustice" 128). In this new discourse of disease, "fitness" was a matter of being free of venereal disease. But it opened the doors to explore other definitions of "fitness" and "unfitness." While she employed the same rhetorical tools as social purity advocates in adopting "protect the pure women" rhetoric, even the more tempered radicalism she espoused later in her life still conformed to several free-love feminist goals: the need for elimination of double standards, a redefinition of what "purity" should be, and the need for sex education for both sexes.

These same goals found their way into Victoria Woodhull's earlier free-love feminism. The discourse of disease provided her not only with new exigence for her critique of marriage but also with a new warrant for her eugenic ideals. In her 1888 pamphlet *Stirpiculture; or, The Scientific Propagation of the Human Race*, Woodhull supported forms of "stirpiculture," or eugenics, using logic similar to the logic behind laws in several states that prevented men inflicted with venereal disease from getting married. She set up a series of propositions, one of which was "Thou shalt not marry when malformed or diseased" (9). We see here the beginnings of the eugenic rhetoric of the early twentieth century that attempted to prevent the "unfit" from procreating. Such discourse had its root in efforts to prevent the spread of venereal disease, but it was shaped for quite different and more sinister ends at the turn of the century. Her rhetoric previewed the kind that doctors produced in response to Morrow's later conclusions about venereal disease as a threat to the family unit and to future generations. Woodhull's text also condemned society's efforts to reform the harms done in the marriage system, noting that they were misguided: "The laws of the United States are constructed to deal with effects only, and do not take into consideration the causes" (*Stirpiculture* 26–27). Many free-love feminists, including Severance and Waisbrooker, shared this sentiment. These reformers believed that only a system where women could choose their husbands freely, not under economic duress, and where their actions and sexual practices would not be dictated by law, would cure society of its ills and, in this new context, would cure society of literal diseases. The discourses coming out of the discipline of bacteriology strengthened their claim that the institution of marriage produced the conditions for disease and also gave them a new argument to apply to their goals. The argument to protect the woman's body from disease, a more conservative goal, gained a feminist spin in free-love texts. It is in texts like Woodhull's and Claflin's that we see more cooperation between social purity and free-love rhetoric.

"Don't Blame Sex"

Other radical reformers, however, rejected all social purity aims attempting to correct inequalities by protecting women. According to these free-love feminists, such rhetoric by social purity advocates, instead of correcting the problems, served to reinforce "diseased" ideologies. For example, in critiquing Frances Willard's rhetoric of home protection and goal to raise the age of consent, Lillian Harman pointed out that Willard reinforced the idea of chastity as one of the highest virtues of women and that arguments to protect women's "honor" only served to enslave them further ("'Age-of-Consent' Symposium: A Protest"). Some free-love feminists feared the turn toward anti-sexuality. Hulda Potter-Loomis, for example, lampooned advocates of "purity" who purported to be above the "vulgar" instincts of sexuality. She critiqued those advocates of abstinence who would view such a life as superior to one that indulged sexual needs. Characterizing such advocates as placing themselves upon the "throne of reason," looking down at those who would dare to embrace sexuality, Potter-Loomis described such a throne as a "cold, barren place, absolutely devoid of every element that is calculated to add to human comfort and satisfaction" (11). She thus contended that the risks involved in sexual behavior did not mean that sexual behavior was at fault. Instead, she urged a renewed examination of the practices that subjugated women sexually.

Potter-Loomis's logic exposed the institution of marriage as a sham that impeded progress and allowed men "ownership" of the "wife's sexual organs" (17, 18). This language, emphasizing that husbands could control their wives' bodies and distancing women from the sexual organs that men controlled, received new urgency by the discourse of disease: husbands who controlled their wives' sexual organs could infect them. Potter-Loomis did not explicitly engage the discourse of disease, but several of her statements evoked this discourse, such as when she referred to the "evils which have grown out of restrictions" (7), a phrasing that suggests disease as the "social evil" being spread by the restrictions inherent in the marriage system. Immediately after calling to mind such evils, Potter-Loomis referenced new divorce laws, which she predicted would not cause significant change. The reference to such laws immediately after the reference to "evils" in the marriage system implies a criticism of the newer divorce laws put in place in order to protect women from husbands infected with venereal disease in the 1880s, a connection similar to Morrow's later arguments.

Potter-Loomis referred to marriage as a "whited sepulcher" sheltering damaging behaviors: "What a 'whited sepulcher' our temple of virtue and morality is and what hypocrites we are who bow before its altar" (21). This New Testament image of the "whited sepulcher" was also used to describe the homes that allowed germs to fester. In an 1883 article in the *North American Review*, Charles Wingate exposed "the unsanitary homes of the rich," showing that germs could attack the homes of the poor and the rich, with inadequate plumbing as a chief cause. After describing houses "of imposing dimensions, palatial in their adornments, and seeming to lack nothing to promote comfort, enjoyment, and health," he went on to proclaim, "A larger number of these houses are mere whited sepulchers, and their luxurious inmates are exposed to constant risk of disease and death" (qtd. in Tomes, *Gospel* 48). The use of this same image reveals that both the home and the institution of marriage sheltered germs of disease, whether it was an actual germ, as in Wingate's discourse, or a metaphorical germ, as in Potter-Loomis's 1890s treatise. As Juliet Severance asserted in 1901, institutional marriage had not succeeded as "the safeguard of virtue" (*Marriage* 4–5).

Like other free-love feminists, Potter-Loomis urged a deeper look into the ways that customs and institutions harmed women. But she also went further than Campbell, Waisbrooker, and Claflin in celebrating sexuality, since she criticized those who championed abstinence as protection, believing "human desire is the true spur to human progress, and we mark our progress by the fulfillment of our desires" (14). Free-love feminists like Potter-Loomis, Woodhull, Forster, and Severance attempted to reframe sexual discourses by showing that it was not sex itself that was "impure" but the way some people practiced it. Advocates for social purity wanted both men and women to reach the same "virtuous" state (read abstinent) in regard to sexuality, while free-love feminists condemned arguments for abstinence because they wanted to critique the social mores that led to unequal applications of "virtue" and the institutions that sheltered men's actions and left women vulnerable. Since they were doing so after the advent of germ theory, their calls for reform became more relevant.

"Body Housekeeping"

The most radical sex reformers seemed to worship sex and the body, making the new discourse of the body an enemy to their aims. However, they still took advantage of the new metaphors created by the discourses of bacteriology and venereal disease for much different ends. Angela Heywood appears to be the most radical free-love feminist, as she was one of the few who advocated abortion. Heywood made two unique arguments that reworked the discourse of disease to radical feminist ends. In an 1887 article titled "Personal Attitudes—Plain Facts," Heywood took aim at the censors of sex speech and charged them with fostering the conditions for disease. Since the censors kept women from knowing about the body, they were keeping them from knowing how to protect it. For Heywood, "ignorance begets disease; but in knowledge Health arrives to teach and to listen" ("Personal Attitudes"). This new line of argument combined the ones found in both physiology and bacteriology discourses: only when women could speak freely about sex could they learn the practices that would maintain health and restrain disease. Such logic was the basis of later sex education reforms, but Heywood employed it to fuel her personal war against censorship. In this way, she molded the conservative discourse of disease to her own radical ends: that language, or more specifically, "obscene" language, provided salvation to women. Her piece "Body Housekeeping—Home Thrift," published in 1893 in the last issue of *The Word*, took her signature confrontational rhetoric and applied it to the right of women to have abortions. In this work, her reconfiguring of abortion not only relied on legal language but also on the new metaphors created by the popularized germ theory of disease.

Heywood presented abortion as a form of "washing" when she asked, "Is it 'proper,' 'polite,' for men, real *he* men, to go to Washington to say, by penal law, fines, and imprisonment, whether woman may continue her natural right to wash, rinse or wipe out her own vaginal body opening,—as well as legislate when she may blow her nose, dry her eyes, or nurse her babe[?]" ("Body Housekeeping—Home Thrift"). Heywood's metaphor likened unwanted pregnancy to a germ in the body that must be washed out. The metaphors about germs that Tomes and scholar JoAnne Brown identify correlate with such logic. Both scholars find that in nineteenth-century discourses of disease, germs were the invaders that needed to be cleansed with proper hygiene. In Heywood's argument, the body is infected by a germ, or stranger, a connection perhaps made possible by August Weismann's use of the word "germ" in the "germ plasm theory of heredity" he asserted in 1883 (see chapter 6). For Heywood, the process of abortion was a means of hygiene; it was compared with the benign act of washing the body. She likened the act of "washing" out the vagina with the common practice of blowing one's nose—both acts done in response to invasion by "germs."

Heywood concluded her argument with another reference to abortion as "body housekeeping": "Sex is not an unheard of or an unfelt fact in any one, and the sooner body housekeeping has rational mention the better. Intelligent acquaintance with, and clear knowledge of ourselves will replace the song of disease with the song of Health, and make home-thrift the rule, instead of the exception" ("Body Housekeeping— Home Thrift"). Her emphasis on the home and metaphor of the body as something that needed cleaning and housekeeping connected with the language used in those campaigns. Thus, in Heywood's portrayal, abortion became "home protection," the same rhetoric employed by those applying science to everyday practices. When we look at her text on "body housekeeping" alongside the rhetoric of "home protection" in the popular discourse arising from germ theory, we see the influence of the new metaphors.

From "Protection" to Liberation and Back to "Protection"

Throughout the century, free-love feminists had critiqued the marriage system, invoking the metaphor of disease. It is no surprise that free-love feminism became more prevalent at the same time that the scientific community was finding out how deeply actual disease had infiltrated the marriage system. The arguments of social purity and free-love feminists were therefore refreshed by the new warrants provided by bacteriology. Science had also emphasized the role of human agency in the war against germs, but it wasn't until Neisser discovered the germ agent in gonorrhea that the same logic applied to venereal disease. As Morrow insisted, the war against venereal diseases needed to be waged in the same way as the war against diseases such as tuberculosis (xxi, 385–87). The discovery of the new disease agent provided a general reform warrant, which could then be applied in numerous ways, helping reformers defeat beliefs that venereal diseases punished immoral women and renewing the exigence for sex education. Neisser's discovery gave reformers a warrant to equate the logic behind the new hygienic rules of disease prevention to the logic behind the sexual reforms they championed. Woodhull illustrated the comparisons they made:

> If there be a cesspool in a street, the neighbours do not hastily cover it up so that it may be hidden from the public view. No; they have the very bottom dredged that their loved ones may not sicken and die from the malaria. But the social and political cesspools may go on gathering in the germs of deadly miasma, while each human soul vies with the other to ignore the fatal effects. (*Stirpiculture* 24)

Medical and social reformers attacked these social and political "cesspools," hoping to check their spread of venereal disease, but it was free-love feminists who revealed the depth of these cesspools and their impact on women. Finally, the new discourses of disease planted the seeds for the eugenic rhetoric that would come to characterize free-love feminist rhetoric in naming disease as a cause for "unfitness" for marriage and breeding. The same discourse that helped them create a greater sense of urgency, making sex a vital topic of discussion, also helped push free-love feminists away from critiquing gendered assumptions and toward advocating reforms with raced, classed, and gendered implications.

5

Embryology: Toward a Eugenic Warrant
for Free-Love Feminism

The first thing to be done is to get rid of the idea that sex in its parts and manifestations is something to be ashamed of. Another has well said: "No one idea has ever fettered the progress of the race and retarded its development to such an extent as the silly superstition that there is something repulsive in the origin of life, something obscene in the process of human reproduction."
—Lois Waisbrooker, *The Fountain of Life*, 1893

When Rachel Campbell was in her teens, she found herself married to a man she called a brute who shocked her with his lewd humor on their wedding night. She also found herself unprepared for recognizing the symptoms of pregnancy and had to rely on her husband, who merely laughed and made "every thing as dreadful and mysterious to her as he could" when he realized what her symptoms meant (M. Johnson 32). Campbell suffered from her ignorance of sexual matters and thus as a free-love feminist promoted sex education so young women would not have to endure the same ordeals. Silence on issues like pregnancy proliferated in the nineteenth-century United States. Women writing in diaries would refer to illness but did not specify that they felt ill from pregnancy, and their children would be shocked by the news of a new sibling (Peavy and Smith 41–42). Free-love feminists made it their mission to challenge such silences, yet they did not speak about the issue of pregnancy in the ways we might think: they did not personalize the issue but discussed pregnancy only in a scientific manner, detailing the conditions under which women would become pregnant and the conditions pregnant women should experience. They also discussed the outcomes of pregnancy. Thus, they kept pregnancy narratives in a scientific context, and new discoveries in the discipline of embryology influenced such narratives.

In her 1893 work *Fountain of Life,* Lois Waisbrooker demonstrated one of the roles embryology filled in free-love feminist arguments: to make sex less "obscene" and "repulsive," the sex act had to be positioned in a scientific perspective as a step in the process of reproduction and a step in the process of evolution. While knowledge of physiology provided the warrants for arguments asserting women's status as sexual beings and bacteriology provided warrants for arguments confirming marriage as a "diseased" institution, the discourse of evolutionary theory combined with the new discipline of embryology and theories of heredity gave free-love feminists arguments on the beneficial results of practicing free love that would be more convincing to their audiences. The developments in embryology, or the study of the development of organisms, could have been read as helping to confirm women's status as child-bearers and to restrict their activities from the public sphere, since these developments emphasized the need to protect women during the sensitive times of conception and gestation. But actually, reformers concerned with sexuality used the new knowledge about embryological development to further their specific women's rights agendas. Stressing the importance of the mother to prenatal development, free-love feminists argued the need for her protection, not from physical or mental activity, but from ignorance, bondage, and brutality. In this new perspective, women's rights and free love become a logical outcome of scientific discoveries.

Nineteenth-Century Embryology

In 1651, William Harvey made the famous statement that "all that is alive comes from the egg" (qtd. in Pinto-Correia 2). This new focus on the egg would resonate in later centuries, but it was in the nineteenth century that embryology emerged as a premier discipline because of the work of the preeminent embryologist Carl Ernst von Baer (1792–1876) and advances in cytology. During the nineteenth century, embryology became a formalized scientific discipline, capitalizing on technological advances in the microscope as well as on theoretical advances such as evolution. Embryology achieved status as the study of development, contributing to knowledge of sexuality and reproduction. Scientists considered the concerns of embryology the source of knowledge for how we got here and where we are going as a species. As von Baer stated in 1828, "The history of development is the true source of light for the investigation of organized bodies" (qtd. in Coleman 36). Similarly, Ernst Haeckel found the study of embryology integral to understanding the present and the future: "Development is now the magic word by means of which we shall solve the riddles by which we are surrounded" (qtd. in Oppenheimer 272). Though optimistic and idealistic in their interpretations of the role of embryology, their focus yielded practical applications. By unlocking the mystery of the embryo, scientists would reveal the mysteries of human descent and open a door that reformers would glide through in their attempts to reconfigure women's roles in evolutionary ascent. The three main questions addressed by nineteenth-century embryology concerned whether the adult organism was preformed or went through a specific process of development—the preformation versus epigenesis debate; whether the development of the embryo reflected the stages of development of a species (known as recapitulation theory); and whether males or females were primarily responsible for the characteristics of the growing organism.

Von Baer contributed to the formation of the discipline of embryology in his study of the mammalian egg in 1828, which showed how organisms develop through a process of differentiation (Bowler and Morus 170–71). Von Baer performed his influential work while holding positions as professor of anatomy and zoology in Vienna, Wurtzburg, and Konigsburg (T. Williams 26). His investigation into the layers of embryos began after his colleague Ignaz Dollinger suggested he study chick embryos. However, this work, which included looking at the blastodermic membrane removed from the yolk, proved expensive, as it required a large number of eggs and someone to oversee the incubator. Von Baer instead chose to develop the work of his friend Christian Pander, who had been investigating the layers of the vertebrate embryo and had found three layers in 1817. Von Baer then theorized that these "germ layers" were central to the development of the embryo and later showed how these distinct membranes developed into the body's separate systems and tissues (Porter and Ogilvie 1.111–12). Von Baer also focused on finding the mammalian ovum. While Harvey had previously sought the mammalian egg in the uterus of a deer, von Baer sought the egg in the ovary of a dog—and found it. This work would be critical to resolving the debates between two camps whose split characterized embryology prior to the nineteenth century.

Von Baer's work on germ layers drove the last nail into the coffin of preformation theory, whose adherents had debated with those supporting epigenesis since the seventeenth century. Preformationists posited that all living organisms were preformed and that there was a primordial organism in which the forms of all succeeding generations were encased. The logic behind preformationism was that nothing could come from nothing (Pinto-Correia xv). On the other hand, epigenesists viewed embryonic development as a process, with each stage as the basis of the next stage in the process (Coleman 35–36). Preformationists were not logically wrong; they understood that spontaneous generation could not exist. However, while their general warrant would be accepted, their specific claim would be rejected by nineteenth-century embryologists. Von Baer's work, for example, helped to show that the embryo went through specific stages in its development. He also refuted the belief that all vertebrate embryos had the same developmental pattern and argued instead that they were merely similar in early stages, which he proved by leaving labels off embryos from different species (Porter and Ogilvie 1.112). He published his influential studies of the mammalian egg in 1827. Scientists who examined the development of different animals proved epigenesis, and support for preformation began to wane (43). Epigenesis thus provided a new warrant—that embryonic development went in distinct stages, each dependent on the previous stage.

Indebted to the work of von Baer, Charles Darwin posited that the stages of development demonstrated the progression of species from lower to higher organisms. Darwin found support for the progression to higher stages through embryonic development, though he clarified, "The embryo in the course of development generally rises in organisation: I use this expression, though I am aware that it is hardly possible to define clearly what is meant by the organisation being higher or lower. But no one probably will dispute that the butterfly is higher than the caterpillar" (*Origin* 356). Darwin saw the products of evolution in an ascending series, which also became an important warrant for reformers.

Another influential philosophy in the study of embryology was recapitulation theory, which proposed that each organism would go through an evolutionary series in its development, from lower to higher forms (Russett 50). The organism would, that is, recapitulate its ancestry in its development. Proponents of recapitulation theory such as Johann Friedrich Meckel (1781–1833) and Ernst Haeckel (1834–1919) believed that they could look to the whole history of the animal phyla to explain the individual organism's development. Meckel said in 1821, "The development of the individual organism obeys the same laws as the development of the whole animal series; that is to say, the higher animal, in its gradual evolution, essentially passes through the permanent organic stages which lie below it" (qtd. in Coleman 50). Haeckel, a professor of zoology responsible for coining the term "ecology," became one of Darwin's most enthusiastic proponents after meeting him in 1866. Haeckel found that Darwin's theories supported his own intense interest in recapitulation. Drawing on the finding that gill pouches existed in both bird and mammal embryos that were not present in the adults of these species (Porter and Ogilvie 1.442–43), Haeckel theorized that "ontogeny (the development of the individual organism) recapitulates phylogeny (the evolutionary history of the species)" (Bowler and Morus 170), the primary tenet of recapitulation theory. A gifted artist, he also produced depictions of species descent to support recapitulation theory, which would later be discredited.[1]

The theory of recapitulation, based on a structure that placed humans at the top of an evolutionary hierarchy, positioned humanity as the intended goal of evolution (Bowler and Morus 153). Proponents of recapitulation theory saw the embryo as the model for evolution, with the embryo literally going through the process of evolution in its development (151–53). While recapitulation had its adherents and detractors, the theory, based on misinterpretation of the laws of parallelism, nevertheless contributed to increased interest in embryology and important findings in the field (Mayr, *Growth* 471, 474). Use of the embryo as a model for evolution in recapitulation theory eventually supplied a line of argument for reformers: the embryo residing within the woman made her an agent of evolution, and she was literally the setting where evolution would take place.

Darwin's question of how changes and variation occurred provided the most important reform warrant. His theory of "descent with modification" placed the occurrence of variations within the embryo, but he was careful to note, "The question is not, at what period of life any variation has been caused, but at what period it is fully displayed" (*Origin* 358). Darwin left the question of agency open, which provided a gap that reformers could enter. His speculation on how variation occurs was of particular significance for later reform rhetoric:

> The cause [of variation between parents and offspring] may have acted, and I believe generally has acted, even before the embryo is formed; and the variation may be due to the male and female sexual elements having been affected by the conditions to which either parent, or their ancestors, have been exposed. Nevertheless an effect thus caused at a very early period, even before the formation of the embryo, may appear late in life; as when a hereditary disease, which appears in old age alone, has been communicated to the offspring from the reproductive element of one parent. (358)

Darwin's theory that the "sexual elements" could be affected, sometimes to the detriment of later offspring, became a central point in reformers' arguments. The lack of precise agency here was also a critical point since reformers were then left to nominate agents that served their argument.

However, it was cytology, the study of cells, that exerted the most influence over the study of embryology, especially concerning the question of whose material, the male's or the female's, contributed most to the formation and characteristics of their offspring. Prior to the nineteenth century, preformationists had split into two camps: "ovists," who believed that the preformed new being was stored in the egg, and "spermists," who believed that the preformed new being was located in the sperm (Pinto-Correia xvi). In classical times, some viewed the influence of the mother as stronger because of the sharing of the blood and blood vessels (Needham 216). Other theories concerned the semen giving "form" to the embryo with the female providing the "shaping" (40). Clearly, whether the influence of the male or the female was emphasized often depended upon gender ideologies (45). Nicolas Venette's influential 1686 sex manual *Tableau de L'amour Conjugal* had ignored the debates between ovists and spermists in favor of the classical views of Hippocrates, who theorized that both male and female produced "seed" through ejaculation that combined to form the offspring, leading to the persistence of the idea that female orgasm was required for conception (Porter and Hall 75–78). The focus on understanding cells in the nineteenth century helped to clarify the process of fertilization.

Cytology allowed scientists to understand the creation of new life as a division of cells and also pointed the way toward understanding how the egg and sperm contributed to the new cell (Bowler and Morus 165). In 1843, embryologists with improved microscopes viewed the sperm interacting with the egg, which showed how fertilization occurred, though the significance of this finding was not realized for several years. In 1855, German embryologist Robert Remak proposed that new cells formed from division of old cells, a refutation of spontaneous generation. Fertilization itself would be illuminated by two different scientists working independently of one another but coming to the same conclusions.

In the 1870s, Oscar Hertwig, a zoologist and professor of anatomy, cytology, and embryology, took a trip to the Mediterranean that led him to study the sea urchin, whose large eggs made cell division easy to study (Gillispie 6.338). He saw the joining of the sperm and the egg and the initial presence of two nuclei, thus observing how the fertilized ovum formed out of material not from one but from both parents. Herman Fol, a biologist studying mollusks, came to the same conclusions, which he published in papers in 1877 and 1879. Cytology, then, pointed the way toward understanding the contributions of both parents, lessening gender biases and forming the basis of later breakthroughs in heredity. The focus on the cell served to further break down the process of reproduction—it could be understood not only at the level of physical interaction of bodies but also at the levels of the cells that composed this material. Thus, as Lois Waisbrooker would claim, what could be obscene about a process that produces cell fusion and division (*Fountain of Life* 24)?

The elite science of embryology dealt with various issues that would find their way into the public consciousness and validate the popular interest in examining sexuality. The discourse then turned to one focusing on influence. Since organisms were not preformed, the possibility that they could be influenced emerged, and it was this idea, along with explanations of fertilization and embryonic development, that moved the discourse toward reform-minded arguments. Depictions of the embryo as the model for evolution and the fact that the embryo grew within the female body eventually provided warrants for women's rights.

From the Science to the Mainstream: The Popularization of Embryology

The popularization of embryology by medical practitioners and physicians in advice books went beyond the fact and definition stases of the scientists, who explained the findings in embryology, to apply the new information to value and action arguments accentuating the importance of women's health and women's rights. Physicians both explained the generation and development of embryos and made arguments for why women should have rights because of their relationship to them. The texts by physicians Russell Trall, John Cowan, and Emma Drake examined in this section relied on several key theories of the scientific community. In describing the stages of development, they based their knowledge on demonstrations like von Baer's, such as Trall's explanations of germ layers. The use of cytology formed the basis for arguments about women's and men's contribution to the new organism. Furthermore, evolutionary theory and recapitulation, both of which relied on a sense of hierarchy, gained presence in the discourses positing the agency of women to influence the growing life. Linking these ideas, physicians popularized embryology and transformed it into a rhetoric of responsibility and agency.

Accommodating Science to Women's Rights

Russell Trall's 1866 *Sexual Physiology: A Scientific and Popular Exposition of the Fundamental Problems in Sociology* not only was a popular source of information on physiology but also included a section on embryology in the middle of the book, between explanations of physiology and the application of physiologic knowledge to sexual practices. Much of his chapter on embryology consists of diagrams and their explanations, as well as quotations from embryologists explaining the process of fetal development. In fact, much of this particular chapter of Trall's is comprised of others' words, with abundant quotations, sometimes lasting for several pages. This practice of quoting at length was common to several popular medical texts I examined that incorporate explanations of embryology. In contrast to his explanations of anatomy and physiology, where he often described and interpreted the anatomy of the body in his own words, Trall appears to be more a conduit for science in this section. Thus, these medical advice texts seem to be popularizations of popularizations. As a science gaining more of an "elite" status in contrast to the more popular science of physiology, practicing physicians may have felt removed from the different methodologies of the new science of embryology, such as the use of more advanced microscopes. Physicians like Trall would have had the ethos to explain how the different parts of the body work and how to prevent and cure disease; the science of embryology, however, breaking down processes to the level of cells, seemed more removed from the actual practice of medicine, thus necessitating use of more prominent authorities on the topic in these popular medical texts. There is much that Trall admitted to ignorance of, including where fertilization occurs (114). He was able, however, to draw on the work of embryologists and cytologists who broke down the processes that occur in the development of the embryo.

Describing the composition of cells to set up his explanation of fertilization, Trall deconstructed the parts of the fertilized cell and detailed how those parts become the embryo. In fact, most of his chapter on embryology discussed development at the level of cells, employing pictures to illustrate cell division and then the development of the embryo, combining two important findings in embryology: epigenesis, or how the embryo develops in stages, and the germ-layer theory that explains how these membranes grow into specific organ systems of the body. The influence of von Baer's work is clear, as is the mid-nineteenth century scientific focus on the cell. Though he used visual diagrams, another common feature in these medical texts, to explain cell division and embryological development, his analogies helped make this process come alive for the reader. For example, Trall explained, "The head is very large in proportion to the body; the trunk is elongated and pointed; the limbs resemble the shoots of vegetables; dark points or lines indicate the existence of the eyes, mouth, and nose, and parallel points indicate the situation of the vertebra. The length is nearly one inch or about ten lines" (115). The shortcomings of a diagram to convey size necessitated such comparisons. Readers would be more able to visualize the dimensions of the fetus and how they altered and aligned. Giving presence to these processes served as an important logical step to then arguing for the rights of women in whom these processes occurred.

Later chapters in *Sexual Physiology* elaborate Trall's feminist interpretation of a woman's influence on the fetus. Similar to free-love feminists, Trall stressed the importance of the health of women to bearing healthy children and argued that women should be subject to conditions that enable them to maintain a healthy lifestyle. Attributing the high numbers of abortions to the fact that women had few rights, he asserted, "Restore woman to health, and give her what God has ordained as her birthright—the control of her own person—and the trade of the abortionist will soon cease" (204). Unlike Emma Drake, Trall did not condemn women for seeking abortions but rather the unequal conditions that led to the need for abortions. His discussions of embryology connected to his arguments for the rights of women, since women were the primary influence on the embryo. Though he clarified that both parents contributed to the new life, he stressed the mother's influence once the egg had been fertilized. This premise became his warrant for women's rights:

> At the moment of impregnation both parties must, to some extent, transmit the lesser or the greater degree of their constitutional peculiarities, thus occasioning the greater or less resemblance to one or the other parent. But, from the moment of conception until birth, the influences of the mother are constant. During this period nothing can affect her injuriously that does not, to some extent, damage her child. (257)

He then highlighted "an unhappy home" or "an unkind husband" as causing "deterioration on the part of the child" (258). Thus, an unpleasant husband was something a woman should be protected from with specific rights, a popular free-love feminist line of argument. He asserted, "The rule, then, for the production of good children is exceedingly simple. *Keep the mother happy and comfortable*" (258; emphasis in original). Under his logic, since a woman could impress feelings and even thoughts on the embryo, she should not be made to have negative feelings and thoughts. She would transmit the best qualities only if given rights and protection from negativity. However, unlike others, notably S. Weir Mitchell, whose "rest cure" the writer Charlotte Perkins Gilman refuted, Trall would not argue that women's confinement was necessary for protection, since he insisted on the importance of exercise and mental stimulation. A pregnant woman, he argued, should have the conditions given to a person with full rights and full "control of her own person," and his chapter on embryological development serves as evidence for this claim.

The "Science" of New Lives

Physician John Cowan's 1889 medical conduct book *The Science of a New Life*, which received an endorsement from Elizabeth Cady Stanton, took the emphasis on embryology to revitalize older beliefs about prenatal influences. A medical reformer who advocated continence, Cowan's ideas of sexuality aligned him with social purity goals. Like Trall, Cowan forefronted women's role in generation to argue for women's rights, but his ideas often seem more like superstition than science because of certain beliefs on prenatal influence. However, his beliefs were premised in scientific principles. Like Trall, Cowan quoted at length from other authorities, most notably a "Professor Dalton," to explain the development of the embryo and also employed analogy to give presence to these processes.

Cowan emphasized how the embryo represented a growing life, a life that could be shaped while in utero. Immediately following the chapter on embryonic development, Cowan stressed the agency of the parents in influencing this growing being: "This minute speck represents an individual who eventually will be temperate, or else a drunkard or glutton; who will be chaste or licentious; whose life will be a success or a failure, depending alone or altogether on what the parents choose to make it" (188). Picking up older ideas on prenatal influence, he particularly emphasized the role of the mother: "It is through the blood of the mother *only* that the body of the child is nourished, its character influenced, and its habits of life formed" (189). Since her blood nourished the fetus, it was her blood that would influence its characteristics. The reformers' ideas on prenatal influence were clearly derived from this line of argument. Cowan summarized, "A man or woman's daily thoughts and actions affect and impress the secretions of the nutritive system, and through this the blood; and in this way, through its reaction on the nervous system, the character of the man increases for better or worse, as may be. It might with truth be said, that a drop of blood represents in its elements the character of the individual who manufactured it" (189). This emphasis on the thoughts of the mother, older advice retold in a scientific register, was exploited by reformers who argued that women should have rights to prevent negative thoughts from influencing the fetus. Cowan's emphasis on the blood shared between mother and child related to larger cultural ideas about how "blood tells" but also alluded to older ideas on the influence of the mother because of blood and blood vessels (Needham 216). While drawing on such developments as the growth and stages of the embryo advocated by epigenesists, the evolutionary hierarchy adhered to by Darwin and Haeckel, and the knowledge of both parents contributing characteristics to the new life, Cowan seemed to reinforce cultural values in his explanations of how parents could actively influence the type of child they conceived and then fostered in fertilization and incubation. His ideas, while compatible with older superstitions, were nevertheless given new "life" by the new scientific developments of the time. For Cowan, a temperate life and attitude before conception and during incubation would create a temperate child, an idea that made his approach particularly attractive to reformers.

Embodying Embryology

Another conservative physician aligned with social purity ideals was Emma Drake, whose 1901 book *What a Young Wife Ought to Know* provided her audience of young women with advice on maintaining health, choosing a husband, caring for a child, and, most of all, pursuing a temperate lifestyle, going further into the genre of a conduct book than other physicians did.[2] Nestled between chapters titled "Ailments of Pregnancy" and "Baby's Wardrobe," "Development of the Foetus" used embryology to impress upon women the importance of their role in sustaining new life and to make an argument against abortion. Where Drake differed from the other physicians was in her more explicit reform agenda within the chapter on embryology. While Cowan and Trall promoted reform agendas at the end of their embryology chapters and then used that knowledge for reform arguments placed later in their texts, Drake interspersed her explanations of development with an antiabortion argument, going into both the definition and action stases. She explained embryology in order to combat the temptation for a woman "to rid herself of the product of conception" (157), beginning the chapter with an emphasis on development:

> How does the tiny speck, so tiny that it cannot be seen with the naked eye, only one hundred and twentieth of an inch in diameter, how does this tiny atom of matter, begin in its growth, continue and develop into the full grown child? This little germ or ovum, the part furnished by the mother, in the creation of a human being, contains the germinal

vesicle, or embryo cell, and the stored up food for the early days of life
after conception takes place. After the ovum leaves the ovary, somewhere
in its journey to the uterus or womb, it is met by the spermatozoon, or
male element of conception, and by their mysterious union the new life
begins. (155–56)

Her narrative underscored the mystery in these processes, which embryology focused on illuminating. It also led into her antiabortion argument
in stressing that this "minute speck" was a growing life. Her explanations
of the stages of development supported her antiabortion goals.[3]

After breaking down the process to the level of cells, Drake ended
with a celebration of the product of this development:

> So the baby grows until it reaches intrauterine maturity, and comes into
> our arms for cherishing. Pity, pity the little one that comes with no love
> to receive it, and pity more the mother of such a child. No woman has
> a right to marry, unless she desires offspring and is willing to fit herself
> for maternity. No man has a right to take upon himself the sacred vows
> that make him husband, unless he comprehends all that it means, and is
> measurably ready to meet its duties and responsibilities. With such prepa-
> ration, and such understanding upon entering matrimony, we should see a
> nobler, stronger race of men and women in the coming generations. (162)

Thus, in Drake's text, the findings of embryology created a rhetoric of responsibility. Unlike Trall and Cowan, she stressed the rights of the child
over the rights of the mother. In free-love feminist arguments, however,
this responsibility was twofold: the woman should have rights so that
she could bear a healthy and happy child, and the child should have the
right to two parents committed to creating a healthy and happy child.
Free-love feminists often gave presence to the rights of the child in order
to argue for the rights of the mother. Drake also highlighted the overall
goal of "a stronger race," positing that this goal would ultimately derive
from an understanding of embryology and women's role in development.

New Applications

Once the science of embryology was popularized in medical advice texts,
each of the important findings of embryology translated into a rhetoric
of women's sexual rights. The triumph of epigenesis over preformation
created a rhetoric focused on influence: since the embryo was no longer
envisioned as a preformed entity, with each characteristic of the adult
predetermined, a new potential opened for agency and influence over that

embryo's characteristics. Recapitulation theory, though controversial and later discredited, contributed the warrant that embryonic development represented the stages of human evolution, which then allowed women to position themselves as both vessels and agents for evolutionary change. Cytology led to the finding that both men and women contribute material equally to a new life, which, under Lamarckian theories of heredity that accepted the transmission of acquired characteristics (discussed in chapter 6), would then aid arguments for providing advancements and education to women so that they too could pass on positive characteristics to the child. While some of these uses of embryology seem like leaps in logic, especially arguments based on prenatal influence, the physicians' texts show how this logic came to dominate reform arguments.

The developments in embryology had one further integral application: the increased knowledge of how and where fertilization occurs increased knowledge of how to prevent conception. Understanding the cycle and movement of the egg reinforced the natural remedies reformist physicians proposed, such as the rhythm method advocated by many physicians. The task of making these methods more efficient would fall to later birth control pioneers, such as Margaret Sanger, but the greater knowledge and practices of birth control would not have been possible were it not for the growing science of embryology.

"Proper" Maternity in Free-Love Feminism

The scientific warrant provided by embryology positioned the pregnant woman as the site of complex development. Complex development requires special treatment. Therefore, reformers argued, potential mothers should be carefully treated. For free-love feminists, this logic amplified their already urgent calls for women's sexual rights. Their focus on the mother's state, not only during fetal development but also during conception, reinforced arguments for pleasurable sex within a "free" sexual union. Free-love feminists urged a "science of proper generation," and in this sense, sexuality, instead of being divorced from maternity, became the amplifier of maternity. They focused on the conditions of women during sexual relationships, conditions that should stress the rights of women to choose their partners, to engage in pleasurable sex, to be knowledgeable about their bodies, and to choose to terminate their relationships with sexual partners regardless of ties by law. These conditions became more urgent by the insights that what affected the mother affected the fetus. Thus, a brutal husband might cause deleterious effects on the future life.

Some of their uses of embryology, though, seem to shift back to old superstitions. For example, Rachel Campbell, in a letter to Mary Florence Johnson, theorized that the deaths of her babies were due to "either a transmitted tendency or a birth-mark due to the infernal nastiness I was forced to witness during pregnancy" (qtd. in M. Johnson 33). She attributed the unhealthy children she bore to her husband's sexual brutality. Her proclamations echoed older ideas about prenatal influence, much like Cowan's theories blended the older superstitions with the new science. The science of embryology, therefore, renewed old warrants in addition to creating new ones, causing some of the uses of embryology in free-love feminist discourse to seem like superstition more than science. But there are indications that the actual science also influenced their discourse. For example, in addition to ideas on prenatal influence, several free-love feminists alluded to recapitulation theory. The recent finding that both men and women contributed material to the new life also renewed their calls for reform and, as we will see in the subsequent chapter, became an important warrant to their eugenic ideas. Embryology gave feminists a more scientific context for arguments they had been asserting for years.

"Like Begets Like"

The warrant that "like begets like" gained a new logic in free-love feminism. "Like" referred not only to physical characteristics but also to mental and emotional ones. Juliet Severance, for example, insisted, "As certainly as like begets like, as surely as temperament, traits of character, complexion, color of eyes and hair are imparted by parents to offspring, so surely is the loathing, the pollution, the hate that filled the mother's mind transmitted to her child" (*Marriage* 29–30). Free-love feminists often posited that the lack of women's sexual self-ownership led to their resentment and hate over their bondage. Severance's use of analogy demonstrated that women should not be subjected to conditions where they would have loathsome thoughts that would transfer to the characteristics of the embryo. If the traits of character, complexion, and color of eyes and hair were transmitted through both parents' material during intercourse and formed the basis of the embryo, why couldn't thoughts and feelings also be transmitted? If the embryo was affected by physical changes and physical conditions of the mother, why couldn't emotional and intellectual conditions also affect the embryo? At this point, scientists had determined that both parents contributed material; what they debated was what that material contained. Preformationists had for many centuries posited that the person was preformed in the embryo, but epigenesis clarified that development went in stages. If the person was not already preformed, then could each stage be affected by outside influences? Darwin was unsure about the possibility and, at times, seemed to endorse it. The medical popularizers discussed above reinforced such possibilities and took for granted that such an influence occurred. Thus, free-love feminist arguments that such influence could occur may not have been a radical interpretation of the scientific discourse of the time.

Victoria Woodhull's arguments also stemmed from the presumption that the embryo could be influenced and its future characteristics shaped, and this warrant featured in her more radical goals for sexual rights for women. Her 1874 *Tried as by Fire* speech based many of its conclusions on the presumption that women, as vessels of embryos, required certain conditions to aid evolution. If women were united in love with the partner of their choice and provided with sex education, they would be more healthy and able to produce "a better race." Thus, Woodhull used the ultimate goal of superior children as her justification for free love while also furthering her emerging eugenic ideals.

Woodhull encapsulated her inquiry into the "two questions in this whole matter of reforming the world," which are "vital and inseparable": "The first is, to discover and develop the science of proper generation, so that all the inherited tendencies may be good; and the second is, that the germ life, once properly begun, may not be subjected to any deleterious influences, either during the period of gestation or development on to adult age" (*Tried* 30). She presented her statements as self-evident:

> There can be a better race only by having better children. If they are bad, good men and women are impossible. There can be better children only through better understanding by women of the processes of gestation, and better methods of rearing and education. These propositions are self-evident, and point directly to the sexual relations as the place to begin the work of improving the race. (29)

These statements had a basis in the warrants produced by the embryologists: that the embryo could be harmed by "deleterious influences" (a claim that would be strong for temperance advocates), such as alcohol, had been established, and it was an example that Woodhull exploited. She extended the logic of the well-known facts of "deleterious influences" to cover more than just substances: since the mother's consumption of substances could harm the embryo, could her consumption of inequality also harm the embryo?

The health of the mother also became integral to free-love feminist arguments, since they maintained that the current conditions of sexual relations harmed women's health. If women were not healthy, then they could not produce healthy children. Thus, a pleasurable sex life to maintain health, an argument backed by physiology, would produce healthy influences on the embryo. In addition, since the embryo was produced by sexual relations, sexual relations were the place to begin improvement. Woodhull presented her logic in stages, but these stages were reversed from arguments in scientific discourses. While scientific arguments started with the elements of conception and gestation and led to the evolution of the race, Woodhull took the evolution of the race for the better as a premise, which then required optimal conditions for the processes of conception and gestation.

Similar to Cowan's, Woodhull's logic focused on situating the mother as the primary influence during gestation. She proposed, "Nothing is more certain than that the mothers can make their children just what they want them to be, limited only by the inherited tendencies of the father" (*Tried* 30). Although scientists were proposing dual influences on the formation of the embryo, in order to argue for women's rights, the woman's role in prenatal influence had to have presence. Woodhull achieved such presence by presenting her statements as self-evident and connecting the embryo growing within the body to the conditions of sexual relations. While men had influence, the woman was the vessel and thus a stronger influence during gestation. Consequently, women had to be protected from harmful influences and possessed the agency to mold the characteristics of future people within their bodies.

Tennessee Claflin also seized the opportunity to place discussions of sex in a new context. For example, her 1871 *Constitutional Equality* speech, once published, included an appendix titled "Children: Their Rights, Privileges and True Relations to Society," where she invoked the questions of women's sexual rights in relation to the children they would bear. Her logic in this and other essays also relied on the "like begets like" warrant that reinterpreted the science to posit that the unequal condition of the mother influenced the child. The section on the rights of children began with the premise that "a series of papers, specifically to women, cannot well be closed without something being said relative to their offspring. We say their offspring, because it is they who, by nature, are appointed to the holy mission of motherhood, and who, by this mission, are directly charged with the care of the embryotic life, upon which so much of future good or ill to it depends" (123). Claflin believed that a discussion of women's rights could not exclude a discussion of their roles as mothers. And while such a warrant featured prominently in Republican motherhood discourse, it now received a scientific basis.[4] She went on to elaborate how "embryotic life" gained its positive or negative influences from what affected the mother; she, therefore, was the vessel that needed more rights to perform her "holy mission."

Claflin quoted medical authority to support her contention that women required positive influences for the gestating embryo, such as a Professor Draper of New York University Medical College, who wrote on prenatal impressions (124–25). Claflin lamented that much reform discourse ignored this vital aspect of women's rights and determined that its absence was due to a reliance on religion as an authority rather than on science (126). She then discussed the conditions of sexual unions, which, she believed, offered a solution for how to mold new life:

> It is scientifically true that the life which develops into the individual life never begins. That is to say, there is no time in which it can be said life begins where there was no life. The structural unit of nucleated protoplasm, which forms the centre around which aggregation proceeds, contains a pulsating life before it takes up this process. As the character of the nerve stimula which this is possessed of and which sustains this evidence of life must depend upon the source from which it proceeds, it is first of all important that the condition of this source should be favorable to the new organism which it is to furnish the nucleus of. In other words, and plainly, the condition of the parents at the time of conception, should be made a matter of prime importance, so that the life principle with which the new organism is to begin its growth should be of the highest order. (128)

Claflin's discussion seems to meld the new science with more spiritualist ideals of "new life," a combination we will also see in the texts of Lois Waisbrooker. It is interesting that Claflin spends so much time enumerating her points in scientific terms before explaining "plainly" what she hopes to accomplish. Following this particular quotation is the assertion that

> cases of partial and total idiocy have been traced to the beastly inebriation of the parents at and previous to the time of conception. On the other extreme, some of the brightest intellects and the most noble and loveable characters the world ever produced owed their happy condition to the peculiarly happy circumstances under which they began life, much of the after portion of the growing process of which having been

under unfavorable circumstances. Many mothers can trace the irritable and nervously-disagreeable condition of their children to their own condition at this time. It must therefore be allowed that the condition under which every child is generated has an important bearing upon the whole future life. (128)

Her logic here demonstrates how she must blend the scientific with what we might call the superstitious to make the argument that "the condition under which every child is generated has an important bearing upon the whole future life." The conclusion from these premises is then that women need proper sexual conditions to produce "the brightest intellects and the most noble and loveable characters."

Claflin did not ignore her ultimate goal of free love, which she defined in the same way as her sister. Since, she believed, "nothing should be held so important as a perfect understanding of the laws which control all things which are involved in the processes of nature relating to reproduction" (134), interrogating the status of women at the time of conception was necessary. She then emphasized her goals of sex education, for potential mothers to understand the ways their bodies worked, and sex emancipation, so that institutional marriage would not impede the "progress" that could occur. She further enumerated the harms that could occur should potential mothers ignore what could become harmful influences on the growing embryo and included the nature of the sexual relations a woman engaged in before the embryo was created as one of those influences (143). Thus, her lengthy discussions of what she saw as "embryology" led to her conclusion that "it is because of this sacredness with which we regard the union of the sexes that we denounce the present marriage systems" (143). By her logic, one who accepted the sexual inequality produced by marriage would then be subject to the kind of influences that would produce "cases of partial and total idiocy" in the children they would bear.

Later in her rhetorical career, Claflin's essay "Maternal Impressions" based its logic around these same premises. This essay contended that the ideas she endorsed in earlier works were no longer a matter of theory; she took the ideas of prenatal influence as scientific fact, not surprisingly given the proliferation of medical texts like Cowan's and Drake's in the late nineteenth century. She referred to studies that proved "the character of the individual is also largely determined by maternal impressions between its conception and birth" (90). Her arguments seem similar to Drake's: "It would seem, therefore, that the character of a child greatly depends upon that of the mother; that the germs of its proclivities may be sown by her before its birth, and that it lies within her power not only to give a bent to its faculties, but also to divert them from hereditary and evil tendencies" (93). She thus emphasized the agency of the mother, who could override any "hereditary" tendencies by providing more positive influences.

This shift in Claflin's rhetoric superseded her free-love ideals. She instead focused on the "duties" of mothers, not in raising their children after birth but in shaping them before their birth. No longer did she give presence to the conditions of sexual relations; she primarily focused on how women had duties to perform, and their most important duties came during gestation. She insisted on the responsibility of women to produce the most positive result from their pregnancies: "She has not only to build up and nurture the highest organism, but she has also to mould its character. Her physique will control her child's; her motions will be communicated to it; her mental and moral capabilities will be largely transferred; her conduct will give a perpetual bias to its life" ("Mothers and Their Duties" 47). She shifted from urging responsibility *toward* women to the responsibility *of* women. In her later texts, responsibility was solely the woman's, since she was the one who held the gestating life. No reference was made to her responsibility to choose the right mate to ensure proper sexual conditions or to the responsibility of the man in giving his sexual partner the most positive conditions. Instead, the rhetoric that she employed to serve her free-love ideals now became the ideal. It was the mother's responsibility, as the vessel of evolution, to conduct herself in the most positive way to ensure a positive product.

Claflin also referred to both evolutionary discourse and recapitulation theory in emphasizing the "duties" of motherhood. For example, she extolled the value of reproduction to evolving the species:

> The function of reproduction is common to all forms of life—to the lowest as to the highest. But the most perfect of each class must be the fittest for the perpetuation of their species. A well-proportioned body, free from organic and hereditary disease, a sound and well-balanced mind, a serene and generous disposition, combined with a good moral and mental training, go to make up the requisites of a good mother. ("Maternal Impressions" 48)

She echoed the earlier rhetoric of Republican motherhood that led to women receiving education: education would make women more effective mothers and would guide their children (read male children) into moral future citizens. However, now that same rhetoric applied not to the mother's value in raising the children but in molding their characters before they were even born. The "requisites of a good mother" focused on the physical characteristics that would make her strong enough to bear healthy specimens, as well as on the moral qualities that Claflin believed would be transmitted to the growing embryo. The result would be the "regeneration of society" that Claflin longed for. Regeneration would not occur from greater education or social reforms but from the task of evolution. In her essay "The Regeneration of Society," she invoked recapitulation theory as her basis: "Just as the foetus has passed through various stages of pre-human life which were once the normal states of our lowly progenitors, so the new-born child begins to pass through the various phases of human life" (57). As the fetus passed through these stages, it was the mother's responsibility to ensure its proper growth. This essay, however, went back to her free-love ideals and critiques of marriage. Since too many "unfit" were being born, she turned to pre-natal influences to produce more of the "fit" (60). But, society tended to dismiss the "fit" if they were born out of conventional marriage and embraced the "unfit" produced within it (61–62). What was needed, then, in Claflin's estimation, was less of a focus on marriage and more of a focus on producing "fit" children, a goal that free-love feminists would endorse with unfortunate results. The "like begets like" warrant then endorsed free love but also led free-love feminists down a dangerous path since in arguing for sexual rights, they emphasized the "duties" of both partners in producing "better children," then emphasized only mothers' responsibilities and ignored the issue of sexual conditions. The "regenerative" rhetoric then regenerated itself into a whole new debate.

Women's Regenerative Power

Other free-love feminists, however, used the premise that women had a unique power in the gestation of children to then argue for the regenerative power of women's sexuality. Such ideas on the power of sexuality to move humanity beyond its present state proliferated in the works of more conservative free-love feminists Lucinda Chandler and Elmina Slenker and the unique free-love feminist Lois Waisbrooker. All three women, as spiritualists and free lovers, subscribed to the idea that sex had a regenerative power, and they defined such regeneration in a different manner from Claflin, who used the term to show how society could be reborn by producing the well born. For Chandler, Slenker, and Waisbrooker, regeneration occurred in a spiritualist sense—the conquering of death—or in an unspecified utopian sense.

Chandler's article "'Cell Wants,' Sex Attraction and the I Am," published in *Lucifer* in 1896, connected cytology to her spiritualist sensibilities. For Chandler, "the relations of sex [involve] the supreme factor of race advancement, [and therefore] it is unwise to overlook or set aside the conditions of individual growth and progress" (3). Chandler's proclamation indicated a eugenic ideal in discussing "race advancement," but she implied a more utopian view of spiritualist regeneration in discussing how sexuality led to "individual growth and progress." She brought the conversation on free love back to individual growth by explicating the connection between "cells," the physical results of sexuality, with the mental and emotional results. That she discussed sexuality at the level of cells but then brought in the emotional and mental aspects as well shows that some free-love feminists reacted to the focus on science by connecting it with more romantic and spiritualist notions. The result, in Chandler's argument, was a free-love feminism intent on shifting the discussion back to the spiritual dimensions of sexuality, but it also participated in the shift toward eugenics by insisting that the spirituality of sexuality would lead to race advancement.

Slenker's arguments, also focusing on the "purifying" power of sexuality, incorporated a scientific focus as well—specifically, the focus on examining sex acts at the level of cells. She devoted her 1887 article in *Lucifer*, "Superiority of the Female," to discussing cells, not morals as the title might indicate. The scientific finding that both men and women contributed material to fertilization led to her focus on cells, but she used it as evidence that females were superior to males, especially since they did not need males except to "furnish his half of the impregnating element" (3). In addition to reducing male contributions to "the impregnating element," she also reduced sexuality to the level of cells, explicating the findings in nineteenth-century cytology to support the superiority of females. Much of the article defined the cell, looking at its status as the "lowest" form of existence and how when combined with other cells, it became a "compound individual," an animal or human. She elaborated on the layers of cells and its components, which she defined as the nucleus and surrounding protoplasm. She also discussed the chemical composition of these parts, the difference between stationary and active cells, and the process (which she got wrong) of cell division. Her lengthy definitions became a story of cells working their way toward conception. She quoted Haeckel's "discoveries" and then moved to a discussion of reproduction and the egg, explaining how the sperm "penetrates the many times larger ovum and mingles with the germinative matter of the cells," but put her own narrative on this process: "Two perfect cells with opposite sexual polarities are thus united by inherent affinity and become one individual, but that individual is no longer a cell but is only a homogeneous mass of protoplasm" (3). Her discussion of "affinity" showed how she was working a more romantic view of the process into the scientific. She ended the article with "This is of course an old story to many of you," indicating that readers of free-love feminist texts would be familiar with the scientific language, "but unless one has it all in a nutshell, the theory of sex is hardly understandable" (3). Her "theory of sex," focused on the superiority of the female element in sex, was thus supported by going back to the level of cells. Hers is an interesting interpretation of the "regenerative" power of sex, mixing the scientific with the romantic and spiritual.

Lois Waisbrooker's perspective on evolution in her 1879 work *From Generation to Regeneration, or The Plain Guide to Naturalism* also combined the ideals of free love and spiritualism in a scientific context. Arguing that the ultimate goal of sex was not the production of better children to advance evolution but rebirth on a spiritual plane as the end of evolution, she nevertheless devoted time to enumerating the conditions that must be present to ensure "regeneration," or spiritual rebirth. While Waisbrooker presented a different ultimate goal in human evolution, her argument shared similarities to Woodhull's and Claflin's in her assumption of woman's integral role in both generation and regeneration.

Waisbrooker's logic was similar to that used by champions of evolution and recapitulation. She stressed understanding the "past history of our planet" to understand the future (*From Generation* 3). She also described "this effort to renew life's cycle" as a "prophecy—one of Nature's hints— an index finger pointing to future possibilities" (4). In referencing this "cycle," she implied the same logic as recapitulation, since recapitulation itself implied the cycle of generation and development repeating earlier cycles. She also referred to an order in development and nature's laws: "Are not Nature's laws uniform in their action, only varying in modes of expression, as manifest through the different orders of life? If so, then the thought of any form of development, when it becomes a fixed and growing belief, must be to the human what the blossom is to the fruit—a pledge of its possibility . . . when the right conditions exist" (5). The references to the uniformity of nature's laws, to variation, and to orders of life implied evolutionary warrants. These warrants set the stage for her later arguments for what conditions should exist for women to exercise their sexuality.

When Waisbrooker posited sex as the means to spiritual rebirth, or regeneration, she connected sex to the generative process. Her argument that the act of sex was the path to regeneration came from her logical connection that since sexual relations were the path to generation, they must also be the path to regeneration. She proposed, "As generation is a tangible physical fact, why should not regeneration be also? Will nature never be able to gestate from matter an organized form which she can perpetuate to the same indwelling life, instead of through a succession of lives, bearing a like form" (6). This point then connected to how better sexual relations could produce better results: "Life, or the base upon which it rests, as we have already seen, comes from sex union, but the character of the life depends upon the nature or condition of the elements thus uniting" (10). As she established in *The Fountain of Life*, the view of sex as repulsive or obscene defined the conditions under which it took place. Consequently, she argued, "We give it its character by the estimate we place upon it" and "The low idea makes the act low and the product low" (*Generation* 11). Thus, she maintained that demeaning sex would produce demeaning results. She also related to free-love feminist arguments on the importance of the conditions under which two people engaged in sex: the conditions must foster equality in status to produce positive results and end in "mutual benefit" (Woodhull, *Tried* 15).

Waisbrooker also employed analogy to discuss the conditions of women during pregnancy. She discussed how, in "the vegetable and animal kingdoms," the conditions for growth affected the nature of that growth, and she pursued that analogy to argue why women needed the proper "soil, climate and culture" to grow:

> If earth, plants, animals, have their spheres, how much more so the human. But we are not yet done with the lower orders of life. To bring the analogies suited to our purpose we must examine the law applying to propagation, gestation and growth. We find that flowers are more beautiful and fruits richer grown in some localities than in others, and that soil, climate and culture have each their influence upon them; but perhaps the animal kingdom will furnish what we need in this direction. (*From Generation* 20–21)

Waisbrooker pointed out that conditions affected the growth of new life in the vegetable and animal kingdom, something Darwin noted as well. She amended the conditions necessary for the human female in elaborating, "Soil, climate, culture, modify the vegetable; so of the animal; but still more so of the human, for here we must have soil, climate, culture suitable to our mental, moral and spiritual natures, as well as the material" (23). Therefore, since human females were more evolved than their components in the animal and vegetable kingdoms, their conditions also required an evolution: they needed conditions necessary for growth beyond just the physical. They also needed mental, moral, and spiritual conditions to ensure growth. She thus had a firm basis for arguing the reforms of free-love feminism.

Waisbrooker's contention on the regenerative power of sex also included the superior power of the female. For example, in an 1898 article titled "Woman's Source of Power," she asserted the belief that if men no longer existed, women would find ways to procreate without them (125), an idea integral to the utopian fiction of the time, such as Charlotte Perkins Gilman's *Herland*. Waisbrooker's assertion received scientific backing: she quoted both Darwin and sexologists Patrick Geddes and J. Arthur Thompson.[5] This belief also led her to prompt women to demand their sexual rights, since "man can do nothing alone" (125). Women could then demand the conditions necessary to produce healthy children that would survive infancy because of the more positive "conditions before and after birth" and even add on some pacifist-feminist goals ("don't make us go through all this trouble to have our healthy sons killed by war" lines of argument). She insisted, "It is man's business, or should be, to furnish for woman the best possible conditions in which to do her work and then leave her to nature and her own soul" (*Anything More, My Lord?* 9). This, then, is the difference between Waisbrooker's arguments and the similar ones of Woodhull and Claflin: it was men's responsibility to leave women alone and to let them have sexual emancipation and whatever other rights they required, not women's responsibility to do her best for the future of her offspring, as Claflin would contend. The rhetoric of responsibility would then shift back, but only once men realized the superiority of the female and gave her what she needs to do her work. Waisbrooker noted, "The quality of the germ can be improved only under improved conditions" (*Anything More, My Lord?* 19), and she defined those conditions as ones women would experience under free love. Waisbrooker's 1897 article "Things as I See Them" summed up her incorporation of embryology into her free-love feminist rhetoric: "The feminine factor is the embodying power. Man quickens, impregnates, woman embodies" (407).

Dissent and Descent

Some free-love feminists who noticed the shift in free-love feminist arguments dissented; they resisted the turn to a rhetoric of responsibility and used the same rhetoric to argue women's lack of responsibility. The findings in embryology produced a renewed focus on maternity, which left anarchist free-love feminists wary. A few women even rejected these new uses of science, not only because they felt the focus on bearing children would eclipse their calls for women's sexual self-ownership (and they did) but also because they felt the science itself lacked specific evidence. However, even as the dissenting voices, they participated in the rhetoric that caused free-love feminism's descent.

Lillian Harman at first seemed to endorse the same lines of argument derived from embryology as those employed by Woodhull and Claflin, for example. In her speech "Some Problems of Social Freedom," delivered to the Legitimation League in England in 1898 and published in both *The Adult* and *Lucifer*, she employed the same line of argument that had as its warrant that marriage produced conditions averse to bearing "better children": "Rarely indeed are free men born of slave mothers. Just so long as we have legally enforced prostitution and rape, so long as the majority of homes are the abiding places of inharmony, degradation, and cruelty, as now, there can be little progress. Marriage is woman's worst enemy, and is therefore the enemy of the race" (126). Her logic here supposed the same prenatal influences as the "like produces like" arguments: women who were exposed to the "inharmony, degradation, and cruelty" of the home because of women's unequal status in sexual relations would transmit undesirable traits through prenatal influence. She thus defined marriage as "woman's worst enemy" and "therefore the enemy of the race," which presupposed that anything that harmed women also harmed the race since women were the agency for generating, or regenerating, the race.

Harman also attacked those who would think they knew better what was best for women than the women themselves. In "The Regeneration of Society," she exclaimed, "The state and the church have undertaken to say how children shall be brought into existence. They have declared that this matter is not one which can safely be left to the parents" (May 20, 145). But the state and church had not produced the desired results; therefore, parents left on their own, or parents who entered sexual relationships without the sanctions of church and state, as they did in free love, had the potential to produce more desirable results. She also rejected church ideologies that encouraged men and women to procreate, saying that they encouraged neglect more than anything else (145). The medical profession also earned her ire since they prevented women from learning about their own bodies and the "best conditions" they needed. With proper sex education in place, parents could "tell of the processes of nature in the development of the embryo with . . . little sense of shame" and thus negate the influences of the church that would have them believe that all processes involved in sex were "unclean" ("What Shall I Say to My Child?"). Harman's logic supposed that under free love, women could ignore the church, state, and mainstream medical profession and thus produce more desirable results.

Harman also took aim at the rhetoric of responsibility that put responsibility on men because it reduced women to procreation and nothing else. She said, "We hear much of the rights and of the responsibility of man to the woman of his choice, and to *his* offspring. Apparently the woman is not in this case to any great extent, except as a sort of machine which shall produce as many children as man in his responsibility, or irresponsibility, shall compel her to bear" ("Regeneration of Society," May 20, 146). She rightly pointed out that some of the rhetoric that even free-love feminists engaged in placed responsibility on men and viewed women as merely "baby machines" who had no choice in the matter. It was this argument that led to her divergence from other free-love feminists discussing prenatal influences. While she conceded that "maternal love is a beautiful emotion, and is necessary to the development of the race," she added, "But it is not the duty of woman to pretend to feel it when she does not. The woman who does not naturally love and sympathize with children should never become a mother, and she will not if properly educated and left free to choose for herself" ("From My Point of View," March 1900). She turned the emphasis in this rhetoric back to the ideal of female choice. Women should realize that they have a choice on whether or not to become mothers and should closely examine their motives behind this choice. She rejected that it was women's duty to procreate, but while insistent on this lack of duty, she still endorsed the same lines of argument that Claflin did when she implied such a duty.

Anarchist feminist Lizzie Holmes also rejected this turn, but, unlike Harman, she also rejected the science of prenatal influence. In her article "Another View of Pre-Natal Influence," published in *Lucifer* in 1895, Holmes rejected several premises that had come to characterize the rhetoric of free love and dominate the pages of *Lucifer*. The first premise was the interpretations of the science of prenatal influence given by both medical authorities and free-love advocates. She provided several examples of women who had never heard of sexual freedom, theories of heredity, or sex education and yet bore healthy children (3). She then posited:

Such illustrations would seem to knock out all the arguments for sex emancipation as well as for stirpiculture. As far as the influence of freedom merely for the children to come, it does. I plead for woman's freedom for her own sake, and for nothing else under the sun, though I do believe that in several generations of free mothers we will see an improvement of the human race. But whether we do or not, I still plead for the right of woman to own herself. (3)

Holmes tried to draw the debate on free love away from prenatal influences and stirpiculture, or eugenics, and back to the focus on women's rights to own her own body. Yet, she still insisted that freeing women would result in the improvement of the race. To the debates on embryology, she added, "All the embryo human being needs is the proper conditions of development, and *to be let alone*" (3). Thus, she would seem to reject the ideas of Woodhull, Claflin, and others who believed free women could assert more positive influences on the growing embryo. Yet, she did not reject the improvement of the race entirely. She hoped to shift the focus to women's improvement, not just for the sake of future offspring, but stated that the race would be improved anyway: "Work, responsibility, care for others, help make her a better woman; they will help make better children" (3). She still relied on certain gender norms, such as the "responsibility" of women and their "care of others," but asserted that women should earn freedom to improve themselves, which would then result in better children: "Let every woman do the very best for herself that she knows and her children will be the best her body is capable of bearing" (3). Even when resisting the new rhetorics of responsibility, it seems free-love feminists still relied on their major premises and goals. The difference is that Holmes posited better children as a result of women's emancipation and not as a reason for it.

Voltairine de Cleyre's voice joined these dissenters, adding to Holmes's arguments by insisting on the lack of proof that free mothers could produce better children. Therefore, she urged free-love advocates to cease relying on arguments that supposed prenatal influence. While she addressed her remarks to Moses Harman in particular, whose pamphlet *Motherhood in Freedom* espoused the same ideas as the ones covered in this chapter but with less feminist influence, her criticisms also applied to women like Waisbrooker. In criticizing their uses of science, de Cleyre actually asserted more of a scientific sensibility in her insistence on proof and her claim that the science itself was still uncertain. She maintained, "The supposition, also, that offspring must necessarily respond to pre-natal influences upon the mother is likewise not only unproven, but frequently given the lie by the most startling contradictions. The whole subject of heredity is so obscure that the entire region of experiment is mere groping" (de Cleyre, "Priestly Control Over Woman"). De Cleyre pointed out how scientists had yet to prove prenatal influence but merely theorized the possibility. Darwin expressed uncertainty when he said, "The variation *may be* due to the male and female sexual elements having been affected by the conditions to which either parent, or their ancestors, have been exposed" (*Origin* 358; emphasis mine). Despite advances in embryology, the exact nature of prenatal influence was left uncertain, but medical writers and reformers took it as scientific truth.[6]

With the exception of de Cleyre, it seems that even free-love feminists who rejected prenatal influence still endorsed the view that one of the goals of free love was the regeneration of the race. These ideas become more problematic when they added theories of heredity to the mix, as discussed in the next chapter. But the descent into eugenic rhetoric did not begin with embryology; it always seemed to be a part of free-love feminists' rhetoric, simply because they could not completely divorce women's sexuality from maternity. As a result, they needed to emphasize the benefits of freedom in sex with maternity.

(R)Evolving Discourses

While the ideas in this discourse, especially those of the physicians and reformers, often recalled older superstitions, to these reformers, the findings in embryology seemed to provide a warrant, justification, and exigence for free love. Associating sex with scientific processes made it more acceptable to argue for sexual rights. Science then assisted in defining the situation, helping to eliminate the constraints on sexual speech and providing an audience united in their belief in the ascent of human life. Waisbrooker theorized, "Judging from [Nature's] past results, she seems to carry her work to a given point, and then to wait for man to interpret her language and cooperate with her in its further development" (*From Generation* 4). Free-love feminists could collaborate with scientists by "interpreting" nature's language, connecting their own personal experiences with sex to these processes. They also become agents "cooperating" with nature. In hereditarian arguments, this "cooperation" became more of a challenge—they attempted to confront and change the course of human development.

The developments in embryology led to a discourse of heredity, but there were key differences between the two: embryology was concerned with the study of the embryo itself and the changes it went through; the science of heredity was concerned with the causes and results of such changes. Embryology established the hierarchies in evolution; heredity theorized how to achieve those higher stages. Embryology showed how both parents' material contributed to the new life; heredity posited how parents could manipulate the characteristics of that new life. These two discourses often overlapped in medical and reform communities.

The logic of free-love feminism, read with embryology as a screen, shows the evolving and revolving nature of their discourse. It evolved from a discourse centered on woman's emancipation and empowerment to a rhetoric focused on her responsibility as a vessel of the "race." It *revolved* in that it went back to older superstitions on prenatal influence and, in some cases, endorsed the very views free-love feminists tried to refute. Yet, I find it hard to dismiss some of their claims on prenatal influence, especially since we have not completely rid ourselves of ideas that we can mold prenatal life. In the twenty-first century, books, CDs, DVDs, and other new media still seek to provide potential mothers with ways to create more intelligent children before they even leave the womb. While the discourse of evolution might be gone from these new rhetorics, is the discourse of eugenics?

6

Heredity: The Disappearing
Reform Warrant

[The] salvation of the world can only come through better children.
—Victoria Woodhull, *Tried as by Fire*, 1874

Instead of child culture I would have the movement called eugenics named woman culture.
—Lois Waisbrooker, *Eugenics; or, Race Culture Lessons*, 1907

Pioneer free-love feminist Mary Gove Nichols had only one daughter who survived infancy. She endured four other pregnancies that resulted in stillbirths and miscarriages. Victoria Claflin Woodhull also knew these hardships; she too had one daughter who survived and gave birth to a mentally challenged son she described as "living death" (*Tried* 27). Both women were not unusual. Many women's rights advocates had large families, suffered miscarriages, or lost children in infancy, and many saw their own mothers experience diminished health after bearing upward of fifteen children. Frances Willard once described the infant mortality rate: "Four hundred thousand babies annually breathe their first and last in the United States—being either so poorly endowed with vital powers or so inadequately nourished and cared for that they can no longer survive. One-third of all the children born depart this life before they reach five years of age" ("Address" 27). It is no surprise, then, that these women came to the question of how they could create stronger, healthier children who would survive infancy. Science seemed to provide them with the answer but would lead them down a dark path. Long before Francis Galton coined the term "eugenics" in 1886 to describe the "science" of breeding, and long before lawmakers used eugenic theories to enforce sterilization in the early twentieth century, nineteenth-century free-love feminists found eugenics an "available means" to argue for sexual rights.

Contemporary feminists often debate the role of nature versus nurture. For them, gender as an inherent or socially constructed characteristic lays the foundation for many theories of social reform. Nineteenth-century feminist activists also took part in this debate, but with a major difference: they tended to attribute everything to nature, or heredity, though environment could affect heredity. Their debates differ from our current "nature versus nurture" debates because of their definition of "nurture." Nineteenth-century thinkers defined "nurture" not only as what occurred after birth in the raising of children but also as what occurred before, in preparation for birth. Debates on heredity and the ability to influence heredity emphasized the goal of producing "superior" or "ideal" children. Just as in the discourse of embryology, in the discourses on heredity, medical writers and reformers stressed the importance of women in creating these ideal offspring. While today's social constructionist feminists reject such determinism, nineteenth-century feminists embraced it.

Toward a Science of Heredity and a Warrant for Women's Rights

From the scientific communities to that of the social reformers, a rhetoric of responsibility emerged. Nineteenth-century thinkers asked, What does the current generation owe to future generations? This chapter asks what happened when a change occurred in their treatment of this question: How do we go from the findings of Lamarck and Darwin to ideas about prenatal influence, to women's rights, to a gendered and racist eugenics? We cannot look at nineteenth-century hereditarian discourse without looking at how it transformed into the idea that we should encourage some and discourage others from reproducing, the principles behind eugenics. Free-love rhetoric often incorporated eugenic ideas: eugenics became a means to argue why women should be given rights. However, a shift occurred at the turn of the twentieth century that diminished the women's rights argument in this discourse. Eugenics became the end in itself, not the means for arguing for women's rights. What happened to cause this shift? The disappearance of the reform warrant supplied by Lamarck's theory of the inheritance of acquired characteristics presents one possible cause of this shift.

Acquired Inheritance in the Theories of Lamarck and Darwin

Nineteenth-century conceptions of "environmental influence" came from the work of Jean-Baptiste Lamarck (1744–1829), whose evolutionary theory prevailed as the dominant theory of heredity for much of the nineteenth century. Lamarck accepted spontaneous generation and published what would become the basis of a theory of heredity in his 1809 work, *Zoological Philosophy*. Lamarck posited that species could adapt to their environment, acquiring new characteristics, and then transfer those acquired characteristics, which would enable them to more easily survive in their environment, to future generations. Lamarck focused on characteristics of the body, such as the long neck of the giraffe, which he presumed had changed to adapt to the environment. Another example that explains Lamarck's theory is the muscles of a weightlifter: the weightlifter would acquire stronger muscles, and the children of the weightlifter would then acquire these through heredity (Bowler and Morus 137). A Lamarckian theory of heredity, then, allowed for the inheritance of acquired characteristics.

Darwin's *The Origin of Species*, published in 1859, also led to theories of heredity in popular literature. For example, when Darwin said, "The variation may be due to the male and female sexual elements having been affected by the conditions to which either parent, or their ancestors, have been exposed. Nevertheless an effect thus caused at a very early period, even before the formation of the embryo, may appear late in life" (*Origin* 358), he provided support for arguments that what affects parents affects offspring. "Conditions to which either parent" were exposed became an important warrant in the logic of free-love feminist arguments, as the preceding chapter demonstrated, but Darwin's statement elaborated embryology since it not only posited an effect during gestation but also implied an effect before fertilization even occurs. Darwin referred to the natural world in these "conditions"; reformers would encompass much more under these "conditions." Similarly, he noted, "It is the opinion of most physiologists that there is no essential difference between a bud and an ovule in their earliest stages of formation, so that, in fact . . . variability may be largely attributed to the ovules or pollen, or to both, having been affected by the treatment of the parent prior to the act of conception" (*Origin* 10). Here, "treatment of the parent" was interpreted by free-love feminists to promote better treatment for women, and there was support for an interpretation of how parents could intervene in the creation of healthier or more desirable children. It was in *The Descent of Man*, however, that Darwin came closer to approaching the hereditarian ideas proliferating in free-love feminist texts.

Clearly influenced by the popular debates provoked by the *Origin*, Darwin adopted a Lamarckian view in his 1871 work, *The Descent of Man*, accounting for environmental influences as well as the influence of habit and surrounding conditions as causes of variation between parents and offspring. He said, "Natural selection had been the chief agent of change, though largely aided by the inherited effects of habit, and slightly by the direct action of the surrounding conditions" (152–53). Like the reformers, Darwin also posited that more than just physical characteristics were transmitted: "Besides special tastes and habits, general intelligence, courage, bad and good temper . . . are certainly transmitted" (110). Social purity and free-love reformers would have been especially interested in his thoughts on how virtuous habits would grow stronger, "becoming perhaps fixed by inheritance" (104). An example relevant to nineteenth-century debates came from discussions of temperance. If the habit of drinking became fixed and produced children with the same habit, the habit of abstaining from drink would also become a fixed tendency. While today we theorize a "gene" for such tendencies, nineteenth-century thinkers did not know the mechanism but assumed that habits became hereditary. Although they never explicitly espoused theories of heredity, both Darwin and Lamarck in their theories of evolution offered the possibility for reform with hereditarian consequences.

Under a Lamarckian view of inheritance, parents who educated themselves would be able to transfer their enhanced intelligence to future generations. A Lamarckian theory of heredity, then, provided exigence for social reform and women's rights: educating women would lead to smarter children, for example. Once this theory of acquired characteristics was combined with Darwin's concept of natural selection and "survival of the fittest" rhetoric, reforms in the name of heredity adopted even more urgency. Though scientists would not state with confidence that both parents contributed material to the new being until Oscar Hertwig and Herman Fol's cell experiments in the mid-1870s, Darwin assumed both parents' material would blend together (Bowler and Morus 195). He did not address, however, how this transference occurred: August Weismann would theorize this agency in the 1880s.

Beyond Lamarck: Weismann and Mendel

Lamarck and Darwin were clearly the most influential theorists on the topic of heredity through much of the nineteenth century, but it was the work of August Weismann (1834–1914) and Gregor Mendel (1822–84) toward the end of the century that would disprove Lamarck, creating a shift in the popular reformist literature with even greater social ramifications in the next century. Although Mendel's work came first, it was not deemed significant until its rediscovery in 1900. It was Weismann's work in the 1880s that would later reveal the significance of Mendel's findings.

Weismann, who had spent his early career studying insects, turned to the theoretical side of science after an eye disease left him unable to perform many of the experiments in his new areas of interest: natural selection and the mechanism for inheritance (Mayr, *Growth* 698). Instead of a science based on his own experiments, Weismann combined the knowledge accumulated in evolutionary biology, embryology, and cytology to refute Lamarckian ideas of inheritance. Although Weismann had previously endorsed these views, his 1883 paper on the topic questioned how habits could be transferred to offspring. Instead, he showed how some of the characteristics attributed to a Lamarckian theory could be better explained by natural selection. However, it was not always considered contradictory in the nineteenth century to believe in both the inheritance of acquired characteristics and natural selection, especially considering that Darwin himself ascribed to Lamarckian ideas. This alliance between the two theories explains why Weismann's conclusions did not completely replace notions of inherited characteristics (Mayr, *One Long Argument* 118–20). Weismann, however, observed a gap in the science of heredity that needed to be filled—the question of a mechanism—and picked up where Lamarck, Darwin, and scientists studying embryology had left off: he proposed a material entity by which hereditary characteristics were transferred.

Influenced by new findings, Weismann suggested that the characteristics of the next generation were stored in what he called the "germ-plasm." However, he isolated this germ-plasm from the rest of the body, leaving little room for the inheritance of acquired characteristics (Bowler and Morus 158, 200). Weismann explained, "The germ-cells are not derived at all, as far as their essential and characteristic substance is concerned, from the body of the individual, but they are derived directly from the parent germ-cell" (Weismann 167–68). Weismann differentiated between the germ cells that held the hereditary material and the soma, or the rest of the body (Mayr, *One Long Argument* 121–22). Since later findings questioned whether germ cells and soma cells could affect each other, Weismann renamed the mechanism the "germ-plasm" rather than "germ-cell." Later writings, mostly from reformers, discussed below, would posit some influence on the germ-plasm, however. Weismann's work proved influential, but it would be the rediscovery of Mendel's work that would move toward resolving nineteenth-century debates over the inheritance of acquired characteristics.

When published in 1865, Mendel's findings failed to cause the explosion of interest that their rediscovery prompted in 1900. The reason for the lack of response was partly a matter of rhetorical situation. At the time, Mendel's findings were not deemed significant since their applications to a theory of heredity went ignored.[1] Mendel himself was not attempting to form a theory of heredity but rather to record the laws of hybridization with his now well-known experiments on pea plants. From these experiments, Mendel found not only that characteristics could be dominant over each other but also that these characteristics were found in pairs, laying the foundation for the theory of genes (Mayr, *Growth* 715). At the time of the publication of his findings, Mendel was unfamiliar with advances in evolutionary biology and cytology. After the rediscovery of his work in 1900, his results, combined with new findings, would lay the foundation for a modern science of heredity.

Lamarck's theories, however, did not completely subside as a result of Mendel's work. Throughout the early twentieth century, neo-Lamarckism often attracted social reformers because accepting Mendel's and Weismann's conclusions negated their arguments that social change could affect subsequent generations through heredity. In fact, Lamarck's theories would not completely disappear until the 1950s (Mayr, *One Long Argument* 120). Early-twentieth-century scientists, however, mostly accepted Mendel, and it is his work that indicates a possible cause of the disappearing reform warrant in feminist arguments.

Social Implications and Applications

Rhetoric in the social sphere not only overlaps but also influences the formation of scientific discourses as much as scientific discourses influence the formation of social reform rhetoric. This reciprocal effect appears in the social theories of Malthus, Spencer, and Galton and their later application by feminist reformers. Theories of heredity derived from Lamarck, Darwin, and Weismann laid the foundation for feminist arguments on the importance of women's physical role as bearers of children, and thus on the rights they should receive, but it was the new scientific ideas combined with their social implications that created a stronger rhetorical situation for free-love feminists to enter.

Thomas Malthus's (1766–1834) theory of population not only provided an impetus to Darwin's theory of natural selection but also created exigence for discussing the problems of population and heredity. Malthus's 1798 "Essay on the Principle of Population" critiqued Enlightenment proposals for how humanity would reach a "happier state of society"

(1.8). He argued that Enlightenment philosophers ignored the crucial premises of his own argument: the necessities of both food and "passion between the sexes" (1.14). Examining the ratio of the increase of the population to the increase in subsistence, he found, "Population, when unchecked, increases in a geometrical ratio. Subsistence increases only in an arithmetical ratio. A slight acquaintance with numbers will show the immensity of the first power in comparison of the second" (1.18). Malthus thus introduced a major premise for later eugenic arguments: the need for checks on the population. His main argument, "that the power of population is indefinitely greater than the power in the earth to produce subsistence for man," provided the basis for Darwin's later work on natural selection (1.17). Malthus's conclusion on the effects of these ratios on the family unit also provided the basis for feminist arguments for smaller families:

> Impelled to the increase of his species by an equally powerful instinct, reason interrupts his career, and asks him whether he may not bring beings into the world, for whom he cannot provide the means of subsistence. In a state of equality, this would be the simple question. In the present state of society, other considerations occur. Will he not lower his rank in life? Will he not subject himself to greater difficulties than he at present feels? Will he not be obliged to labour harder? and if he has a large family, will his utmost exertions enable him to support them? May he not see his offspring in rags and misery, and clamouring for bread that he cannot give them? And may he not be reduced to the grating necessity of forfeiting his independence, and of being obliged to the sparing hand of charity for support? (2.22)

Malthus sparked debate in many reform circles, including *Lucifer*, which published several exchanges on his theories and debates over whether the poor should procreate when they could not provide for their offspring. In introducing competition for survival, Malthus built the foundation for later arguments: How could humanity check its reproduction to ensure enough sustenance for the growing population? Would the human race actually *de*volve if subsistence diminished? Who would win the competition for survival? How could parents produce offspring "fit" to win?

Influenced by Malthus, social scientist Herbert Spencer, a prolific writer beginning at midcentury, also criticized Enlightenment philosophies of human nature, preferring instead to view the course of humanity as a long process of adaptation to environment. However, Spencer concluded in his 1852 essay "A Theory of Population" that the growth of the population and its struggle for resources encouraged rather than constrained the ability of humanity to reach perfection (*Selected Writings* xxi). Using the model of evolution as a branching tree in his 1851 work *Social Statistics*, Spencer found that "progress, therefore, is not an accident, but a necessity. Instead of civilization being artificial, it is a part of nature; all of a piece with the development of the embryo or the unfolding of a flower" (*Selected Writings* 13). Since species are influenced by their surrounding conditions, Spencer viewed civilization as the most important influence on human evolution. To Spencer, humanity, the species, the family, and civilization were evolving organisms. Applying evolutionary theory to the idea that civilizations are what instigate the upward progression of humanity, Spencer embraced a Lamarckian view and introduced the key concept, usually attributed to Darwin, of "survival of the fittest" in his 1864 work, *Principles of Biology*. Many free-love feminists would quote Spencer's work, ignoring its more gendered connotations and instead focusing on this specific application of Darwin.[2]

Darwin's cousin Francis Galton (1822–1911), another pivotal figure in the debates over heredity in the nineteenth century, was interested in proving hereditarian determinism. His 1869 work, *Hereditary Genius: An Inquiry into its Laws and Consequences*, attempted to solidify the importance of heredity through observing how intelligence occurs in successive generations of certain families. In its preface, Galton claims to introduce the "law of deviation from an average" into discussions of heredity. Galton's key contributions to reform arguments, however, were his contentions that humanity has a tendency to degeneration if left unchecked and that conscientious breeding could check this decline and produce more intelligent offspring. He compared the breeding of dogs and horses to the breeding of human children, an analogy that often recurs in this discourse. He also postulated that human breeding could aim for more specific goals to "produce a highly-gifted race of men by judicious marriages during several consecutive generations" (1), a line of argument that played a key role in free-love feminist arguments. Galton's emphasis on the responsibility of parents to future generations, as when he said, "Each generation has enormous power over the natural gifts of those that follow" (1), also appeared in feminist discourse of the same time period. This rhetoric of responsibility to the next generation already existed in some feminist writings before Galton but gained more popularity afterward. Though Galton himself did not believe in the inheritance of acquired characteristics, reformers who combined Galton's observations with their own Lamarckian views had a warrant for social reforms.

Galton is also credited with coining the term "eugenics" in 1886, though the theory behind eugenics had existed before his formal naming of it. Eugenics, or the idea of improving the race through selective breeding, blended together the science of Darwin and Lamarck, and later of Weismann and Mendel, with the social theories of Malthus, Spencer, and Galton. Eugenic theories went from encouraging the "superior" to reproduce, known as "positive eugenics," to discouraging, or even forcing, the "unfit" from reproducing, known as "negative eugenics."[3] Eugenic practices, such as sterilization, became institutionalized through laws in the early twentieth century, such as the 1927 Supreme Court decision upholding sterilization of the "feeble-minded" (English, *Unnatural Selections* 13). Yet, nineteenth-century free-love feminists often invoked the theories behind eugenics long before laws were enacted in its name and even before Galton gave the concept a new name. Free-love communes often practiced forms of eugenics, called stirpiculture, such as John Humphrey Noyes's Oneida community, where men and women deemed worthy were paired to reproduce.

It is tempting to dismiss eugenics because of its subsequently discredited nature and its racist applications, but historian Nancy Stepan warns against characterizing eugenics as a "pseudoscience," since many prominent scientists were involved (5). The theory of eugenics provides insight into how scientific theories affected and were affected by popular value systems. Eugenics also reveals nineteenth-century concerns about imperialism, immigration, and race, as well as how such theories could be altered for different purposes.

When do hereditarian discourse and the focus on relieving future suffering become eugenic? One of the central questions of this chapter concerns this shift from reformers discussing heredity to advocating more eugenic outcomes. When Lamarckian theories of heredity were more popular, eugenics only scantly resembled the insidious theory we currently know it as because of twentieth-century practices and its popularity with racist policies (such as compulsory sterilization of certain groups). Lamarckian theories, combined with a eugenic goal, seemed to provide scientific credence to social reforms. Changes in education and in marriage laws could be justified in the name of evolution and progress, since the material that built future generations would improve. Eugenics left its mark on social reform discourse, and the benefit of superior offspring became a driving force behind many reforms. The shift between these two discourses of heredity and eugenics occurred when arguments moved from the cause and value stases, where heredity was theorized and celebrated, to the action stasis, where specific eugenic reforms were introduced. That is, it was when reformers shifted from the value to the action stasis in discussing heredity that hereditarian rhetoric became eugenic.

Medical Popularizations and the Power of Heredity

Popular medical advice books also participated in, and may have contributed to, this shift in stasis from cause and value to action, resulting in a shift in the aims of hereditarian discourse. Nineteenth-century physicians had already noted the importance of heredity in diagnosing patients and taking their histories, a popular methodology, as shown by critic Susan Wells's examination of the "heart history" in nineteenth-century women physicians' texts and by physician Clelia Mosher's late-nineteenth-century sexuality questionnaire.[4] Combined with feminist goals, some of these advice books shifted into more explicitly eugenic discourse. Medical advice books and essays by physicians Russell Trall, John Cowan, Elizabeth Blackwell, and Emma Drake often combined the disciplines of physiology, bacteriology, and embryology in the ultimate goal of advising women on the best choices to make to produce "fit" offspring. For these physicians, making lifestyle decisions on diet and sex were important not only to women's health but to the health of future generations not yet conceived.

From Superstition to Science . . . and Back to Superstition

Like his chapters on embryology, Russell Trall's discussion of heredity in his 1866 popular medical advice book also involved a feminist sensibility. For example, his chapter "Regulation of the Number of Offspring" begins with a statement on "woman's rights" to choose when and under what circumstances to have children, similar to "voluntary motherhood" arguments. He also blamed the lack of women's rights for stillbirths, the prevalence of venereal diseases, and the "depravities" of the current generation. He asserted, "And when her supremacy is fully recognized, there will soon be an end of stillbirths, and of frail and malformed offspring who can seldom be reared to an adult age, or, if they can, are only curses to themselves and to the world" (203). His arguments reflected those of free-love feminists: if women were not given rights, how could they be expected to bear healthy children who would further the goals of evolution? His argument also reflected many of the feminist reformers' claims that diseases and weaknesses in children were the result of the mothers' limitations, since their status confined them to situations where their own health suffered.

Trall further advocated women's rights by emphasizing the importance of a woman's choice of partner and of her sexual pleasure in producing more "fit" children. Although the idea that women must experience orgasm to conceive had been refuted by this time, women's orgasm was now represented as a means to producing superior children. Trall noted that conception did not require female orgasm but enumerated its benefits when he discussed the conditions under which children should be conceived. He argued that since the characteristics that formed the growing being were transferred at conception, the conditions at conception must be of a certain kind to yield positive results. These conditions included women who desired sex with their husbands, since no "offspring [can] be as perfect as it should be unless the act is both desired and enjoyed by both parties. This rule or law, for it is a law of Nature, at once suggests the conditions which are necessary to insure this result" (245). Trall also defined these conditions as including both women and men who experienced pleasure during conception and who were "in their best bodily and mental condition when the fruitful orgasm is experienced" (254). Trall believed that "children are often from birth stamped through their whole organization with the depravities, propensities, infirmities, eccentricities, and disordered conditions which one or both parents exercised during the act of reproduction" (xiii). Thus, Trall combined nineteenth-century ideals of "romantic love" with the idea that parents could make impressions on the fertilized egg: if both parents had full rights and experienced "at-one-ment" during the act of conception (232), what would be transmitted to the child would less likely result in "depravities, propensities, infirmities, eccentricities, and disordered conditions" for the future generation. This blaming of social ills on heredity and emphasis on women's rights in order to perfect the qualities passed on to the offspring recur in medical texts.

Physician John Cowan's 1889 book, *The Science of a New Life,* was based on the premise that parents could consciously influence the characteristics of their future children, a view owing much to embryology, but he also based his hereditarian ideas on a Lamarckian perspective. Like many social reformers, Cowan believed that the responsibility for reform lay with parents rather than with reformers and temperance workers (21). He participated in a rhetoric of responsibility that attributed both good and bad characteristics and actions in offspring to their parents' behavior. However, unlike our current rhetoric of responsibility that emphasizes the way parents rear their children, this rhetoric of responsibility concentrated on actions taken by the parents before the child was born—often before the child was even conceived. If a child was imperfect, it must have been because of hereditary or prenatal influence.

Cowan even urged parents to choose the profession of their child before he or she was born, listing professions and the corresponding actions, thoughts, and readings likely to produce a child who would become this type of professional (151). For example, he advised that if parents wanted their child to be a geologist, they should travel, go for long walks, and read appropriate books in preparing to have such a child (156). His advice in this area recalls older ideas about the influence pregnant women have over the unborn, even to the point that images the pregnant woman views will affect the offspring's appearance (166). He also advised parents to prepare their future offspring for professions regardless of sex, since females could be inventors too (154).

Women's rights became a central part of Cowan's hereditarian ideology, since he believed that if children were not propagated under the right conditions, they could not be reared under the right conditions (131–32). He advocated female choice in a partner, which had its warrant in Darwin's sexual selection theory, as well as choice in when to have sex (109). However, *The Science of a New Life* did not focus responsibility for better children solely on women. For example, Cowan devoted sections in his advice book to what men should abstain from, such as alcohol and meat, since both men and women could influence future generations through their current habits.[5] For Cowan, it was not only the actual characteristics passed on through heredity that influenced the offspring but also the surrounding conditions and agency of both parents before conception and before birth. He adhered to the nineteenth-century ideology that there was no such thing as a "self-made man" (155)—it was all determined before birth.

Heredity and the Power of Habit

Elizabeth Blackwell's 1894 work, *The Human Element in Sex*, centered on the power of the will and the power of habit, which informed her hereditarian discourse. Blackwell conceded that many theories of heredity lacked scientific proof, but, following Lamarck and Darwin, she believed that habits could become tendencies transferred to future generations. Darwin had speculated, "Natural selection had been the chief agent of change, though largely aided by the inherited effects of habit, and slightly by the direct action of the surrounding conditions" (*Descent* 152–53), and his reference to "the inherited effects of habit" provided the warrant for Blackwell's contention that the power of the will could help humans change their tendencies, which would then become modified through habit and become hereditary (*Human Element* 61). Her social purity aims are apparent in these beliefs, since the tendencies and habits she discussed concerned temperance and the power of the will. The power of the will, to Blackwell and many others before her, was what separated humanity from lower evolutionary stages.

Blackwell also participated in the growing connection between the rhetoric used to discuss heredity and the rhetoric used to argue for women's rights. Referring to women as "mothers of the race" (30), she highlighted the role of women's health in the production of a "vigorous healthy race" (*Essays* 253). As the woman's body was the vessel in which this race would be bred, Blackwell theorized that the uterus was "capable of containing a perfect child" (*Human Element* 29). She showed that deficiencies in the child were not the result of its prenatal housing and set up her argument for how both parents could achieve that "perfect child" through a temperate lifestyle. Blackwell combined arguments warranted by physiology, bacteriology, embryology and heredity: she established what the female body was capable of, noted how venereal disease led to "degenerations" and how purity could result in more perfect children, and discussed improvement in the race as the ultimate result of these lifestyle choices.

Blackwell's rhetoric also anticipated more racist eugenics in her discussions of heredity and self-sovereignty. Stephanie Athey's 2000 study of the rhetoric of eugenics in nineteenth-century feminism asserts that the rhetoric of female self-sovereignty, or the right of women to control their own bodies, often privileged white women. When discussing the power of the mind over the body, or the power of the will over the control of venereal disease, Blackwell noted, "We should uproot our whole national life and destroy the characteristics of the Anglo-Saxon race, if we gave up this natural right of sovereignty over our own bodies" (*Essays* 125). Like other reformers of the time, Blackwell placed women's control or rule over their own bodies as the key to race progress; if women could not control their own bodies, the tendency toward degeneration would continue. This argument reflected the growing trend of hereditary discussions contributing to nationalistic discourse. Blackwell argued that sex education was vital to the growth of a nation (239) because of the central function of the family in society (204). Thus, the role of heredity became crucial not only in the health and well-being of individual families and future generations but also in the survival of a nation. This logic reflects many of the changes occurring in the late nineteenth century and how eugenics combined hereditarian, nationalistic, and feminist arguments.

Heredity and a Rhetoric of Responsibility

While Blackwell's essays often focused more on purity arguments, us-ing hereditarian arguments as part of her case for moral responsibility, physician Emma Drake, also a social purity advocate, focused more on moral responsibility as a case for attention to heredity. In other words, hereditarian arguments were the claim, rather than the support, in her writing. Drake's 1901 advice book, *What a Young Wife Ought to Know*, includes a chapter titled "The Moral Responsibility of Parents in Hered-ity," and her text explicitly quoted both Galton and Darwin for evidence. Drake began the chapter with a quotation from Galton on parents' moral responsibility to the next generation, which becomes a key feature of her argument. For Drake, parents were responsible not only for bringing up their children once they had been born but also for the character-istics they transmitted to the children before they were born. She then introduced a quotation from Darwin on how both parents contribute characteristics to the new life. Unlike Blackwell, who acknowledged that heredity was not yet an exact science, Drake believed the opposite: "We might go on indefinitely making quotations from undisputed authorities on this great science of heredity, for to-day it has become almost an exact science" (137). Drake hailed Darwin and Galton as "undisputed authori-ties" in this science and also referred to Weismann's theories when she quoted a Dr. Holbrook, who said, "'Every child born into the world is essentially an experiment; we cannot tell what its chief characteristics will be; these depend upon the potentialities stored up in the germ-plasm'" (143–44). This quotation both references the germ-plasm theory of heredity and incorporates social values. Thus, Drake's writings show how the newer knowledge of the sciences was combined with older ideas on heredity at the turn of the century. Though Weismann's ideas, which negated the possibility for influence from the parents' habits, had gained more popularity by this time, many still believed parents' lifestyle could influence future generations.[6]

Drake insisted that both parents contributed characteristics to the new life, drawing on newer scientific knowledge, but also insisted that the mother was a stronger influence, since it was her body that held the new life:

> That both in the law and the gospel of heredity, of the two parents, the mother has a far greater influence we believe firmly; yet this does not relieve the father from responsibility. The germ from him, which is "bone of his bone, flesh of his flesh," contributed to the formation of the child

in its beginning, must be of high nature and cultivation, seed from a noble sire, or the little life is dwarfed from the outset, and the mother must expend much precious time and strength in making good the terrible deficiencies which such a beginning entails, and then mourn that so much can never be overcome. (138)

Drake's word choices signify a combination of the scientific and the social: the science is "the law" and social values "the gospel." The gender roles implied—the man supplying a germ that must be cultivated and corrected by the woman—also demonstrates how social values were derived from scientific discoveries: both parents contribute, but the woman is more important in molding the new life. Drake directed young women on their choice of a mate throughout the book and also focused on the responsibilities they had to change themselves, saying, "Begin by weeding out the habits and tendencies that you would not wish to transmit, and by cultivating the qualities and accomplishments, which you would delight to see repeated in your children" (145). Her advice is both part of her rhetoric of responsibility and a conduct edict, such as when she insisted, "Children have become what they were trained to be in intrauterine life" (144). She also combined scientific ideas with anecdotal evidence in her advice. For instance, in her book she told a story about a traveler who met a family of several "coarse, boorish" sons and one "refined" daughter. When asked about the difference, the mother attributed the difference not to gender but to her reading of Scott's *Lady of the Lake* while pregnant with the daughter, which she believed helped to mold the child's refined character (142–43). Drake's combination of older, even ancient, ideas with newer ones on heredity and prenatal influence shows the status of the discourse at this particular point in time, when Mendel's work was just beginning to become more well-known, though not yet incorporated. Drake's logic also begins to sound more familiar to the modern reader, such as her ideas about listening to classical music and reading to the unborn.

These four texts by Trall, Cowan, Blackwell, and Drake demonstrate the hybrid nature of medical advice texts, since they start with explanations of the body and its processes and end with advice on conduct that will aid these processes and produce better offspring. Each text also illustrates the status of hereditarian knowledge at its particular time. Trall had no knowledge of Weismann, so his hypothesis of how characteristics are transferred focused on conditions of the body that affected it; for him, the feelings of pleasure experienced by the parents during the act of conception impressed themselves on the embryo. Two happy, healthy, and self-owning parents would result in healthy, happy, self-owning (and less depraved) offspring. Cowan, writing when embryology became more popular, believed influences on the embryo could mold its future characteristics. Both men implied Lamarckian and Darwinian ideas in their rhetoric of self-improvement for the sake of future generations. Blackwell, writing at a time when fears of venereal disease caused fears of "degeneration" in future offspring, focused on how to avoid these degenerating influences through a life of purity motivated by the will. Finally, Drake, with her purity ideals and her knowledge of Weismann, created a rhetoric of responsibility focused on how women could make the best decisions to ensure that the germ transferred and cultivated would become the more refined offspring desired. It is in these four texts that we see the discourses of evolution, physiology, bacteriology, and embryology combined into a new rhetoric of heredity that reformers in several social movements, including free-love feminism, exploited in emphasizing the rights of women in sexual practices and motherhood.

Women Elevating "the Race": Eugenics in Free-Love Feminism

What feminist historians call the argument from expediency, or the argument from difference, focused on giving women rights since they are different from men; one of their differences was their refining role in begetting and raising children. Nan Johnson's study of nineteenth-century women's rhetoric shows how women rhetors often positioned themselves as "mothers-of-the-nation" in their ethical appeals, arguing to extend their sphere of influence on the basis of the values of "Republican motherhood" (113). These are familiar arguments. But something is added to these arguments when we look at them through the lens of nineteenth-century hereditarian discourse. Free-love feminist rhetors participated in, and may have even instigated, the intense focus on progress through better children and stressed the position of women as a key factor in that progress. Women could argue for rights on the basis of their status as mothers of the race because of the intense focus on science in the popular realm. The mothers of the race logical appeals led to material reforms, such as laws testing men for venereal disease before a marriage license was granted, changes in the age of consent, and more liberal divorce laws. This "scientized" rhetoric was often convincing to nineteenth-century audiences. But using an appeal to mothers of the race led to eugenics superseding feminist aims. In earlier free-love feminist texts, the type of eugenics advocated asserted a woman's right to choose a partner that would help her bear offspring that would survive infancy. Many rights fell under this mantra. However, toward the late nineteenth century, eugenic discourses become more racist and more deterministic.[7] The new consciousness of disease transmission and its effects on degeneration also influenced this discourse. Later feminist advocates of eugenics, instead of using eugenic arguments for feminist ends, created arguments that championed more "negative" eugenics than "positive" eugenics. Eugenics became the end in itself rather than the means to argue for feminist reforms.

Eugenics and Feminism in Nineteenth-Century America

Free-love feminist arguments that incorporated hereditarian ideas were not unique in nineteenth-century feminism. Frances Willard, an advocate of social purity, espoused similar ideas using similar warrants in her discourse on "scientific motherhood," a revision of the popular "voluntary motherhood" arguments. The focus on heredity allowed Willard to create stronger urgency for the reforms she championed. Her interest in abolishing alcoholic beverages, for example, had added backing when many believed that alcoholism could be passed through heredity. She also promoted eugenics in statements like, "It seems to be a law of nature that quantity decreases as quality improves" ("Address" 27). Willard urged attention to producing a "better quality" of children and thus shifted from the value stasis in enumerating the benefits of attention to heredity and critiquing the status of women and children to the action stasis in urging fewer children to produce better children—a shift into eugenic rhetoric.

Eugenic rhetoric also spread to the racial uplift movement, even before W. E. B. DuBois urged the "talented tenth" to reproduce in a 1922 issue of *The Crisis*, because, he argued, "the Negro" needed to "breed for an object" and must breed "for brains, for efficiency, for beauty" (qtd. in English, "W. E. B. DuBois's Family Crisis" 293). Although some nineteenth-century science aimed to use such discourse to promote determinism and the inferiority of the black race, nineteenth-century women arguing for racial uplift used the discourse of heredity to promote positive changes and to show how improvement in the current generation would benefit future generations. Women, once again, were the vessels for evolution and racial uplift, as demonstrated by Anna Julia Cooper's goal to elevate womanhood in her 1886 speech "Womanhood: A Vital Element in the Regeneration and Progress of a Race." Cooper (c. 1858–1964), a prolific speaker on racial uplift, indicated eugenic arguments that relied on a Lamarckian ideal of inheritance. Stephanie Athey suggests that Cooper borrowed the rhetoric of female self-sovereignty popular with white women activists and rewrote it to include black women (para. 31). Thus, some of the language Cooper used to describe women's importance to racial uplift is similar to the language of free-love feminists. Also similar is the way that Cooper forefronted the role of women in evolution, as when she referred to "[woman's] influence on the individual personality, and through her on the society and civilization which she vitalizes and inspires" ("Womanhood" 60). Cooper's statement also evokes the focus on prenatal influences in this discourse; like Emma Drake, Cooper emphasized the role of women in shaping the personality of the fetus. But Cooper also connected that influence to the larger "civilization which [woman] vitalizes and inspires" in an argument that posited women's "civilizing" influence in the public sphere (60). Cooper thus connected this popular argument on women's moral influence to the emerging eugenic discourses in her contention that women's influence would also be a "vital element in the regeneration and progress of a race." Only women could check the "narrow, sickly and stunted growth" of a nation and a race that had "degenerated" because of their treatment of women (58). Thus, the "degeneration" was due not to inherent unfitness but to Lamarckian inheritance from the lower status of women.

Cooper brought a unique argument into the discussion of heredity by accounting for the legacy of institutionalized racism and slavery. These, she argued, have had detrimental effects on the race, which have become inherited. Athey's reading of Cooper's "What Are We Worth" speech shows how Cooper insisted on viewing "degeneration" not as inherent but as a result of the conditions of slavery (para. 52–53). Cooper's work used the language of heredity and eugenics in emphasizing "the hope in germ of a staunch, helpful, regenerating womanhood on which, primarily, rests the foundation stones of our future as a race" to advocate the role of women in racial uplift ("Womanhood" 62). Her eugenic arguments are the support, or the warrant, rather than the claim: she was arguing primarily to honor the role of women in racial uplift and used eugenic premises on women's influence as support. However, Athey notes that "when Cooper asserts women's control in reproduction, she does not entirely disrupt the eugenic claim that efficient and proper reproduction is (black) woman's chief value to the state" (para. 59), a criticism that free-love feminists resisting eugenics would also make.

Another rhetor in the racial uplift movement, Adella Hunt Logan, was more explicit in her use of eugenics. Logan (1863–1915) was raised in Hancock County, Georgia, part of a large "free family of color." Her parents, a white father and African American mother, could not marry, since laws in Georgia restricted interracial marriages at the time. Logan, one of nine children, was well educated and became certified as a teacher in Hancock County when she was only sixteen years old (Alexander 169). She later attended Atlanta University and taught for several years at Tuskegee. Logan challenged racial and gender stereotypes throughout her life and advocated equality and women's suffrage. But after suffering from depression, a result of her despondence at social equality, she ended her own life in 1915 (Alexander 194). Family friend W. E. B. DuBois remembered Logan as one of the "voices from within the veil" (qtd. in Alexander 194).[8] In 1897, Logan delivered an address significantly titled "Prenatal and Hereditary Influences" at the Second Conference for the Study of Problems Concerning Negro City Life in Atlanta. Logan was the only woman speaker at the conference not relegated to the separate women's meeting (S. Logan, *"We are Coming"* 169), which signifies the powerful status of hereditarian arguments at the time. Referencing hereditarian thought of the late nineteenth century, Logan used a Lamarckian warrant on the inheritance of acquired characteristics to argue for women's rights, since improving women's status and nurturing their intellectual pursuits would lead to better results in the children they bore.

Logan highlighted women's unique roles in the creation of better children, but she also stressed that the characteristics of future children would be influenced by both the mother and father: "Before the body is ready to begin life as a separate being, as a new personality, it is molded and cast by the combined traits of the father and the mother from whom this new creature must draw its individual existence. And the intellectual and ethical cast will follow as closely the law, 'Like begets like,' as will the physical" (A. Logan 212). This statement, refreshed by the findings of embryology in the late nineteenth century that both parents contributed material to a new life, also contained an implicit argument for women's rights: if the woman influences the future life and molds it before its birth in physical, intellectual, and ethical characteristics, women should thus have rights that nurture and maintain their intellectual pursuits. But Logan also specified that both parents were responsible for hereditary characteristics, drawing on the same arguments used in embryology texts. In addition, she made arguments similar to Woodhull's and Claflin's when she stressed heredity and the treatment of women as the basis for moral deficiencies: "To no one source more than the conditions attendant upon pregnant women can the cause of physical or moral evil be traced. The unborn child draws its physical and in large measure its intellectual and ethical make-up from its father and its mother. Not from the mother alone, as many suppose, but from both" (213). Thus, Logan's women's rights argument, while stressing the unique role of the woman, placed responsibility on both parents. She continued, "Both parents contribute to the possibilities for health, good or bad, and furnish the germs for character creation and development just as certainly as they together originate physical life" (213). Since it was an established scientific fact in the nineteenth century that both parents contributed hereditary material, uplift, Logan argued, needed to occur for both genders. And that uplift needed to account for the prenatal influences operating on the mother, which the father affected since he had influence and, as the free-love advocates would claim, physical, legal, and emotional control over the mother.

Since medical popularizations stressed the importance of prenatal influence in molding the characteristics of the unborn, Logan capitalized on their logic, adding her women's rights argument. She emphasized, "Let it be distinctly understood that the development of germ life depends upon the original germ and equally upon the culture and treatment of that germ:—in short, teach that the prenatal development of the child depends largely on whatever affects the mother" (214). Under her logic, a woman should not be subjected to conditions that would cause her to think negative thoughts that would make an impression on the embryo: "Few women seem to appreciate the fact that the sensitive embryo receives the impression made upon the mind of the mother" (214). In this discourse, the husband could be the cause of those negative thoughts. Logan described how the father might resent the unborn as an additional mouth to feed, which could then create negative thoughts in the mother that would make a negative impression on the embryo (213–14). Thus, both parents had a responsibility in prenatal influence.

To drive home her point, Logan employed an image often evoked in free-love feminist rhetoric: "If the pregnant woman is constantly wishing that her unborn child were dead or that the man who has given her this burden,—as she has learned in chagrin to regard the child,—were dead; who can wonder that out of such murderous thought there should come in very truth a murderer!" (214). Mary Gove Nichols had used a similar line of argument almost fifty years earlier. Free-love feminists often argued that the inequalities and conditions fostered by the marriage system created murderous thoughts in women, which could then be transferred to unborn children. They employed this rather unusual notion to then argue that women should receive equality that would prevent them from harboring such thoughts and resentments. Free-love feminists took this causal argument even further, maintaining that it was the brutality with which men treated their wives during sexual unions that would cause such murderous thoughts; thus, women needed partnerships based on equality and pleasurable sex in order to prevent such feelings. Logan employed this logic not to argue for sexual rights but for the importance of women as bearers of the future generation in the goal of uplifting the black race.

Throughout her speech, Logan urged attention to the "silent, but powerful, thing known as heredity" (212), blaming heredity for individuals "prone to the social sin" (211), and applied Lamarck's theory of acquired characteristics (which had yet to fall out of favor, despite Weismann's refutations) when she invoked the "like begets like" warrant to argue that mental, moral, and physical characteristics were transferred to the offspring:

> [T]he intellectual and ethical cast will follow as closely the law, "Like begets like," as will the physical. We do not expect to find the children of white parentage having black faces or kinky hair, nor the children of black ancestry having fair brows, blue eyes, and flaxen locks. It would be just as unreasonable to expect the intellectual and ethical characteristics of children to be radically unlike those of their ancestors as it would be to expect their physical features to be radically different. (212)

Thus, potential parents had to ensure that they could transfer positive "intellectual and ethical characteristics" to their children; if they did so, racial uplift could occur. Logan, like Anna Julia Cooper before her, highlighted the role women played in racial uplift because of their status as the vessels for future generations.

It seems that Cooper and Logan (and DuBois) supported what are called "positive" eugenic arguments in that they urged reproduction of "positive" qualities rather than discouraged those they would deem "unfit" from reproducing. However, as the subsequent analysis shows, the line between "positive" and "negative" eugenics is a slim one and may even be a false demarcation. When urging the reproduction of positive qualities, is there not a sense that there are other, more negative outcomes that should be prevented? Logan's speech implied such arguments in her focus on the crime that could be prevented through more attention to heredity and prenatal influences. For Logan, it seems eugenics is the claim rather than the support of her argument, mirroring the shift occurring in women's rhetoric in other social movements, such as free love. Cooper, though, did not allow eugenics to supersede her women's rights goals to the same extent by keeping eugenic arguments as the support rather than the claim. Neither Cooper nor Logan explicitly addressed sexuality or sexual practices, though there was some implied critique, especially by Cooper, of the ways that the community, especially the church, had given an "impure character to the marriage relation, especially fitted to reflect discredit on woman" ("Womanhood" 56). Reading their hereditarian arguments, though, alongside free-love feminist arguments and noting their marked similarities reveals that one of their reasons for employing eugenic lines of argument was to reclaim black women's sexuality. Cooper, especially, in drawing on the rhetoric of female self-sovereignty, framed her arguments within a discourse that audiences would have recognized as one that involved a reclaiming of women's sexuality. Logan, in referencing the brutality of men toward their wives, also indicated a critique of sexual practices.

That eugenic arguments proliferated in women's rhetoric across social movements shows that free-love feminists were not alone in turning to eugenic lines of argument as a powerful influence on their audiences. However, many of these women, in both the racial uplift and free-love movements, seemed to ignore the race and class issues their discourse evoked. For Cooper, Logan, and DuBois, social class was tied to their arguments for black people of a higher class status to reproduce, an implication they often ignored in their arguments. For free-love feminists, the issue of race was either ignored or dealt with problematically. Most, if not all, free-love feminists limited their calls for sexual self-ownership to white women. Thus, when they spoke of uplifting "the race" in their eugenic arguments, we can assume they meant the white race. Even when they did account for race in their claims, as Lillian Harman did, their handling of race was problematic. Though some of the uses of eugenics in the following analyses seem less problematic than the eugenics of the early twentieth century, we can see how their arguments led to the later, more hard-line eugenic arguments because of their inattention to important issues.

Heredity and the "Free" Lover

Juliet Severance's free-love feminism explicitly addressed the question that would become a vital part of later, more sinister, eugenic discourse: fitness for reproduction. Her 1881 pamphlet and lecture, *A Lecture on Life and Health, or How to Live a Century* began by referring to loved ones lost, using the deaths of children as an exigence for her eugenic thought (3–4).

That is, she defined the rhetorical situation calling for eugenics, not in racial terms, but in response to the high infant mortality rate. She then harshly condemned the conditions that result in infant mortality to introduce her main argument:

> Are we fit to reproduce? This is the question! How many fathers and mothers ever think of, much less seriously consider, this question? They see puny, sickly, half-made-up children born to them, living out a few years of miserable existence and then, with streaming eyes and lacerated hearts, they place their little forms around which cluster so many tender memories and loving associations, beneath the sod and call it a dispensation of Providence. It should be said that every child who dies, *had better never* have been born. Aye more: Those who live to grow up filled with disease and pain, a constant burden to themselves [and] all around them, *should* never have been born and *would* never had their parents been instructed in the grand law of parentage. (5; emphasis in original)[9]

Severance's rhetoric seems to draw attention to the elephant in the room: the idea that if there are some people "fit" to reproduce, there are others who are "unfit." However, free-love feminists did not always define "unfitness" as inherent. Severance, for example, defined "unfitness" as resulting from marriage laws and practices that proscribed women's choices in mates and allowed husbands to dominate, and legally own, their wives, which created obstacles to securing the best "conditions" for creating healthy children. She then shifted from elaborating the law's role in ensuring proper conditions for "proper parentage" to the woman's role, which she could fulfill only if the law allowed her. She also incorporated definitions of "unfitness" from social purity advocates. For example, like Blackwell and Drake, Severance urged women to observe the habits of potential sex partners to ensure that they did not have undesirable habits, such as drinking or smoking, that any children they would have would inherit (9). She also incited women to ask of their potential partners, "Are you as pure and free from the effects of social vice as you expect me to be?" (9), critiquing the double standard and aligning her stand with the new rhetoric that occurred after the discovery of the prevalence of venereal disease in women. Finally, she required that women take responsibility for the kinds of unions they sought, asking potential partners:

> Is the attachment between us worthy to be called love? and will it secure the transmission of our best instead of worst qualities; is either of us induced to this association for any reason, other than that of love?

Is either of us seeking any selfish gratification incompatible with proper parentage? Do I seek a home, position, fortune, or any other thing more than a father for my children and a lover for myself . . . [?] (9)

This popular demand for love between the parents was given new urgency due to texts like Trall's, who focused on "at-one-ment" during the act of conception (232). Severance thus positioned free love as a "prerequisite for proper parentage" (*Lecture on Life* 6), because only then would they transmit their best qualities to their children. She defined "fitness" as a quality inherent in the relationship between parents rather than in individuals.

Severance's 1886 essay "Farmers' Wives" expanded her eugenic arguments with an appropriate context to compare the breeding of animals to the breeding of humans. The setting of the farm, she believed, illustrated how women, and the work that they did, lacked respect and agency. In this sense, free-love feminists moved away from what they saw as the more elitist views of suffragists to address how rural women experienced their material conditions. Severance called attention to the plight of the farmer's wife whose work kept the farm productive but who suffered high infant mortality while the animals breeding received care and attention:

The farmer does not apply his knowledge of heredity to the propagation of his own species. If he is proposing to raise a thoroughbred colt, he is very careful that the prospective mother has every favorable condition. She must not be overworked or worried and must be carefully groomed and fed, but how little attention he pays to the conditions of the prospective mother of his children. She may toil and worry and bring into existence half gestated children, the majority dying before maturity and yet nothing seems to be thought of it. It is a "visitation of Providence," and that ends the matter. (275)

Severance took aim at those who would attribute the high infant mortality to issues other than women's rights and revealed the hypocrisy of the marriage institution and also the material reality rural women faced. Her comparison also recalled Darwin's analogy to the breeder in the *Origin of Species*, but she added to that discussion by highlighting how rural women on farms presented a unique position on women's rights, because of the (over)work that they did, and also theorized that these women could do more than women in cities in helping shed light on heredity: "Farmers' wives have better opportunities for incorporating the more advanced ideas into the character of their children, than do mothers living in cities, for fashionable society with its falsities and foibles, its castes and false standards, neutralizes to a great extent the effect of any sensible ideas upon practical living" (282). She valorized such women, since they lived a more practical reality that would seemingly avoid the more restrictive strictures placed on upper-class women that Gove Nichols had also condemned. Severance also idealized more attentive breeding, claiming that it could create a world where people would die only of "old age or accidents" (276). In this sense, her argument shows how free-love feminists adapted the utopian ideas integral to free love at midcentury to a more scientific age. Women's rights, however, remained a major part of her version of eugenics. She opined, "To the women of the nation, enfranchised, educated, elevated, do I look for salvation from the evils that fill our penitentiaries, our asylums, our dram-shops and brothels. Not by legislation, but by and through an enlightened mother-hood, in which she will refuse to propagate children unless of a healthy, intelligent, moral paternity" (283). Theories of acquired characteristics and prenatal influence convinced Severance that reform should take place in the womb, not in the halls of Congress. Free love, then, became her panacea for all social problems.

These two works by Severance indicate a strong leaning toward eugenics in her rhetoric. In these texts, she saw eugenics as an all-encompassing solution and disdained those who would try to use law to attempt reforms. Yet, not all of her works contained eugenic thought, which indicates how and why she employed these specific lines of argument in these two works. In other works, such as her 1901 treatise *Marriage*, she asserted that women's rights would lead to better children almost as an afterthought, mentioning the benefit of better children toward the end of her argument promoting the practice of free love. The timing of this argument is also significant: the 1901 text incorporated eugenics less as the inheritance of acquired characteristics fell out of favor in the scientific community.

Similar to Severance, Victoria Woodhull maintained, "[Marriage] stands directly in the way of any improvement in the race, insisting upon conditions under which improvement is impossible" (*Tried* 7) because marriage does not always guarantee "mutual love" and "reciprocal benefit" in sexual relationships (15). In her 1873 and 1874 speeches, where she argued for sex education, the abolition of marriage, and the practice of free love, we see her logic: healthy women produced healthy children; and women knowledgeable about sex would know how to maintain their health and how to achieve sexual pleasure, which would result in more favorable offspring since pleasurable sex produced orgasm, which, as

Trall believed, produced conditions optimal for parents to transfer their best characteristics to their children. Showing that marriage was not the source of "superior" children, she argued, "A woman who bears a dozen or less scraggy, scrawny, puny, half-made-up children, by a legal father, is a disgrace to her sex and a curse to the community; while she who bears as many perfect specimens of humanity, no matter if it be by as many different fathers is an honor to womanhood and a blessing to the world" (30). Her arguments started to move toward "negative" eugenics, since she characterized some children as "disgraceful." Under her logic, there were people who should not reproduce, but in the 1870s, she characterized these people as those stuck together by law and necessity rather than by love.

Clearly influenced by the rhetoric of "fitness" coming from Spencer, whom she quoted in her 1874 speech, Woodhull even used her own mentally challenged son to illustrate the harmful results of marriages where women uneducated about sex and heredity were forced to submit to brutal husbands without "mutual love" and "reciprocal benefit": "My boy, now nineteen years of age, who should have been my pride and joy, has never been blessed by the dawning of reasoning. I was married at fourteen, ignorant of every thing that related to my maternal functions. For this ignorance, and because I knew no better than to surrender my maternal functions to a drunken man, I am cursed with this living death" (27). Her rhetoric reveals the "fit" and "unfit" mentality in eugenic logic, but she expanded the definitions of "fit" and "unfit" to include a feminist argument: give women rights and sex education, and they will no longer bear children who suffer a "living death."

However, Woodhull did not endorse all applications of eugenics. Responding to the Oneida free-love community's practice of "stirpiculture"[10] in her 1873 speech, she clarified that this type of eugenics would not produce "superior" children. She characterized their belief: "When a woman desires a child she should select for its parent, some person, who, from physical health and perfectness, should be something like an ideal man" (*Elixir* 11). But she continued, "I utterly repudiate all such stirpiculture as this. I do not believe it possible for a woman to produce her best child, except by the man whom she loves best and for whom she has the keenest sexual desire" (11). Woodhull and Severance both agreed that the key ingredient in the formula for a healthy and intelligent child was not the characteristics of its parents but the conditions under which the child was produced. For them, the love between parents would create a happy and stable environment, and those feelings would allow the transference of favorable qualities to a healthy child, due to environmental and prenatal influence. Free-love feminists seemed to reinterpret the degree of environmental influence on heredity in order to create a theory compatible with their radical reforms but found a basis for their logic in the medical discourse of the time.

Though Woodhull's earlier arguments suggested eugenics as a means and a result of feminist reform, her later arguments de-emphasized the feminist arguments and instead emphasized eugenic arguments, to the point where eugenics became the end in itself rather than a benefit of giving women rights. She thus illustrates the shift occurring in free-love logic: in using eugenic ideologies to justify free love, these rhetors became so enmeshed in it that eugenic ideologies started to supersede other aims. The discourse seems to lend itself to this shift: if one is going to argue that creating better children is an important end, how far does one have to go to then argue that certain groups of people should be prevented from propagating the species? The implied arguments of "negative" eugenics featured in earlier discourse then began to take over free-love feminists' version of eugenics. Woodhull's 1891 book *The Rapid Multiplication of the Unfit* illustrates in its title this shift. Though Woodhull had attempted to redefine who was "fit" and "unfit" in earlier speeches, focusing not on physical or mental characteristics but on the relationship between parents, her definitions got away from her. *The Rapid Multiplication of the Unfit* acknowledged social causes of "unfitness," noting that social conditions produced unhealthy bodies that then produced unhealthy children (10), but a sense that "unfitness" was hereditary prevailed: "The best minds of to-day have accepted the fact that if superior people are desired, they must be bred; and if imbeciles, criminals, paupers, and otherwise unfit are undesirable citizens they must not be bred" (38). Here, Woodhull expressed a determinism not found in her earlier works, and the women's rights arguments received less emphasis while the case for eugenics received more. She also demonstrated how easy it was for these rhetors to go from advocating "positive" eugenics to "negative" eugenics, perhaps illustrating that the difference between the two was negligible.

Tennessee Claflin's eugenic rhetoric also reveals the shifts in free-love feminist arguments. Like her sister, her eugenic arguments appeared earlier than the time that most historians find eugenics emerging. Her 1871 *Constitutional Equality* speech mentioned several points that implied eugenic lines of argument. Going from the assertion that men and women needed to be equal in the "union of the sexes" to an argument for the economic equality of men and women, so that no woman would need to count on marriage for support, she then ended that passage by blaming marriage for the "puny, imperfect, even idiotic children the world is filled with" (42–43). She concluded, "They come simply from the relations existing between the father and mother which should have prevented their union" (43). She also evoked women as the mothers of the race and attacked the treatment of women bearing such a burden: "The mothers of humanity are treated in the matter of maternity more like brutes than humans; while the mothers of brutes are treated more like human beings than brutes" (63). It is noteworthy that she called on the "mothers of humanity" rather than on the mothers of the race, which indicates the nature of free-love feminism at the time. They had yet to shift to more racist eugenics. Claflin also referred to the "perfecting process," and in this speech, such a process could not begin without women's full equality—including suffrage, economic stability, and free love.

Claflin's rhetoric also underwent shifts. For example, in *Constitutional Equality*, she praised motherhood as "the most holy of all the functions woman is capable of" but clarified that it was not women's only mission in life and that women and men needed to be equal in having "spheres" outside of the home to which they could devote their attention (47–48). In much of her writings, she still focused on sexual conditions, since, like Severance, she believed "like begets like, even in our feelings, thoughts, and actions" (Claflin, "Maternal Impressions" 90). The regeneration of society could occur only if women were not subjected to negative "feelings, thoughts, and actions" likely to be produced by their status as the sexual slaves of men. They therefore needed sexual emancipation to produce more positive results. Yet, in later speeches, she seemed to hold up motherhood as the only mission of women, such as in her essay "Maternity," where she evoked the logic that women's rights would clear out the asylums and jails to show that the current method of breeding had not produced the desired results, logic Severance and Woodhull also employed. To solve the problem, she again offered women's rights as the answer, but her argument did not place eugenics as the outcome of women's rights but as the reason for it. This essay also evoked a revised "Republican motherhood" argument as she pleaded for education for women so they could instruct their daughters on proper choices to make in sexual relations (35). I see her argument as similar to the arguments for expediency at some points since she used women's status as mothers to argue for their rights. However, the nature of her arguments changed, another case of eugenic lines of argument overshadowing women's rights discourse.

In a move contrary to anarchist free-love feminists, Claflin later supported intervention by the state in claiming that no one should be able to be married without a "medical certificate of their fitness" ("Social Injustice" 128). Her proposal matched social purity advocates' efforts to protect women from venereal disease. Yet, while promoting a principle that seemed contrary to free-love ideology, she nevertheless asserted her platform against marriage in the same essay, calling upon eugenic thought: "[M]arriage alone—that is our conventional system of marriage—cannot justify the reproduction of human beings. For under this system the unfit increase and multiply with every sanction and encouragement that law and custom can give them, and fill the world with the weak, the vicious, and the insane" (119). "Unfitness" for marriage went hand-in-hand with arguments that conventional marriage would produce more of the "unfit." She also used eugenics to support her plea for eliminating the stigma against "illegitimate children," since such children "so far from being inferior, are frequently if not generally superior to those born in wedlock" (117). The problematic language of the "superior" and "inferior" common to eugenic rhetoric served a more liberating agenda here. Claflin's eugenics in this essay still seemed somewhat less racist (though still raced) than later uses of eugenics, especially since she evoked the health of women as a consequence of attention to eugenics: "If, however, married women had full control of their maternal functions, few cases would occur where they would have more than two or three children, with an ample duration of time between the birth of each, and thus their offspring would be as strong and healthy as those of the others, provided they were equally healthy themselves" (117). "Fitness" here became a matter of health, and few feminists would disagree with the idea that bearing too many children put a strain on women's health. Thus, the attention to producing "healthier," more "fit" children had positive consequences for the discourse of women's health.

Like later free-love feminists discussed below, Claflin also expressed wariness that eugenic thought would turn to discouraging the poor from having children. She devoted an essay to the question, which also provided the essay's title: "Should the Poor Marry?" This essay critiqued the conditions under which children may be reared in poverty, but she concluded that excluding the poor from marriage, and thus from the only legal outlet for sexuality, would turn marriage into more of an elitist institution than it currently was. Claflin, who once delineated the harms done by marriage, now encouraged the state, if only to negate the rhetoric of the "unfit" that some reformers, like her own sister, had begun to support. Claflin's eugenic premise, then, did not take over her women's rights agenda to the same extent as her sister's. Claflin's rhetoric, however, did shift from using eugenics only implicitly to exerting more explicit eugenic logic and to bringing in the fit/unfit, superior/inferior mentality that came to characterize eugenic rhetoric in the late nineteenth century.

These women's eugenic rhetoric was not unique, and in fact eugenic rhetoric proliferated in the pages of free-love periodicals. *Woodhull & Claflin's Weekly*, for example, published many articles on the topic, as early as 1873, with such pieces as "The Causes of Physical Degeneracy," and even earlier, with the 1870 editorial "Social Evils: Regeneration a Necessity of Proper Generation" and an article by Stephen Pearl Andrews published in the same year, "Stirpiculture, Scientific Propagation: Improvement of the Breeds of Men." Lucinda Chandler also contributed articles arguing for women's rights and "wise motherhood" based on improving "the race." Angela Heywood, a singular perspective in free-love feminism, evoked stirpiculture as the salvation of humanity in *The Word* and insisted that one of the central reforms of "sexual self-government" should be children "well-conceived and well-born" ("Morality of Free Love"). It seems that even those who did not write explicitly about eugenics found it became part of their free-love feminism. Was eugenic thought, then, always a part of free-love feminism? Was being "free" of church and state control a prelude to surrendering sexuality to the cause of "uplifting" and "regenerating" the race? Or was it an argument for expediency that took on a life of its own? Not all free-love feminists were comfortable with such reasoning, yet, even while critiquing it, they still subscribed to some of its main tenets.

What about Women's Freedom? Ambiguous Eugenic Arguments

Lois Waisbrooker was one free-love feminist who critiqued the shift from free-love advocacy to a more purely eugenic discourse, and she put a different spin on hereditarian ideas in her 1907 book on eugenics. Waisbrooker did not always resist such a discourse; in fact, she actively participated in it. Such a view of her rhetoric runs contrary to that of other scholars who place her in complete opposition to eugenics, such as Joanne Passet (*Sex Radicals* 178), Hal Sears, and Angus McLaren, who believe that eugenics mostly featured in male free-love discourse, with the females as opponents of it. In Waisbrooker's pamphlet *The Temperance Folly; or, Who's the Worst*, written around 1900,[11] she attacked temperance workers "who attempt to redeem the world by dealing with effects instead of the causes which produce them" (1) and named hereditary and prenatal influences as two of these causes. She insisted, "No well born child,—one born of a happy, satisfied, well conditioned mother—will ever become a drunkard" (2). Similarly, in her 1893 book *Fountain of Life*, she argued that for a race to be "well born" and to clear out jails, social reforms "must supply women with the very best conditions" (81). Advocating the "well born" as the solution to the temperance problem, and also recalling free-love feminist arguments for "satisfied" mothers, did not indicate a resistance to eugenics but an endorsement.

Waisbrooker, however, allowed eugenic thought into her discourse only so far as it supported her radical views. She sympathized with the plight of women who had to bear children "the half of which must die before maturity, because of conditions both before and after birth," and to bear "inmates for prisons and asylums . . . gestated under conditions that make them naturally weak and criminal" ("Woman's Source of Power"). Her ideas here allude to two lines of argument popular in eugenic thought: that weaker children would die early in infancy and that heredity and prenatal influence produced the "naturally weak and criminal"—"nature" over "nurture."

Her sympathy for such women, however, did not extend to their use of contraceptives, which she deemed unnatural. Refuting Annie Besant, a British birth control advocate, Waisbrooker agreed that limiting conception was desirable but believed that contraceptives would only enslave women more:

> I do not say that I would blame a woman for using preventives if she has no other way of escaping unwelcome motherhood, neither would I blame a woman for killing a man if it was the only way in which she could prevent a violation of her person, but these are emergency measures, not panaceas for great evils. The general use of "checks" might possibly lessen prostitution outside of marriage, but it would tend to increase it on the inside, for with no fear of offspring man would make claims the more insistently. (*Anything More, My Lord?* 10–11)

Her refutation reacted both to birth control as the panacea for women's rights and to the prevailing thought that birth control would prevent the "unfit." Her reference to "checks" on the population also reveals how birth control advocates used Malthus's theories as justification for their aims. Waisbrooker, on the other hand, saw economics as the motivation behind birth control movements, and she attacked Besant's claim that birth control would help the poor by allowing them to limit their families, a claim Margaret Sanger would also make. Waisbrooker asked why it was the poor who had to limit their families and not the "royalty," who had children whom the poor must support (*Anything More, My Lord?* 12). Instead, she countered, "Why not limit the income of lord Derby and the earl of Pembroke, and yet further, why did they not limit the family of the queen?" (12). For Waisbrooker, "contracepts," or contraceptive devices, were crude and "unnatural." Instead, she believed that under sexual freedom, women would be able to prevent unwanted pregnancies without the use of such devices. She promoted continence as the ideal method, since women had not yet attained sexual freedom, but qualified that continence worked only with an enlightened and willing male ("Woman's Power"). She also startled the readers of *Lucifer* with her exclamation, "I cannot speak for other women, but were I thirty instead of seventy, and life's strong tide demanded expression I would seek self-relief before I would enter into a sex relation with a man and scientific appliances between" (125). To the advocates of contracepts, she asked why they placed the responsibility for preventing conception on women (*Anything More, My Lord?* 7–8). Once again, she brought the argument on birth control back to the economic conditions of women, concluding, "Contracepts and charity are both efforts to cover up the wrongs of our present economic system by trying to fit people to conditions instead of conditions to the people" (8). For Waisbrooker, on the economic margins for most of her life, economics and sex were the basis of women's oppression. While she supported women's options to limit their families, she did not support contraceptives as birth control, nor did she support encouraging the poor to limit their families.

Waisbrooker, however, not immune to the power of eugenic arguments, based her eugenic logic in a Lamarckian theory of heredity. In her 1907 book *Eugenics; or, Race Culture Lessons*, published the same year that *Lucifer*'s name changed to the *American Journal of Eugenics*, she responded to the increasing use of eugenic arguments to justify reforms and that urged women to change their practices to produce better children. She refuted these ideas, drawing from, but reinterpreting, theories of heredity that stressed the power of habit, such as Blackwell's. Waisbrooker maintained that if a woman changed her habits only to produce a better child, the child would not inherit that changed tendency. Instead, she urged, the woman must change for herself. For example, she noted that if a woman stopped drinking for the benefit of her child, her child would still be born with a tendency to drink. However, if the woman stopped drinking for the benefit of herself, her child would not be born with a tendency to drink. For Waisbrooker, if the woman changed the habit and altered her own self, she would transmit that tendency to her children. In her logic, the warrant of "like produces like" meant that a woman had to change herself for herself; otherwise, such superficial changes would not create a "like" result. She implored women, "You are the material out of which the race is built, and only as you live for yourself do you live for the race" (*Eugenics* 10). She compared the womb to a chemist's lab (10) and also recalled Darwin's focus on the effects of habit on future generations. Like Blackwell, Waisbrooker emphasized the power of habit and the power women had to change themselves for the better. Therefore, even though she critiqued the way some free-love advocates used eugenics, Waisbrooker did not entirely condemn eugenic ideology, since she did not critique the goal itself of producing an improved race. Waisbrooker's main critique of the type of eugenics expounded by some free-love advocates lay in their means rather than their end. As she insisted, "The transformation from sex slavery to living for the next generation is not freedom" (65).

Lillian Harman's eugenic rhetoric produced similar ambiguity, as she seemed to both condemn it and participate in it. At her father's death, she memorialized his work by noting his contributions to eugenics (*Moses Harman* 1). Her writings also included arguments that women should limit the number of children they bore because of limits on resources ("Radical Women—And Others"), a Malthusian premise, and arguments that sex education would aid in the issue of elevating the race. She mused, "The salvation of our race must rest in the hand of our descendants. Hence the necessity of the proper instruction in the sacredness of the sexual functions" ("Regeneration" 154). Thus, she seemed to support the eugenic turn in free-love rhetoric, yet she also espoused ideas that ran counter to her father's ideologies. Her protest against eugenics lay in its negative implications. For example, she condemned the "insolence of our self-vaunted 'superior race' in arrogating to itself the ability and the right to regulate the lives of the 'inferior races'" ("From My Point of View," January 1900). It seems that Harman supported eugenics only in its "positive" connotations, and not interpretations that would have "inferior races" refrain from breeding.

In fact, Harman's writings on eugenics forefronted the racial issues that other free-love feminists ignored. Her writings on race, though, produced similar ambiguity. On the one hand, she remained the only free-love feminist to explicitly include black women in her call for women to own their own bodies, but on the other hand, she implied black

women's inferiority. "The Regeneration of Society," the speech and essay she produced in 1899, argued for women's sexual freedom as the
"salvation" of the race and a necessary step in evolution. At one point,
she discussed miscegenation laws as a failure, citing evidence that there
were few "full-blooded negro[es]" and that in most, "the Caucasian blood
predominates" (154), which indicates that she subscribed to the same
racist ideologies that produced "negative" eugenics. She continued:

> Instead of leaving women, white and black, in possession of their own
> bodies, with freedom to accept or reject any proposition from any man,
> the black woman was the slave of the master whose name she bore, just
> as the white wife took the name of the husband and belonged to him.
> Neither white nor black woman belonged to herself. I do not mean to
> assert that the absence of law would have prevented miscegenation; but
> I do maintain that the law did not prevent it. I am also confident that
> had the black woman been free, even though ignorant, there would not
> have been as great a mixture of the blood of the African and Caucasian
> races as exists today. In presenting these facts I do not wish to be under-
> stood as either advocating or opposing miscegenation. I merely use the
> illustration to show how utterly powerless such laws are to accomplish
> their purpose. (154)

Harman endorsed several rhetorics that she would seem at first to condemn. She disdained the rhetoric of eugenics that would hold one race
higher than another, but she then participated in it by placing white
women higher than the black women she deemed "ignorant" and by
implying racial mixing as an undesirable result of slavery. Other free-love
feminists seemed to skirt around the issue of what "race" they wished
to elevate, the human race or the white race. Once the question of race
became more explicit, as it did in Harman's speech, the more sinister
rhetoric of eugenics emerged.

Waisbrooker and Harman represent the ambiguity of this stage of
free-love feminism: they resisted eugenics yet did not deny its major
premises. Both women viewed sex as a means of elevating "the race,"
however they defined it. They denied that maternity should be the chief
function of women but argued for women's sexual freedom with the logic
that it would, either immediately or eventually, produce better children.
I find the timing of these arguments important when looking at them
alongside the developments of hereditarian science: Waisbrooker and
Harman wrote many of these texts in the 1890s and the beginning of
the twentieth century, the same time that the Lamarckian warrant of

the inheritance of acquired characteristics began to lose more ground. Thus, the warrant that improvements in women's condition, mental or physical, would become inherited conditions was beginning to disappear. Therefore, arguments for eugenics started to become more about inherent "fitness" and "unfitness," because improvements could not become hereditary. The ambiguous nature of the science led to similar ambiguity in free-love arguments. And though some dissented, they could not escape the rhetorical force of eugenic logic.

Dissenting from the Descent into Eugenic Rhetoric

Even the free-love feminists who more explicitly dissented from the descent of free-love feminism into eugenic rhetoric struggled with their refutations. They did not dissent based on fear of negative eugenics—not entirely—but on the same grounds as Waisbrooker attempted: that a focus on "enlightened," "wise," or "scientific" motherhood would enslave women in a different way than marriage. They might be "free" of the sexual bondage that marriage entailed only to be enslaved to maternity and their "duty" to "elevate the race." In a time when many women had not only the power but also the means to achieve smaller families, fears of "race suicide" emerged—and these charges were usually aimed at white women. Women, then, were attacked for neglecting their "duty" to bear children who would be the "salvation of the race." Even Moses Harman, who championed women's rights throughout his lifetime, had begun to let eugenics dominate his arguments. In fact, after delivering an 1896 speech titled "Motherhood in Freedom," Harman faced objections by several women present, including Lucinda Chandler and Lillie D. White, who protested that "the duties and responsibilities of Fatherhood were ignored, and that it was unjust to woman to hold her alone responsible for the results of maternity" ("Motherhood in Freedom"). The logic of the objections was not the eugenic claim of "elevating the race" but women's specific role.

White and her sister Lizzie Holmes brought a class-based critique to the eugenics that free-love advocates championed, and they continually wrote to *Lucifer* to critique Moses Harman's theory of eugenics. Both women had once promoted Harman as a leader in the cause of women's rights but objected to his descent into eugenic rhetoric on the basis that his eugenics would enslave women and marginalize the poor. They were uneasy with the claim that helping the poor to limit their families would lessen the "rapid multiplication of the unfit." Responding to Harman's call for "fewer and better children," they rejected the claim that the poor should limit their families as an "absurd" solution "for economic evils" and instead called for an investigation into the economic conditions that produced children condemned to starvation (White, "Population and Economics"; Holmes, "Fewer and Better Children"). White and Holmes resisted both "negative eugenics" because of its marginalization of the poor and "positive eugenics" encouraging more privileged women to breed. Responding to the "race suicide" charge aimed at upper-class women who chose to have fewer children, White noted that women had been given more opportunities and that insisting that they have children to "better the race" forced them back into servitude ("Various Voices," August 1899). Finally, Holmes cited a study that negated "positive eugenics":

> The leading scientists of the world now assert that habits, traits, disease or vices are not transmitted from parents to children. Robert Owen proved, by taking at random a number of children from the slums of London and placing them in the best possible conditions, that heredity has very little influence as against conditions. Weakness may be inherited—a weak father and mother cannot produce strong, sturdy offspring. ("Population" 229)

Holmes's arguments demonstrated how relying on the inheritance of acquired characteristics as a warrant for eugenic logic would fail, since science no longer recognized that warrant—Lamarck's theories had already begun to wane.

The refutations of Holmes and White seem to explain how and why free-love feminism began to decline. Holmes characterized the stand of *Lucifer* and its editor as "Women ought to be free in order that fewer and better children may be born" ("Population" 229). Unlike other free-love feminists, she asserted that women's rights should not be won based on their status as mothers, with proclamations like "To my mind, the freeing of women, the placing of women on the footing of a human being, equal by no more, with all other human beings of whatever sex, for her own sake, is sufficient. I need no further excuse or reason for pleading woman's emancipation" (230). She also asserted that when sex reformers "claim that in these demands the whole of the sex question is involved, or when they claim that woman should be more honored, more privileged, more reverenced than man, or that motherhood is her highest and best function, I must protest" ("More of the Problem"), and added, "I have no universal panacea to apply" and "Free love and varietism do not, for me, solve the question at all" (342). Her objection encapsulated the problems with free-love rhetors at the time: they not only proposed that free love would solve multiple problems but also relegated women to motherhood and forgot about their sexual freedom, the formative tenet of the philosophy of free love they had initially supported. Women's sexual emancipation used to be the end of their argument, or the conclusion from their premises. Now, it was simply one means to get an "elevated race."

Voltairine de Cleyre also resisted the turn to eugenics, and she hit the proponents with the same tool they were using to support it: science. De Cleyre's 1900 article in *Lucifer* attempted to shine some reality on the idealistic notions that free women would produce a race of superior children by pointing out that the science did not exist to support such a claim. She noted how women enslaved in marriage could produce liberal and even radical thinkers ("Love in Freedom"), which disputed the inheritance of such characteristics. She also pointed to the inheritance of disease and the focus on health in eugenic rhetoric with "I see that the children of diseased parents are frequently models of healthy physique; that the daughters of health are often the mothers of disease" (226). Developments in science had shown that not all diseases were inherited and that physical characteristics acquired during one's life, such as a healthy physique, would not necessarily be passed to the offspring. De Cleyre concluded, "Therefore I say that while there may be a law of heredity, discovering which we may be able to control the mental, moral and physical, dowry of offspring; while it is more than likely that free selection will play an important part in the functioning of such law, we have as yet discovered no such law" (226). De Cleyre's approach supported the science of the time: inherited characteristics could not be passed on through heredity. Some advocates, like Waisbrooker, clung to the warrant of the inheritance of acquired characteristics because it justified women's rights reform. The science supporting them was disappearing, hence the disappearance of women's rights arguments from eugenic discourse. The efforts of Holmes, White, and de Cleyre at resisting the eugenic rhetoric of *Lucifer* were unsuccessful; in 1907, *Lucifer* became the *American Journal of Eugenics*.

The New Sex "Radicalism"

Free-love feminists of the 1850s to 1880s had reversed conservative discourses to argue for radical causes; by the turn of the century, they used radical discourse to argue for the conservative cause of eugenics. Whether the cause of such a shift was the disappearance of the Lamarckian warrant or the overwhelming nature of the rhetoric of eugenics itself, the story of free-love feminism ends on a sad note, when sexual freedom aims had turned into a discourse that would justify many twentieth-century atrocities. The shift from arguing for women's rights using eugenics to simply arguing for eugenics fully occurred after the turn of the century. Looking at this shift alongside the discoveries of science reveals a parallel: it was after the rediscovery of Mendel's work, which verified Weismann's conclusions disproving the inheritance of acquired characteristics, that a shift fully occurred from women's rights to eugenics. Though Margaret Sanger later employed eugenics as justification for birth control, it was a different kind of eugenics, more focused on discouraging the "unfit" from breeding than on encouraging women to better themselves to create better children. Once Lamarck's theory of acquired characteristics became less accepted, the arguments for social reforms to improve the next generation received less presence in the discourse, since an "improved person" would not be able to pass these improvements on to the next generation through the body. There was thus no longer any need to argue for specific improvements in parents or in conditions during sexual intercourse.

Waisbrooker proposed, "Instead of child culture I would have the movement called eugenics named woman culture" (*Eugenics* 17). From the work of Lamarck and Darwin to the free-love feminists who used their conclusions as a warrant, a "child culture" emerged, celebrating the next generation as the means to human evolution. Free-love feminists created a "woman culture" out of a theory of eugenics that often resulted in raced, classed, and gendered discourse. The argument from difference, long examined by scholars of women's rhetoric, became a mothers of the race discourse, showing that women could use arguments from difference with a basis in science to actually support women's rights. Reading these women's arguments alongside the findings in science and their interpretations by physicians shows the complicated nature of eugenic arguments in free-love feminism. We can see the new dimensions of arguments based in "Republican motherhood" and how the ethical appeals of the "mothers of the nation" were transformed into the logical appeals of the mothers of the race.

The new "sex radicalism," epitomized by Dora Forster's 1905 eponymous work, insisted:

> The monogamous system does not now fulfill the function of reproducing the race, as regards Americans of Anglo-Saxon stock; and even some upholders of orthodox marriage, like Roosevelt, are beginning to see that there is something wrong when married women so often entirely

refuse to be "as ladies love to be who love their lords." It can hardly be doubted that the system which checks free motherhood by persecution also checks the almost instinctive desire for maternity within marriage; and that free unions, and a sane and instructed public opinion in regard to sex duly honoring maternity, will accomplish what blundering coercion has failed to do. On this question, women will have the last word. (20)

They didn't.

CONCLUSION

Historiography and Feminist Uses of Eugenics

[T]hose who want sex-science will get it.

Dora Forster, *Sex Radicalism*, 1905

Recovering free-love feminism, and moving it from a "fringe" movement to a multifaceted, multivoiced social movement, has required me to continually interrogate both my own practices and the larger feminist goals of recovery. Many feminist rhetorical scholars have analyzed the ways in which women of the nineteenth century negotiated agency to allow themselves to speak. Free-love feminists' challenges would have been amplified by their salacious subject, but when we look at their rhetoric in the context of the larger conversation occurring over sexuality in the nineteenth-century United States, we can see that some of these women may have taken their right to speak about sex as a given. In fact, when looking at the texts aimed at like-minded audiences, as many of their texts were, we find that such negotiation strategies were minimal. That is, they constructed a community of like-minded individuals as audiences of their pamphlets and speeches, and since they had such audiences through periodicals and free-love societies, they made fewer negotiations to speak about sex. Mary Gove Nichols and Victoria Woodhull entered into such negotiations in speeches to larger audiences, but their texts to the free-love or spiritualist communities did not make such concessions.[1] Furthermore, when we look at the practices of these women against the scientific discourses of the time, we see that they entered an ongoing conversation and did not often feel the need to justify their presence in such a conversation. That physicians had made giving "your history" a vital tool in understanding sexual maladies and practices supported such a contention. Therefore, they found agency in both the community of like-minded individuals and the science itself—their shared logic, based in science, provided their right to speak about sex.

Much feminist recovery has highlighted the belief of Karlyn Kohrs Campbell, who says, "Because of the challenges to women advocates posed by agency and subjectivity, the most significant contributions of criticism have come from work that explores the ways that women negotiated the assumption of the role of rhetor" ("Consciousness-Raising" 51). The work of recovery has necessitated attention to these negotiations because of the traditional lack of female rhetors in the rhetorical tradition. In fact, much feminist recovery work has been based on this principle, reading the rhetoric of women as overcoming the challenges to their speech. Many feminist historiographers have called for new methods as a lenses to viewing women's speech, since traditional—read male—methods often ignore the specific situations and challenges faced by women rhetors. But, in seeking new methods and focusing on how women assumed the agency to speak and negotiated the challenges to practicing rhetoric, could we ignore other approaches to such texts? Could we overlook the argumentative techniques that could help us learn more about feminist sources of argument, such as science?

Recovering a Silenced Movement

I first came to this topic through a text by the most "visible," from a recovery standpoint, free-love feminist, Victoria Woodhull. In an excerpt in Miriam Schneir's *Feminism* anthology, I encountered a woman outspoken about sex and sexuality at a time when women's speech faced restrictions based on their gender. After several trips to the library, I had her life, in all its fragments and scandals, in front of me, along with her texts, and planned a project on the rhetorical concessions necessary for her seemingly isolated and taboo feminist message. But I kept coming back to certain sections in her 1874 *Tried as by Fire* speech: Why was she talking about woman owning herself? Why quote Herbert Spencer and Charles Darwin for such a message? Where did the arguments that certain standards are "violated in no species but man" come from? Why was she arguing that free love would produce "superior children" and reduce diseases in women that she blamed on unhealthy sexual practices? Who was this John Scudder physician she quoted that asserted the same views in a time when many physicians worked to define women's bodies as passionless? The logic of her statements intrigued me and led me to other questions: What did she know and what didn't she know about human sexuality and anatomy? Are her arguments "weird," as one historian would claim, or was she misinterpreting, intentionally or unintentionally, the science of the time? I began my research into these questions by recovering other free-love texts from nineteenth-century America. I expected to uncover a few isolated radicals but instead found many women arguing the same points as Woodhull, or, in some cases, arguing even more radical points. While Woodhull's body of work proved easy to recover, with several biographies, anthologies, and works readily available on microfilm, other free-love feminists proved more elusive. Thanks to Joanne Passet's recovery work, I found other women in the free-love movement, and research on women like Juliet Severance and Lois Waisbrooker led me to still other women, such as Angela Heywood and the elusive Hulda Potter-Loomis. Often I found unknown texts like Potter-Loomis's on the same reel as a text by Severance or Waisbrooker. The last stages of my recovery work concerned the free-love periodicals, where I saw a rich discourse community conversing with each other, disproving any claim that free-love texts were isolated acts of radicalism.

My research also directed me to a rich body of texts on sexuality coming from the medical community, especially texts on "sexual physiology." These two discourse communities discussing sexuality then led to my research question on whether there was a connection between free lovers' and medical writers' discussions of female sexuality, two viewpoints I did not think compatible. The medical texts mostly proved easier to find. Arno Press released many reprints of nineteenth-century medical texts in the 1970s, and that is how I obtained copies of Trall's and Blackwell's texts on sexual physiology. I also received marriage manuals dug up from the attics of colleagues, who unearthed interesting texts, like Emma Drake's *What a Young Wife Ought to Know*, when they heard about my topic. I was also interested in finding the John Scudder text, since Woodhull quoted him in her 1874 speech, and I wanted to see if she was misrepresenting his ideas to suit her own agenda. His text proved key, since it obviously espoused feminist ideals and Woodhull used his arguments to support her own.

As I read these medical texts, a different picture emerged. Many feminist scholars have critiqued nineteenth-century medicine and noted their participation in ideologies of female inferiority and oppression. However, instead of supporting women's oppression and denying their sexuality, many of these medical texts supported women's rights and affirmed their sexuality. Whether they ascribed to one view or the other was not based on gender—both male and female physicians were in both camps. These texts challenged the image of the "chaste" or "passionless" Victorian woman. Even when they urged more temperate sexual indulgence, these physicians did not deny that women had sexual feelings that should be indulged. These texts, however, had a particularly interesting status as medical popularizations of science: Trall, Blackwell, and Scudder reflected the scientific understanding of the body of their particular time periods and applied science to advice on lifestyle choices. But since these medical texts were intermediary texts, I found I needed to go back to science to explain their conceptions of female sexuality. I then hypothesized that science was providing the knowledge from which free-love feminists conceived female sexuality. I proposed to read these women's rhetorical strategies against the context of the science of the time.

My own reading practices throughout this process confirmed my hypothesis on the importance of reading these texts against science. Early on, I was confused about Woodhull's strategies in discussing "superior" children as a benefit of free love and about other rhetors arguing that social reforms that improved the mother's condition would produce "superior" children. But once I read about the influence of Lamarckian theories of the inheritance of acquired characteristics and found more eugenic arguments in medical advice texts, I was able to contextualize the reformers' premise that reforms would improve future generations through heredity. Similarly, definitions of disease in Gove Nichols's and Severance's texts confused me until I learned about vitalism, a scientific theory that defined the body as affected by a "vital" force (and that a lack of that force led to disease). Thus, my reading about nineteenth-century science helped me make sense of what seemed like strange claims by free-love feminists.

During this process, I encountered many texts with eugenic lines of argument, a finding that disturbed my preconceptions. As I shared my findings, I found colleagues equally flummoxed by the turn to eugenics in this rhetoric; they wanted to automatically dismiss such rhetoric as inherently racist and were surprised to see it did not always seem to center on the classic fit/unfit dichotomy but on women's health. Was free-love feminist eugenics, then, a different kind of eugenics than the more racist applications of the twentieth century? Several scholars have written about eugenics in this movement, positing that the eugenics that emerged during this time period was quite different from later interpretations. For example, Pam McAllister, who recovered and republished Waisbrooker's utopian novel *A Sex Revolution* in the 1970s, found herself disturbed by Waisbrooker's references to "perfecting the race" but concluded that "her notion of eugenics seems well-intentioned" (11). Linda Gordon notes of such discourse, "Eugenics had not yet become a movement in itself. Feminists used eugenics arguments as if they instinctively felt that arguments based solely on women's rights had not enough power to conquer conservative and religious scruples about reproduction. So they combined eugenics and feminism to produce evocative, romantic visions of perfect motherhood" ("Voluntary Motherhood" 17). Joanne Passet characterizes the turn to eugenics as an outcome of the argument that love between parents would produce more "superior" children, and Passet defines such "superiority" as "healthier, purer, and happier offspring, untainted by their parents' anger and selfishness" (*Sex Radicals* 165). Passet and Hal Sears acknowledge that such a definition was supported by the hereditarian ideas of the time; for example, Sears explains that what he calls "anarchist eugenics" meant that free women and men would produce free children and that "this belief depended upon the prevalent notion that a child's character could be prenatally influenced; a mother's submission to sexist laws, it was believed, would affect the unborn child" (121).

Looking back at the use of embryology as a warrant in free-love feminism and at similar arguments occurring in other discourse communities, such as racial uplift, we can see that free-love feminists' claims were not about the mothers producing a similar breed of sex slaves but about their inferior status causing hateful thoughts that would transfer negative characteristics to the child. The conversation on eugenics occurring in the scientific and medical communities supported the beliefs of free lovers, and while we may not see those beliefs as "science" today, to nineteenth-century thinkers, it was science. Sears is also careful to distinguish "anarchist eugenics" from "the later prescriptive eugenics of the Progressive Era" (121), and other scholars such as Angus McClaren agree with him that "anarchist eugenics" seems more benign and less racist (533). McClaren also distinguishes this form of eugenics from the eugenic theories of Francis Galton and asserts that the anarchists lost ground to those who "turned their 'science' to even more transparently self-serving purposes" (546). (McClaren and Sears also characterize eugenics as an exclusively male phenomenon in free-love texts.) In distinguishing free-love advocates' eugenic arguments from Galton or from later eugenics, we may also ignore the raced consequences of free-love rhetoric. Their rhetoric always implied raced consequences, though these became more racist as they followed their own logic to more dangerous ends.

Whether they call it "anarchist eugenics," as Sears does, or "eugenic feminism," as Stephanie Athey does, it seems that scholars found a different kind of eugenic argument. Michael Perry, who anthologized

Woodhull's speeches in 2005, theorizes that Woodhull was in fact the first eugenicist (*Lady Eugenist* 8), but he does not read her in the context of science or against other free-love feminists of the time. Mary Gove Nichols's texts, published in the 1850s, also contain eugenic implications, indicated by the title of her 1854 work (with T. L. Nichols) *Marriage: Its History, Character, and Results; its Sanctities, and its Profanities; its Science and its Facts. Demonstrating its Influence, as a Civilized Institution, of the Happiness of the Individual and the Progress of the Race.* She also blamed hereditary deficiencies and the sexual slavery of women for "depraved" children. Thus, she indicated eugenic lines of argument long before the insidious theory was given a name. Consequently, was free-love feminist rhetoric eugenic all along?

Free-love feminists were not alone among nineteenth-century feminists in turning to eugenic lines of argument. I found eugenics in the social purity discourse of Frances Willard and in the racial uplift discourse of Adella Hunt Logan, whose speech on the topic is included in an appendix in Shirley Logan's study *"We are Coming": The Persuasive Discourse of Nineteenth-Century Black Women.* Eugenic lines of argument, then, proliferated in other feminist movements, and these rhetors are surely not isolated occurrences. Why, then, has this particularly prolific line of argument by nineteenth-century women gone unexamined?

I've found that free-love feminism was always a raced discourse, as it positioned sexuality in a particular frame and ignored sexual self-sovereignty as a raced assumption, but was it always a racist discourse? What did free-love feminists mean when they referred to "progress in the race"? Physician Elizabeth Blackwell, for example, specified Caucasians when she engaged in mothers-of-the-race discourse: "We should uproot our whole national life and destroy the characteristics of the Anglo-Saxon race, if we gave up this natural right of sovereignty over our own bodies" (*Essays* 125). Blackwell connected the free-love feminist tenet of women's self-sovereignty with a "racial purity" line of argument, showing that she did not mean "humanity" when she specified "progress in the race." Her rhetoric also reacted to the growing nationalistic discourse of eugenics, also found in texts by Willard and Anna Julia Cooper. Free-love feminists participated in this element of the discourse as well, with the argument that we can judge a nation's progress by their treatment of women. Tennessee Claflin, for example, insisted, "The nearer [woman] is to the condition of slave, the more generally degraded is the whole nation" ("Women and Progress" 49). Thus, another appeal of eugenic rhetoric was its emphasis on progress, which free-love feminists applied to women's position. In recovering these eugenic lines of argument and analyzing eugenic rhetoric in feminist texts, I do not seek to excuse their use of eugenics but attempt to understand the confluence of factors that led to its use by feminists. Eugenic rhetoric appealed to feminists in an era when Republican motherhood arguments ceased their effectiveness. Whether they initiated it because of the high mortality rate among infants or because such arguments had more appeal to audiences, these feminists unknowingly participated in a discourse that would result in many atrocities in the twentieth century. I'm not sure their rhetoric is so different from twentieth-century applications, though. They might not have employed it to the same racist purposes, but the implications were there. Such findings also offer another reason for the absence of free-love feminists in recovery efforts.

Implications for Recovery

Why recover this movement, then? Why recover women's rhetorics that we cannot—and should not—celebrate? We want to celebrate some of their achievements, especially since they broke barriers for women's speech and produced arguments that would later become prominent in sexual liberation movements of the twentieth century. And, much of the work of feminist recovery in the field of rhetoric has warranted celebration. But the absence of nineteenth-century feminists who used eugenics and other unpopular stances indicates that we may still recover women with admirable qualities and agendas that fit our own definitions of feminism. Have free-love feminist texts gone ignored because of these issues, or because the issues are not as simple as "here are some racist feminists"? Are we, perhaps, sanitizing feminist histories of rhetoric?

Carol Mattingly's important insights on her recovery of temperance rhetors indicate two possibilities for the absence of such rhetoric from feminist efforts of recovery. First, their feminism is not our feminism. She points out:

> In our initial efforts, we have, not surprisingly, appreciated those historical figures who most resemble academic feminists—those who seemed to share our investment in confrontational and assertive approaches—at the expense of others worthy of our attention. This problem was complicated, I think, because historians also felt the need to prove the credibility of the women they promoted. ("Telling Evidence" 100–101)

Free-love feminists not only had a different kind of feminism than contemporary feminists but had several goals that would prove to be problematic. Feminist rhetoricians have wanted to "prove the credibility of the women they promoted" but also wanted to prove the worthiness of their rhetoric. Karlyn Kohrs Campbell has also noted that recovery work has had to contend with beliefs about rhetorical theory and criticism that would seem to contradict our efforts. She, and others, believe that rhetorical theory itself has excluded some women's practices because "constraints on who may speak, on what issues, in what sites, on what occasions and using what styles and appeals have been the primary means by which women (and others) have been excluded from rhetorical action" ("Consciousness-Raising" 48). Furthermore, she contends, "Women were partially or completely silenced for centuries; then the women who dared to break these barriers were silenced in turn by rhetorical historians and critics and theorists" ("Biesecker" 158). In ignoring women who do not match our agendas to celebrate women's challenges to the rhetorical tradition and in ignoring women whose beliefs diverge from our own, are we perpetuating the same silencing?

Mattingly's other important observation about the temperance movement as a failed movement also applies to free-love feminists. There are many ways in which we can view them as failed rhetors, not only in their free-love goals but also in their reconceptions of women's sexual physiology. For example, in the 1840s, Gove Nichols argued how physiology did not prevent women from doing more strenuous work, arguments Clelia Mosher made in the early twentieth century. Gove Nichols, then, failed in conveying that message. The arguments of Woodhull and Severance found their way into the birth control rhetoric of Margaret Sanger, because they did not succeed in their goals. The logic and strategies of their texts, good and bad, both reflected and influenced later, more visible and influential feminist reformers. They also failed to uphold the feminist values they initially championed when they let eugenics supersede their aims.

Finally, we could think about whether it was their use of science that distances us from their rhetorical practices. As feminists, we may view science as an inherently gendered discourse. Could science as a source of their arguments place them in the more "masculine" framework in contrast to the "feminine style" of invention and delivery that Campbell and Lindal Buchanan theorize? Or, once again, is it simply that we feel the need to celebrate the rhetorical practices we recover?

Looking at this dark side of feminist history, what do we learn? We can employ Krista Ratcliffe's model of rhetorical listening, "with the intent to understand not just the claims but the rhetorical negotiations of understanding as well" (28). Listening to the voices of free-love feminists, we uncover an uncomfortable aspect of feminist history that we should not ignore. In discussing her feminist recovery work, Christine Mason Sutherland says, "I do not believe that research can be justified only in terms of its practical value today. That said, however, I believe nonetheless that we can learn from the wisdom of these early women writers" (120). Recovering the story of nineteenth-century free-love feminists, we learn not from their wisdom but from their mistakes.

NOTES

BIBLIOGRAPHY

INDEX

NOTES

Introduction: The Unlikely Rhetorical Allies of Science and Free-Love Feminism

1. Moses Harman, editor of *Lucifer*, renumbered volumes of the periodical, starting at volume 1, around 1890. He may have even started a new numbering system every time he moved *Lucifer*'s offices (from Valley Falls to Topeka and then to Chicago).

1. The Season of Battle: The Rhetoric of Free-Love Feminism in Nineteenth-Century America

1. Passet provides a helpful overview of free-love periodicals (*Sex Radicals* 174–75). The free-love commune Berlin Heights produced several periodicals from 1856 to 1859. Other periodicals with editors included in this project are Thomas and Mary Gove Nichols's *Nichols' Monthly* (1855–57), Edwin C. Walker and Lillian Harman's *Fair Play* (1888–1908), and Lois Waisbrooker's *Foundation Principles* (1893–94) and *Clothed with the Sun* (1900–1902).

2. Spurlock describes the perfectionist free lovers as a "women's liberation movement with few women leaders" and attributes this lack to "an artifact of either the culture or the sources. Perhaps, on the one hand, both men and women were so accustomed to having male leaders that men naturally took command of the movement. Though free lovers condemned marriage, most were married themselves. Wives might join husbands in repudiating male domination, even though they personally adopted a subordinate role" (*Free Love* 183).

3. Gutierrez explains about the philosophy of spiritualism: "The dead were not instantly perfected but rather progressed in heaven, climbing the ladder of heavens as they became more knowledgeable and spiritually refined. Heaven was open to all, reflecting the self-identity of the young republic as a meritocracy" (190). Sears reveals the basis of spiritualism's appeal to the people of the nineteenth century: "Spiritualism acted as a device to accommodate Americans to the exigencies of technological change; it promised that the same forces that caused upheaval in their lives (symbolized, for instance, by electricity), allowed them benefits, two in particular—victory over the ultimate alienation called death, and liberation from sexual and familial constrictions" (20). Sears also names spiritualism, along with feminism and free love, as one of the three "infidelisms" of nineteenth-century society (6–7). Goldsmith's biography of Victoria Woodhull is also helpful for a background in spiritualism and its connections to radical reform movements. Finally, the work of McGarry has elaborated the connection between spiritualism, free love, and free speech.

4. Helpful background studies on the water-cure medical sect include Weiss and Kemble's 1967 study, *The Great American Water-Cure Craze*, and Cayleff's 1987 study of the feminist aspects of water cure, *Wash and Be Healed*.

5. For more biographical information on Gove Nichols, see Silver-Isenstadt's 2002 *Shameless* as well as Passet's *Sex Radicals*.

6. In his analysis of *The Bostonians*, scholar Alfred Habegger does not name the free-love advocate satirized by James as Woodhull but does offer some insight into James's motives. He relates how Henry James Jr. was humiliated when *Woodhull & Claflin's Weekly* published a letter of his father's on the Beecher-Tilton scandal, where he said: "I marry my wife under the impression that she is literally perfect, and is going to exhaust my capacity of desire ever after. Ere long I discover my mistake" (qtd. in Habegger 331). *The Bostonians'* satire resulted from James's humiliation, as well as his discomfort with his father's radical politics (335).

7. Woodhull's scandalous life has long interested biographers, and it is difficult to separate fact from fiction in accounts of her life. Johnston's 1967 biography, *Mrs. Satan*, for example, reports the more scandalous side of Woodhull's public persona. Several recent biographies have given more insight into the life of this controversial figure, including Underhill's *The Woman Who Ran for President* and Gabriel's *Notorious Victoria*.

8. Frisken says of the nomination of Woodhull and Douglass, "The party's political coupling of one of the century's most disreputable white women with one of its most respectable black men was more a provocative gesture than a bid for electoral success. . . . [I]t is instructive to view the Woodhull/Douglass ticket as the effort of a group . . . to address the most pressing social questions of Reconstruction—racial and sexual equality" (*Victoria Woodhull's Sexual Revolution* 56). Documents also support the symbolic nature of Woodhull's nomination. For example, in a letter addressed to Woodhull from the "Victoria League," the Equal Rights Party stressed the ideology behind the nomination rather than a desire to get her elected. Party members opined, "We shall urge all women who possess the political qualifications of other citizens . . . to assume and exercise the right of suffrage without further hesitation and delay. We ask you to become the standard-bearer of this idea before the people, and for this purpose nominate you as our candidate for President of the United States, to be voted for in 1872 by the combined suffrages of both sexes" (Woodhull, *Correspondence* 1). The letter makes no mention of her actually campaigning for president; it is clear they chose her as a voice for women's suffrage rather than as a legitimate candidate.

9. Discussing the question of Woodhull's authorship, Frisken concludes, "It is nearly impossible to recover Woodhull as a historical actor in her own right. Her own personal papers are fragmentary and heavily edited. We will never know for certain who really wrote the lectures, speeches, letters, and articles attributed to her. They were almost never written in her own hand, and she later repudiated many" (*Victoria Woodhull's Sexual Revolution* 10). Several historians have noted similarities between her later speeches, written and delivered after her break with Blood and Andrews, and the earlier speeches attributed to them. For example, biographer Lois Beachy Underhill notes that Woodhull's *Tried as by Fire* speech bears several distinct stylistic characteristics that indicate Woodhull herself wrote a majority of it (259). Another writer points out, "In fact, since Woodhull became increasingly strident in her views of utopia after she became separated from her ghost writers, one may conclude that either she learned something profound and lasting from them or else the American lectures contained a good deal of Woodhull's views to begin with" (Gutierrez 192). While we can never know the extent of Woodhull's contributions to the speeches attributed to her, we can surmise that many represented her views at that particular time (though she later changed her views). We might also apply Buchanan's revised concept of delivery

(131–58), which accounts for collaboration, to analysis of Woodhull's texts. Since the rhetorical techniques in her earlier speeches continued to be used by Woodhull long after her association with these men ended, I conclude that she did have input into these speeches, even when she collaborated with others.

10. Frisken conjectures that Woodhull "benefited from new trends in public speaking after the Civil War. The public lecture, once a forum for intellectual enlightenment, had gradually shifted into a venue for popular entertainment" (*Victoria Woodhull's Sexual Revolution* 118). Ray has examined how the genre of the public lecture shifted from educational purposes to entertainment. Though audiences most likely attended Woodhull's lectures for their entertainment value, they became participants in her reformist agendas.

11. See Frisken ("Sex in Politics" and *Victoria Woodhull's Sexual Revolution*) and Horowitz ("Victoria Woodhull") for more on Woodhull's brushes with Comstock and his obscenity laws. These historians show how Comstock's pursuit of Woodhull became a personal vendetta.

12. Male historians of the free-love movement often diminish Woodhull's contributions, choosing instead to see her as a dangerous figure in the movement. Spurlock characterizes Woodhull as causing the end of a positive relationship with the suffragists, saying, "Victoria Woodhull's notoriety added to the public reputation of free love as a sinister movement and hurried the end of the free love movement's cooperation with the women's movement" (*Free Love* 216). Sears also blames Woodhull for negative interpretations of the movement: "Victoria Woodhull's free-love agitation in the early seventies marked the end of the serious and widespread discussion of sexual alternatives in nineteenth-century America" (23).

13. Claflin made several references to herself as a physician because of her experiences with faith healing and magnetic healing. She did not, however, practice medicine, and even the more alternative medical sects of the nineteenth century would not have called her a physician.

14. Though they earned some acclaim from newspaper writers who found the lady stockbrokers a novelty, they also earned censure for invading the male enclave of Wall Street. In one of her speeches, Claflin recalled how her male clients asked her to conduct her business with them in writing, since they feared her visits to their firms would damage their reputations (*Ethics* 21).

15. Frisken's work has analyzed the reception of Woodhull's exploits in the popular press during this period, and to a lesser extent Claflin's, offering some interesting details about the press's obsession with the sisters.

16. No biography of Severance exists, and Passet is the only scholar to treat her at length. Additional background material on Severance comes from her obituary in the *New York Times* ("Dr. Juliet Severance Dies").

17. *Lucifer* quoted a review from *Boston Ideas* that called Severance's book *Marriage* "a fearless, straightforward presentation of a subject whose social perplexities need scientific attention. It is a mighty arraignment of the legal institution of marriage and faithfully states the exact condition of things known to prevail only too broadly in our land as well as in all the world" ("Says 'Boston Ideas'—"). Praising her eloquence, the review says, "Dr. Severance's address is keen, sarcastic, incisive—characterized by just those elements that cause her words to penetrate determinedly to the attention of all readers. She is in deadly earnest and she makes her points so plainly and unmistakably as to cause the sensitive to shudder" (198).

18. While no comprehensive biography of Angela Heywood exists, Battan's and McElroy's works have illuminated her life.

19. Blatt observes, "[Ezra Heywood's] writing style was scholarly, and it is possible that his prose, choice of vocabulary, and frequent, lengthy footnotes made him inaccessible to many. No doubt his writings on free love, which achieved much greater notoriety, had a far wider, although still limited, impact" (52). Sears also compares Angela's writing style to the more dry and scholarly style of Ezra's writing: "A singular woman among a remarkable group, Angela Heywood managed to transcend the Victorian consciousness of the period to a greater degree than any other sex radical. If Ezra sometimes intoned praises to the joys of love and sex, Angela exploded in melodies, filling *The Word* with flowing columns of impressionistic prose that enlisted the intellect to the service of the emotions. She did much to give *The Word* its characteristic style" (172).

20. In an 1887 letter, Rachel Campbell, for example, condemned Angela Heywood's speech, especially since Ezra was the one jailed for it: "It is cowardly to court danger & defy law when the suffering falls on another. I am out of all patience with her; if she wants too much to say words that offend decent people, let her go to a brothel & say them over and over until she is satisfied" (qtd. in McElroy, *Individualist Feminism* 53). The editors of *Foote's Health Monthly*, a radical medical periodical, also berated her for her "nasty" tongue and decried the circumstances that led to Ezra's imprisonment: "Sending Mr. Heywood to the penitentiary a few years was not a fair deal; but the real object was to punish indirectly Mrs. Heywood for a dreadful speech which she made in Boston, which the authorities had not the courage to deal directly with her for. So now it would appear that again the authorities have attempted to punish Mrs. Heywood who is really the guilty person, by arresting her husband." They added, "If the Vice Society is disposed to proceed against Mrs. Heywood herself on the charge of insanity, and can make out a good case, perhaps they might succeed in putting her into the madhouse, but we would pity Comstock . . . if she lived to get out" (qtd. in McElroy, *Individualist Feminism* 29).

21. Biographical details on Campbell come from works written by other free-love advocates after her death, including Mary Florence Johnson's tribute and a tribute by *Lucifer* entitled "Knowledge Better Than Faith," which praised Campbell for never wavering from her spiritualist ideals, even on her deathbed (2).

22. Waisbrooker's life has been chronicled by Pam McAllister, in her introduction to the reprint of *A Sex Revolution*, and Joanne Passet. Passet's article "Power through Print" provides the most extensive biography of Waisbrooker.

23. Dr. Edward Bond Foote (1829–1906) and his son of the same name (1854–1912) contributed to the free-love cause, raising money for some of those arrested under the Comstock law and publishing their ideas in their periodical, *Dr. Foote's Health Monthly*. They supported women's rights, free love, and birth control and thus also became targets of Comstock. Sears has a helpful section on the Footes (184–97), and Wood's 2008 article, "Prescription for a Periodical," highlights the contributions of these radical doctors. Cronin's 2006 article on obscenity laws and the free-love debate also discusses the contributions of the Footes.

24. Chandler endured tragedies early in her life, including an illness that cut short her formal education at the age of thirteen and the loss of her only child, a son who drowned when he was three (Leach 87). She became part of an active community of reformers in Vineland, New Jersey, and joined women studying the emerging discipline

of "social science." She helped form a moral education society in Boston, held a post in the National Woman Suffrage Association in 1877, and lobbied for the end of coverture laws ("Lucinda B. Chandler"). Leach's section on Chandler in *True Love and Perfect Union* (85–92) is the most helpful biography of her.

25. Slenker briefly edited the *Water-Cure Journal* and was a regular contributor to *Dr. Foote's Health Monthly* and *Lucifer*. She spent a year in prison for a letter deemed obscene by Comstock, but the charges were then dismissed by a Virginia court (Wood 38). She was also the only free-love feminist to publish articles on free thought aimed at children, and she produced a periodical for young people called *The Little Freethinker* from 1892 to 1898 (Passet, "Freethought Children's Literature" 110). Helpful biographies of Slenker can be found in Passet ("Freethought Children's Literature"), Sears (204–22), and Wood.

26. McKinley's writings on Lizzie Holmes contain the only biography of this radical reformer. Little is known about her early years or about her radical family.

27. The Haymarket massacre occurred in Chicago in 1886, when police arrived to break up a labor rally in Haymarket Square. At the arrival of more than 100 policemen, an unknown anarchist let off a bomb in the crowd. The police then fired upon the crowd, killing several more people. Several men were arrested for the incident; four men, including Albert Parsons, were hanged, two received life sentences, and one killed himself in prison.

28. McKinley analyzes Holmes's novel in "Free Love and Domesticity," finding that it represents the ambivalence of Holmes's free love-feminism. Passet also analyzes the novel in *Sex Radicals*.

29. Avrich produced an excellent biography of de Cleyre in 1978. Articles in *Lucifer* in 1903 recount her ideas on not pursuing the man who shot her. Another helpful analysis of de Cleyre is DeLamotte's "Refashioning the Mind."

30. Biographical details on Lillie D. White are even more elusive than details on her sister Lizzie Holmes. I was able to ascertain, from a 1900 article in *Lucifer*, that she had a son; the article noted that a new print run of White's pamphlet *The Coming Woman* was delayed because she had left for Louisiana "to attend her sick son" ("Light Bearer Library, No. 8"). I obtained her geographical locations from letters she wrote from Halstead, Kansas, and Chicago, Illinois ("Letters from Friends"; "Various Voices," August 1899).

31. There are several excellent secondary works analyzing Comstock's war on free speech and the reaction of the free lovers. Frisken and Horowitz have both documented Comstock's almost personal battle with Woodhull. McGarry's 2000 article notes the effects of spiritualism on the debates on free speech and sexuality. Wood's "Prescription for a Periodical" focuses on how medical periodicals, particularly the work of Dr. Foote and his son, earned the ire of Comstock. Cronin's "The Liberty to Argue Freely" gives the free lovers their due in documenting their crusade for free speech. I also enjoyed Piercy's fictionalized account of the Comstock crusade in her novel *Sex Wars: A Novel of Gilded Age New York*, which features Comstock, Woodhull, and Susan B. Anthony as characters.

2. Evolutionary Theory: (R)Evolutionary Rhetorics in the Free-Love Movement

1. Many writers have elaborated on the unique language and use of metaphor by Darwin. Bulhof finds that Darwin's analogies helped his readers connect to "the processes

of living nature" (72). John Angus Campbell's extensive studies of Darwin have shown the many tools of language Darwin brought to elaborate his theories. These tools improved the accessibility of Darwin's work, but Campbell shows how the reader must think critically about them ("Why Was Darwin Believed?" 212–13), which indicates that Darwin provided agency to his readers. Campbell elaborates such techniques and the impact of Darwin's rhetoric in other works, such as "Charles Darwin" and "Revisioning the *Origin*" (with Ryan K. Clark). On Darwin's appeal, see "Mr. Darwin and His Readers" by Crismore and Farnsworth.

2. Frankel's analysis of the waning of sexual selection theory notes the contributions of Julian Huxley in the early 1900s, who assigned a more passive role to the female. In Huxley's view, females did not choose but were "stimulated to action" (qtd. in Frankel 168). Other scientists shared Huxley's views and challenged Darwin's notion of female choice by positing physiological sexual excitement in females (163). She was not receptive to the male but to his sperm (166). They thus believed that it was not "mate choice" but "reproductive efficiency" driving the sexual relations, making sexual selection a form of natural selection (167), and endorsed the idea that women are controlled by their sexual organs.

3. On the shifts in Darwin's views, Claeys clarifies:

> In the mid-1860s Darwin himself became in effect a Social Darwinist, and came increasingly to hope that the optimal outcome of human natural selection would be the triumph of "the intellectual and moral" races over the "lower and more degraded ones." It must be stressed that this was not the inevitable outcome of thve logic of *The Origin of Species* nor the only path Darwin might have trod but the specific result of his reaction to a variety of critics and fellow philosophers. In this sense too, then, "Social Darwinism" was not as such "Darwinian" but the result of Darwin's acceptance of other interpretations of evolutionary theory, some of which were incorporated into the *Descent of Man*. (237)

4. Conway explains how Spencer used evolutionary theory to assert women's inferior development in relation to men: "Spencer attempted to give scientific authority to the romantic view of women as intuitive and irrational" (141–42). Conway also notes Spencer's lack of knowledge about biology, leading him to gendered conclusions about evolution and fertilization, for example (140–41). His views would be refuted by later scientific developments.

5. I was unable to locate any biographical information on Potter-Loomis. I did find one reference to her as an opponent of the death penalty.

6. Forster is another free-love feminist whose origins remain elusive. Scholar Angus McLaren provides biographical background on Forster's husband, Robert Bird Kerr, a lawyer originally from Edinburgh, but notes, "Little is known of Dora Forster. She claimed that she was active in the English campaign for women's education and appears to have been acquainted with the English feminist Lady Florence Dixie. . . . In Kerr's obituaries there is no reference to Forster other than mention of the fact that she followed him to Canada" (537n). Forster first resided in Britain and then Canada but became interested in the free-love movement in the United States, believing "America . . . is the field in which the sex problem will be worked out both theoretically and practically" (Forster, *Sex Radicalism* 38). In 1898, she and her husband began contributing articles to radical periodicals, including *Lucifer* and Canadian periodicals (McLaren

529), and both created a stir with their articles. (Kerr, in fact, caused a backlash among free-love feminists with his eugenic ideas; though many free-love feminists supported eugenics, they rejected Kerr's ideas because his focus in promoting eugenics was not the sexual emancipation of women.) Forster may have been accused of parroting her husband's ideals, leading to this statement in *Lucifer*: "Let me say that I should never dream of accepting a philosophy of sex from any individual, least of all from a man. My beliefs are my own, founded upon my own observations and experience of life, and my own reading" ("Varietism"). Her rhetoric certainly indicates her self-proclaimed status as "an emancipated woman of the new time." Originally a series of articles in *Lucifer* that led to one of Moses Harman's arrests for distributing "obscenity," her 1905 pamphlet *Sex Radicalism as seen by an Emancipated Woman of the New Time* was as radical as its name would indicate, often volatile in its rhetoric, rebuking the "great stupid public" for their puritanical mores and taking unpopular views, even among free-love feminists, on topics like masturbation, eugenics, and variety.

3. Physiology: Rewriting the Body and Sexual Desire

1. On the popularity of Gove's lectures, Skinner notes, "Despite the novelty of a woman speaking on anatomy and physiology, *The Graham Journal of Health and Longevity* reports that Gove's first lecture drew a crowd of nearly two thousand women" ("'She Will Have Science'" 245).

2. Horowitz names "reform physiology" as a specific genre of medical texts and highlights the focus on reform in the medical profession (*Rereading Sex* 86). Taylor's *The Medical Profession and Social Reform*, Michael Gordon's "From an Unfortunate Necessity to a Cult of Mutual Orgasm," and Haller and Haller's *The Physician and Sexuality in Victorian America* are also helpful in illuminating this shift.

3. Helpful backgrounds on the scientific study of physiology in the nineteenth century include Coleman's *Biology in the Nineteenth Century*, Fye's *The Development of American Physiology*, Thomas S. Hall's *History of General Physiology*, and Locy's *Biology and Its Makers*.

4. Showalter and Showalter explain that Edward Clarke and Henry Maudsley (who produced similar work using interpretations of the law of conservation of energy to reinforce sexist views) "were not presenting new ideas; they merely publicized the new scientific evidence for prejudices which had existed throughout the century" (43).

5. British physician Elizabeth Garrett Anderson challenged the depth of Clarke's research in *The Fortnightly Review*'s ongoing discussion of his work in 1874. Clelia Duel Mosher's later 1923 work, *Woman's Physical Freedom*, also challenged Clarke's study. Countering the idea that women's physiology justified their inequality with men, she pointed out that menstruation and menopause, long employed as valid reasons to keep women from actively engaging in the workforce, were not naturally painful and that lifestyle choices caused these natural bodily functions to become painful. Like many "reform physiologists" of the nineteenth century, Mosher established that knowledge of physiology would help to free women, and her arguments relied on the evidence she had collected through her studies: "What I am about to say in regard to the function of menstruation is based on the study of more than 2,000 women during 12,000 menstrual periods. The observations and work in physiologic and hygiene laboratories have extended over a period of 30 years" (19). Her data was certainly more extensive than Clarke's previous study, which included a very small number of participants. She

also used a chart to support an argument for women's fashions as a cause of women's ill health rather than their physiology and concluded, "An extraordinarily close correlation was found between the fashion of dress and the menstrual disability of women. As the skirt grew shorter and narrower and the waist grew larger, the functional health of women improved. . . . We should rejoice in the freedom of the modern girl with her large normal waist" (30–31). Mosher, like Gove and Trall, urged women to take responsibility for their own health and well-being, since her research showed that "many of the disabilities of menstruation and the change of life are due to removable and preventable causes, viz., bad hygiene" (50). She drove the final nail in the coffin of Clarke's argument:

> Only yesterday women went to college at great personal sacrifice. And dire were the predictions of the evil results to her health and to the race. Characterized as "hermaphrodite in mind," and "divested of her sex," the college woman failed to develop the anticipated evils. She was found to be rather healthier than her sisters who did not go to college, to marry as other women of her class, and to bear a rather larger number of healthy children. (14)

She also quoted several students from Vassar College, where Clarke reportedly drew the subjects of his study. Consequently, Mosher refuted Clarke's argument, ending the lengthy nineteenth-century debates about women's physiology and their social roles.

6. Horowitz's study of sexual mores in the nineteenth century reveals the complicated debate on how the "Victorians" viewed sexuality in nineteenth-century America. Theriot's and Morantz-Sanchez's work is also helpful in re-visioning how women responded to the medical profession's dictates on women's bodies. Both scholars elaborate how medical women contested views of women's health and physiology. The emerging field of gynecology, however, perpetuated antifeminist views of women's bodies. Donnison's *Midwives and Medical Men* and McGregor's *From Midwives to Medicine* detail these challenges and debates.

7. Porter and Hall explain that Venette's text actually espoused more liberating philosophies on female sexuality than did many nineteenth-century manuals:

> Preoccupation with such charged issues as the virginity of brides and proof of paternity stemmed, [Venette] believed, from outmoded notions of honour that thwart Nature's purposes. The compassionate doctor urges charity and tolerance. In any case, no tests of paternity, legitimacy, chastity, virginity and pregnancy are infallible. If your bride hasn't a maidenhead, that could be for many reasons— hymens are easily ruptured by horse-riding. If she does not shed blood on her wedding night, do not fear: many virgins do not bleed. Venette is even prepared to give brides-to-be advice on simulating virginity: abstain for a while and use styptics, and the vagina will contract. Indeed he tells how brides can trick husbands, using dried blood inserted into the vagina on the wedding night. (80–81)

8. Homeopathic medical movements such as water cure had their own medical schools and philosophies of health different from the "allopaths," their term for the dominant medical culture, or the non-homeopathic medical sects (the "allopathic" physicians did not seem to use this name for themselves).

9. The multiple meanings of physiology in the nineteenth century also played a role in the debates over "obscenity" in medical texts. Horowitz points out that some

writers even marketed erotic literature by claiming that their work was "physiology," not obscenity (*Rereading Sex* 272). (Mary Gove Nichols's husband, Thomas L. Nichols, may have been one such writer.) Some medical writers also marketed advice on birth control as scientific discussions of physiology, which drew the attention of lawmakers concerned about obscenity (272). Texts by reform physiologists often critiqued the traditional marriage system and sometimes even endorsed free love; they consequently became threats to the status quo and challenged "obscenity" laws. Physician Frederick Hollick even went on trial in 1846 for obscenity because of his frank discussion of sexuality in his books and lectures. Since Hollick also advocated women's right to express their sexuality, his trial illustrates how the conversation over sexuality escalated. The key focus of his trial was distinguishing illicit sexual speech from scientific medical information about the body (Haynes 557). In some cases, it seems to be the political rights they were advocating, such as rights to birth control, rather than the physiologic information they were conveying that landed "reform physiologists" in hot water. Since some "reform physiologists," such as Thomas and Mary Gove Nichols, also advocated free love, "physiology" could then suggest a different meaning, one associated with radical ideals and persons. Haynes explains:

> Listeners and readers [of physiology texts], especially married women, relished many of the promises that underlay lecture topics: women's capability to control their own health, the importance of equal access to scientific and medical education, prescriptions for sexual health that highlighted women's agency and contraceptive advice. The self-consciously masculine drive to overthrow "medical monopoly" and make "every man his own doctor" that had animated Jacksonian health reformers such as John C. Gunn and Sylvester Graham had merged, by midcentury, with explicitly feminist goals. (544)

10. In her study of the Hollick trial, Haynes points out, "Hollick argued that frequent sexual pleasure constituted a *physiological necessity* for all postpubescent human beings, regardless of gender or marital status, a stance that he insisted was medical but that his enemies deemed obscene" (543; emphasis in original).

11. Horowitz has examined the "anti-masturbation" genre of texts more closely. Gove often published texts in this genre aimed at both men and women.

12. In Maines's study of the use of electricity and the vibrator to treat "hysteria," she asserts, "When marital sex was unsatisfying and masturbation discouraged or forbidden, female sexuality, I suggest, asserted itself through one of the few acceptable outlets: the symptoms of hysteroneurasthenic disorders" (5). Her conclusions link the rise in diagnoses of "hysteria" with prescriptive ideologies of women's sexuality.

13. Interestingly, Trall's *Sexual Physiology* is one of the books often mentioned in Walters's *Primers for Prudery*. Walters picks out the quotations from Trall that would seem to support the traditional view of "Victorian repression." Blatt also portrays Trall as a sexual conservative who nevertheless became a target of Comstock because of *Sexual Physiology* (116), which was one of the books that precipitated one of Ezra Heywood's arrests for obscenity because he mailed it. However, while Trall did advocate "temperate sexual indulgence" (232), not much else in his book supports such a reading. For example, Trall also said that abstinence was not always the healthiest option for birth control (206). Furthermore, his advice that women should achieve orgasm as a natural result of the sex act also countered the "prudish" reading.

14. In "Sexual Ideology and Sexual Physiology," historians Connell and Hunt group Blackwell's ideas on female sexuality together with physician William Acton's, who believed that women had no sexual feelings (27).

15. For a more in-depth reading of Gove Nichols's novel, see Keetley, who connects the themes in the novel to Gove Nichols's medical writing.

16. Linda Gordon says, "Slenker, the toughest and most crusty of all the 'sex-haters,' dared to explore and take seriously her own longings, thereby revealing herself to be a sex-lover in disguise" (*Moral Property* 64).

17. Alice Stockham, the author of *Karezza*, was a physician who advocated continence, or refraining from orgasm, for both males and females in her treatise on sex.

4. Bacteriology: Marriage as a "Diseased" Institution

1. Geison's *The Private Science of Louis Pasteur* elaborates Pasteur's biography and discoveries and presents Pasteur as an accomplished rhetor.

2. Arnold Levine summarizes Koch's famous postulates: "(1) the organism must be regularly found in the lesions of the disease, (2) the organism must be isolated in a pure culture (hence the need for sterile techniques), (3) inoculation of such a culture of pure organisms into the host should initiate the disease, and (4) the organism must be recovered once again from the lesions of this host" (qtd. in Fahnestock, *Rhetorical Figures* 162).

3. The *Oxford English Dictionary* notes one use of "germ" as associated with a "virus" in an 1803 medical journal. "Germ" as synonymous with "bacteria" began in the 1870s (the *OED Online* documents the use of "germ" by Tyndall as synonymous with "bacteria").

4. Scudder, born in Harrison, Ohio, turned to the study of medicine after the deaths of his three infant children (Garraty and Carnes 19.541–542). Scudder studied under Milton Thomas at the Eclectic Medical Institute in Cincinnati, where he later became a professor after graduating in 1856 (19.542). Three of Scudder's sons later followed in his footsteps, becoming eclectic practitioners (19.543).

5. Eclecticism combined the philosophies of allopathic and homeopathic medicines. See J. Ben Nichols's 1895 article, "The Eclectic Medical System," and Haller's 1999 study, *A Profile in Alternative Medicine*.

6. Blackwell's stance on germ theory was shared by another nineteenth-century pioneering female physician, Marie Elizabeth Zakrzewska, who feared that germ theory would replace a focus on prevention and hygiene (Tuchman 122–23). However, Blackwell did include an appendix to "Medical Responsibility" from gynecologist T. Gaillard Thomas, who discussed both the gonococcus germ and the latency period.

7. Engs is one scholar who portrays the social purity movement as anti-sexuality, but she may be concentrating on the "Comstockian" adherents of "social purity" and not on the feminist adherents. Feminist social purity reformers took a more complicated stance on sexuality, not arguing for complete abstinence but for more of a temperate sexual indulgence.

8. Birth control advocate Margaret Sanger would be influenced by Morrow's studies. In her 1920 text, *What Every Girl Should Know*, a collection of essays from her column in the *New York Call*, she used Morrow's findings to create more urgency to talk about the topic: "When a few years ago Dr. Morrow stated that there is more venereal disease among innocent, virtuous wives, than among prostitutes, this statement should have resounded throughout the walls of every home in the land, instead of which it is kept

intact within the covers of large volumes, where only those wearing cap and gown have access to it" (67). Sanger here illustrates how medical practitioners still used the danger posed to "innocent, virtuous wives" as an exigence for greater efforts at sex education. She also emphasized the importance of communicating information to the public, rather than keeping it within the medical community. Finally, Sanger drew on the eugenic implications of the discourse of disease, calling both gonorrhea and syphilis "social dangers" because of their effects on offspring (80). Her rhetoric demonstrates how the key features of the discourse of disease in the late nineteenth century survived in new reform discourse of the twentieth century.

9. Such a law was passed in Michigan in 1899 (Brandt 19–20), and by 1922, thirteen states had laws restricting marriage licenses to men infected with venereal diseases (Engs 146). These laws did not require testing for women. Thus, the shift from viewing women as inherently diseased and the sole carriers responsible for disease transmission to blaming men had occurred.

5. Embryology: Toward a Eugenic Warrant for Free-Love Feminism

1. Haeckel drew images to show the comparative development of different species of embryos to support theories of evolution and recapitulation, but many of his images were later contested, and Haeckel was accused of fabrication to support evolution (Hopwood).

2. Drake published marital advice books throughout the late nineteenth and early twentieth centuries that often espoused social purity and eugenic ideals. Drake's *What a Young Wife Ought to Know* was part of the "Self in Sex" series. According to Skinner, Drake was one of only two women to write books in this series ("'Purity of Truth'" 117).

3. Skinner also elaborates on the nature of the antiabortion arguments in Drake's texts. She points out the conundrum Drake must have faced in even alluding to abortion and characterizes her rhetoric as a rhetoric of sex education: "Drake does not advise mothers to speak with their daughters about abortion specifically; instead, she suggests they discuss the sanctity of marriage and motherhood, a roundabout way of introducing the topic that protects Drake's ethos while simultaneously modeling a conversational approach for mothers hesitant to broach such a delicate topic with their own children" ("'Purity of Truth'" 108). She goes on to explain, "Drake's emphasis in this passage on teaching daughters (and implicitly, Drake's readers) is evidence of an important thread running through women physicians' medical advice texts: Conveying information, even about such sinister subjects as abortion, is better than protecting one's daughters from that information because informed women are more likely to make moral decisions" (108). Some of these rhetorical strategies also apply to male physicians, such as Trall and Cowan.

4. Frisken notes the same about what she calls Woodhull's "Darwinian motherhood": "Unlike the republican mothers of the early 1800s, Woodhull's Darwinian motherhood emphasized biology rather than education as women's contribution to humanity" (*Victoria Woodhull's Sexual Revolution* 136).

5. Conway's reading of Geddes and Thompson's *Evolution of Sex* reveals their antifeminist leanings (140–54). She elaborates how their evolutionary theory reified gender stereotypes and reinforced female inferiority. That Waisbrooker quoted them as an authority does not negate their antifeminist influence, but it does show that feminists at the time took what was useful out of their theory and ignored what was not.

6. As late as 1906, science had yet to take a definitive stance on prenatal influence. Sears cites the work of Havelock Ellis, whose study of sexology would influence the

next decades. Of his work, he notes, "In volume 5 (1906) of his *Studies in the Psychology of Sex*, Havelock Ellis traced the historical genesis of prenatal beliefs, reviewed current professional opinion, and cited reputable reports of apparent prenatal influence. He cautiously concluded that while definite effects of maternal influence upon the fetus had not been proven, neither had they been positively disproven" (123).

6. Heredity: The Disappearing Reform Warrant

1. Bowler and Morus attribute the difference in the reception of Mendel's ideas in 1900 to the changes that occurred between their publication and rediscovery: among these changes were the failure of recapitulation theory and an increased interest in eugenics (199–200). Thus, Mendel's work was given new significance because of social reform discourse. Wynn has proposed that it was Mendel's inattention to audience in his use of mathematical formulae that led to the poor reception of his 1865 article (5). It is clear that the scientific community was not ready for Mendel's theories when they were first published but recognized their significance due to the changes in rhetorical situation and in audience.

2. The elimination of the theory of acquired characteristics refuted some of Spencer's antifeminist interpretations:

> The inheritance of acquired characteristics permitted Spencer to explain the existing stereotypes of female character as though these were the forms of femininity evolved by male-domination since primitive times. He could thus give scientific authority to the romantic view of women as intuitive and irrational. Once environmental factors were removed as major sources of variation, evolutionary theorists were compelled to look for other explanations of the supposed psychic differences between the sexes, and other ways to explain the undoubted social fact of the inferiority of women. (Conway 141–42)

3. Hasian's 1996 study, *The Rhetoric of Eugenics in Anglo-American Thought*, provides more detailed analyses of "positive" and "negative" eugenics.

4. Mosher asked respondents for details on their grandparents and parents, including the age they married, their health, and diseases in the family. She also asked about "any prenatal influences before your birth" in the section on the respondents' mothers' information.

5. Cowan's warning to abstain from both alcohol and meat reveals the influence of Sylvester Graham and many water-cure ideologies on his text. I have been unable to trace the particular medical sect Cowan belonged to, but he was clearly influenced by the more reformist and homeopathic sects.

6. Skinner notes that Drake's *What a Young Wife Ought to Know* was republished even in 1936 ("'Purity of Truth'" 104), a time when its science was clearly outdated.

7. Richardson's 2003 study of the same discourse in British feminist texts notes that in England, eugenics became a discourse centered on class rather than on race.

8. Alexander's *Ambiguous Lives* provides additional biography of Logan and her family. (Alexander is a descendent of Logan.)

9. The same passage is also included in Severance's 1886 work "Farmers' Wives," indicating that both the lines of argument she employed and the wording she expressed held currency for a women's rights audience.

10. The term "stirpiculture," an early form of eugenics practiced by utopian free lover John Humphrey Noyes, is an especially significant choice of term because of the root "stirps," which can be used to describe the branch of a family and is also used in zoology as a term of classification (*OED Online*).

11. No date appears on this pamphlet. However, Waisbrooker referenced writing it just before her seventy-fourth birthday and referenced the publication of *A Sex Revolution* seven years earlier, putting its date around 1900.

Conclusion: Historiography and Feminist Uses of Eugenics

1. Both Gove Nichols and Woodhull employed the line of argument that they were speaking on the subject only because others would not and promoted their goals as educational. Thus, they justified speaking about sex by blaming others for their silence about sex. Woodhull's *Tried as by Fire* speech, given on a lecture tour, employed such arguments to counter accusations of impropriety. Other speeches given to spiritualist communities, such as 1874's *The Scare-Crows of Sexual Slavery* and 1873's *The Elixir of Life*, did not make similar negotiations.

BIBLIOGRAPHY

Alexander, Adele Logan. *Ambiguous Lives: Free Women of Color in Rural Georgia, 1789–1879*. Fayetteville: U of Arkansas P, 1991.

Anderson, Elizabeth Garrett. "Sex in Mind and Education: A Reply." *Fortnightly Review* 15 (1874). Reprinted in Rowold 54–68.

Andrews, Stephen Pearl. "Stirpiculture, Scientific Propagation: Improvement of the Breeds of Men." *Woodhull & Claflin's Weekly*, September 17, 1870, 9–10.

Andrews, Stephen Pearl, Horace Greeley, and Henry James. *Love, Marriage, and Divorce, and the Sovereignty of the Individual: A Discussion*. 2nd ed. Boston, 1889.

"An Appeal." *Lucifer, the Light Bearer* 9.25 (April 22, 1892): 2.

Appel, Toby A. "Physiology in American Women's Colleges: The Rise and Decline of a Female Subculture." *History of Women in the Sciences: Readings from Isis*. Ed. Sally Gregory Kohlstedt. Chicago: U of Chicago P, 1999. 305–36.

Athey, Stephanie. "Eugenic Feminisms in Late Nineteenth-Century America: Reading Race in Victoria Woodhull, Frances Willard, Anna Julia Cooper, and Ida B. Wells." *Genders* 31 (2000): 98 paragraphs. <http://www.genders.org/>.

"Autonomistic Marriage Practicalized." *Lucifer, the Light Bearer* 4.27 (October 1, 1886): 1.

"Autonomy—Self Law: What Are Its Demands." *Lucifer, the Light Bearer* 4.24 (September 10, 1886): 2.

Avrich, Paul. *An American Anarchist: The Life of Voltairine de Cleyre*. Princeton: Princeton UP, 1978.

Barry, Francis. "Crudities Criticized—No. 8." *Lucifer, the Light Bearer* 3.9 (March 4, 1899): 70.

———. "Crudities Criticized—No. 9." *Lucifer, the Light Bearer* 4.13 (April 7, 1900): 101.

———. "Has Frank Barry Gone Back?" *Lucifer, the Light Bearer* 11.47 (March 15, 1895): 4.

———. "Who Were the Pioneers—Who Wrote the Platform?" *Lucifer, the Light Bearer* 2.44 (November 5, 1898): 355.

Battan, Jesse. "The 'Rights' of Husbands and the 'Duties' of Wives: Power and Desire in the American Bedroom, 1850–1910." *Journal of Family History* 24.2 (April 1999): 165–86.

———. "'The Word Made Flesh': Language, Authority, and Sexual Desire in Late Nineteenth-Century America." *American Sexual Politics: Sex, Gender, and Race since the Civil War*. Ed. John C. Fout and Maura Shaw Tantillo. Chicago: U of Chicago P, 1993. 101–22.

———. "'You Cannot Fix the Scarlet Letter upon My Breast': Women Reading, Writing, and Reshaping the Sexual Culture of Victorian America." *Journal of Social History* 37.3 (2004): 601–24.

Beer, Gillian. Introduction. *The Origin of Species*. By Charles Darwin. Oxford: Oxford UP, 1996. vii–xxviii.

Bitzer, Lloyd. "The Rhetorical Situation." *Philosophy and Rhetoric* 1.1 (1968): 217–27.

Blackwell, Elizabeth. *Essays in Medical Sociology.* Reprint, 1902 ed. New York: Arno, 1972.

——. *The Human Element in Sex: Being a Medical Inquiry into the Relation of Sexual Physiology to Christian Morality by Dr. Elizabeth Blackwell.* London: J. and A. Churchill, 1894.

——. "Medical Responsibility in Relation to the Contagious Disease Acts." Blackwell, *Essays in Medical Sociology* 83–112.

——. "Rescue Work in Relation to Prostitution and Disease." Blackwell, *Essays in Medical Sociology* 113–32.

Blatt, Martin Henry. *Free Love and Anarchism: The Biography of Ezra Heywood.* Urbana: U of Illinois P, 1989.

Bowler, Peter J., and Iwan Rhys Morus. *Making Modern Science: A Historical Survey.* Chicago: U of Chicago P, 2005.

Brandt, Allan M. *No Magic Bullet: A Social History of Venereal Disease in the United States since 1880.* New York: Oxford UP, 1985.

Brigati, A. J., ed. *The Voltairine de Cleyre Reader.* Oakland, CA: AK, 2004.

Brown, JoAnne. "Crime, Commerce, and Contagionism: The Political Language of Public Health and the Popularization of Germ Theory in the United States, 1870–1950." Walters, *Scientific Authority* 53–81.

Buchanan, Lindal. *Regendering Delivery: The Fifth Canon and Antebellum Women Rhetors.* Carbondale: Southern Illinois UP, 2005.

Bulhof, Ilse N. *The Language of Science: A Study of the Relationship between Literature and Science in the Perspective of a Hermeneutical Ontology, with a Case Study of Darwin's* The Origin of Species. New York: Brill, 1992.

Bullough, Vern. *Science in the Bedroom: A History of Sex Research.* New York: Basic, 1994.

Burke, Kenneth. *A Rhetoric of Motives.* Berkeley: U of California P, 1969.

Campbell, John Angus. "Charles Darwin: Rhetorician of Science." *Landmark Essays on Rhetoric of Science.* Ed. Randy Allen Harris. Hillsdale, NJ: Erlbaum, 1997. 3–17.

——. "Why Was Darwin Believed? Darwin's Origin and the Problem of Intellectual Revolution." *Configurations: A Journal of Literature, Science, and Technology* 11.2 (Spring 2003): 203–37.

Campbell, John Angus, and Ryan K. Clark. "Revisioning the *Origin*: Tracing Inventional Agency through Genetic Inquiry." *Technical Communication Quarterly* 14.3 (Summer 2005): 287–93.

Campbell, Karlyn Kohrs. "Biesecker Cannot Speak for Her Either." *Philosophy and Rhetoric* 26.2 (1993): 153–59.

——. "Consciousness-Raising: Linking Theory, Criticism, and Practice." *Rhetoric Society Quarterly* 32.1 (2002): 45–64.

——. *A Critical Study of Early Feminist Rhetoric.* Vol. 1 of *Man Cannot Speak for Her.* Westport, CT: Greenwood, 1989.

Campbell, Rachel. "A Criticism: With Comments by Rachel Campbell." *Our New Humanity* 1.1 (December 1895): 85–87.

——. *The Prodigal Daughter; Or, The Price of Virtue.* Valley Falls, KS: Lucifer, 1888.

——. "Sex Ethics No. 2." *Lucifer, the Light Bearer* 9.28 (May 20, 1892): 6.

Cantor, Geoffrey, and Sally Shuttleworth, eds. *Science Serialized: Representations of the Sciences in Nineteenth-Century Periodicals.* Cambridge, MA: MIT P, 2004.

"The Causes of Physical Degeneracy." *Woodhull & Claflin's Weekly*, March 29, 1873, 9–10.

Cayleff, Susan E. *Wash and Be Healed: The Water-Cure Movement and Women's Health.* Philadelphia: Temple UP, 1987.

Chandler, Lucinda. "'Cell Wants,' Sex Attraction and the I Am." *Lucifer, the Light Bearer* 13.15 (September 18, 1896): 3.

———. "The Requirements of Natural Morality." *Lucifer, the Light Bearer* 4.10 (June 4, 1886): 1.

———. "Wise Motherhood." *Lucifer, the Light Bearer* 4.47 (March 11, 1887): 1.

———. "Woman Is Irresponsible by Her Legal Status." *Lucifer, the Light Bearer* 12.10 (July 26, 1895): 2.

Chandler, Lucinda, et al. "Woman's Plea for Justice." *Lucifer, the Light Bearer* 7.29 (December 6, 1889): 1–2.

Claeys, Gregory. "The 'Survival of the Fittest' and the Origins of Social Darwinism." *Journal of the History of Ideas* 61.2 (April 2000): 223–40.

Claflin, Tennie C. "Advice to Parents." Claflin, *Talks and Essays* 3.128–47.

———. *Constitutional Equality, a Right of Women; or, A Consideration of the Various Relations which She Sustains as a Necessary Part of the Body of Society and Humanity; with Her Duties to Herself—Together with a Review of the Constitution of the United States, Showing that the Rights to Vote is Guaranteed to All Citizens. Also a Review of the Rights of Children.* New York: Woodhull, Claflin, & Co., 1871.

———. "The Degradation of the Sexes, I." Claflin, *Talks and Essays* 3.36–47.

———. "The Degradation of the Sexes, II." Claflin, *Talks and Essays* 3.48–57.

———. *Essays on Social Topics.* London: Roxburghe, c. 1873.

———. *The Ethics of Sexual Equality, A Lecture Delivered by Tennie C. Claflin, at the Academy of Music, New York, March 29, 1872.* New York: Woodhull & Claflin, 1873.

———. "Illegitimacy." Claflin, *Talks and Essays* 3.84–102.

———. "Maternal Impressions." Claflin, *Talks and Essays* 4.90–95.

———. "Maternity." Claflin, *Talks and Essays* 1.24–38.

———. "Modesty." Claflin, *Talks and Essays* 1.18–23.

———. "Mothers and Their Duties." Claflin, *Talks and Essays* 1.47–53.

———. "One of the Evils of Society." Claflin, *Talks and Essays* 3.121–27.

———. "The Regeneration of Society." Claflin, *Talks and Essays* 1.54–65.

———. "A Short History of Marriage." Claflin, *Talks and Essays* 2.7–40.

———. "Should the Poor Marry?" Claflin, *Talks and Essays* 3.19–27.

———. "Social Injustice." Claflin, *Talks and Essays* 4.116–33.

———. *Talks and Essays.* 4 vols. Westminster: Roxburghe, 1897.

———. "Virtue: What It Is and What It Isn't." *Woodhull & Claflin's Weekly*, December 23, 1871, 7.

———. "Who Should Propose?" Claflin, *Talks and Essays* 2.48–55.

———. "Woman's Purity." Claflin, *Talks and Essays* 3.109–15.

———. "Women and Progress." Claflin, *Talks and Essays* 4.49–55.

Clarke, Edward. *Sex in Education: A Fair Chance for Girls.* 1873. Boston: James R. Osgood, 1874.

Coleman, William. *Biology in the Nineteenth Century: Problems of Form, Function, and Transformation.* Cambridge: Cambridge UP, 1977.

Cole-Wilcox, Elsie. "The Limitation of Population, and Woman's Freedom." *Lucifer, the Light Bearer* 1.15 (April 14, 1897): 114.

Connell, Erin, and Alan Hunt. "Sexual Ideology and Sexual Physiology in the Discourses of Sex Advice Literature." *Canadian Journal of Human Sexuality* 15.1 (2006): 23–45.

Conway, Jill. "Stereotypes of Femininity in a Theory of Sexual Evolution." Vicinus 140–54.

Cooper, Anna Julia. "Womanhood: A Vital Element in the Regeneration and Progress of a Race." S. Logan, *With Pen and Voice* 53–74.

Cott, Nancy. "Passionlessness: An Interpretation of Victorian Sexual Ideology, 1790–1850." *A Heritage of Her Own: Toward a New Social History of American Women.* Ed. Nancy Cott and Elizabeth Pleck. New York: Simon and Schuster, 1979. 162–81.

Cowan, John. *The Science of a New Life.* New York: John B. Alden, 1889.

Crismore, Avon, and Rodney Farnsworth. "Mr. Darwin and His Readers: Exploring Interpersonal Metadiscourse as a Dimension of Ethos." *Rhetoric Review* 8.1 (Autumn 1989): 91–112.

Cronin, Mary M. "The Liberty to Argue Freely: Nineteenth-Century Obscenity Prosecutions and the Emergence of Modern Libertarian Free Speech Discourse." *Journalism and Communication Monographs* 8.3 (Autumn 2006): 163–219.

Darwin, Charles. *The Descent of Man and Selection in Relation to Sex.* Princeton: Princeton UP, 1981.

———. *The Origin of Species.* Ed. Gillian Beer. Oxford: Oxford UP, 1996.

Dawson, Gowan, Richard Noakes, and Jonathan R. Topham. Introduction. *Science in the Nineteenth-Century Periodical: Reading the Magazine of Nature.* Ed. Geoffrey Cantor et al. Cambridge: Cambridge UP, 2004. 1–34.

De Cleyre, Voltairine. "Love in Freedom." *Lucifer, the Light Bearer* 4.29 (July 28, 1900): 226.

———. "Priestly Control over Woman." *Lucifer, the Light Bearer* 2.14 (April 6, 1898): 110.

———. "Sex Slavery." Brigati 93–103.

———. "They Who Marry Do Ill." Brigati 11–20.

———. "Unchaining the Lower Animal." *Lucifer, the Light Bearer* 10.31 (June 14, 1893): 3.

———. "A Word from Voltairine de Cleyre." *Lucifer, the Light Bearer* 6.51 (January 1, 1903): 404.

Degler, Carl. "What Ought to Be and What Was: Women's Sexuality in the Nineteenth Century." Leavitt, *Women and Health* 192–212.

De Kruif, Paul. *Microbe Hunters.* New York: Harcourt, Brace, 1926.

DeLamotte, Eugenia. "Refashioning the Mind: The Revolutionary Rhetoric of Voltairine de Cleyre." *Legacy* 20.1–2 (2003): 153–74.

D'Emilio, John, and Estelle B. Freedman. *Intimate Matters: A History of Sexuality in America.* New York: Harper and Row, 1988.

"Dissatisfaction." *Lucifer, the Light Bearer* 10.24 (May 19, 1893): 2.

Donawerth, Jane, ed. *Rhetorical Theory by Women before 1900.* Lanham, MD: Rowman and Littlefield, 2002.

Donnison, Jean. *Midwives and Medical Men: A History of Inter-professional Rivalries and Women's Rights.* New York: Schocken, 1977.

Drake, Emma F. Angell. *What a Young Wife Ought to Know.* Philadelphia: Vir, 1901.

"Dr. Juliet Severance Dies." *New York Times*, September 4, 1919. *New York Times Online.* November 16, 2009.

English, Daylanne. *Unnatural Selections: Eugenics in American Modernism and the Harlem Renaissance.* Chapel Hill: U of North Carolina P, 2004.

———. "W. E. B. DuBois's Family Crisis." *American Literature* 72.2 (June 2000): 291–319.

Engs, Ruth Clifford. *Clean Living Movements: American Cycles of Health Reform.* Westport, CT: Praeger, 2000.

Erskine, Fiona. "*The Origin of Species* and the Science of Female Inferiority." *Charles Darwin's* The Origin of Species: *New Interdisciplinary Essays.* Ed. David Amigoni and Jeff Wallace. Manchester: Manchester UP, 1995. 95–121.

Fahnestock, Jeanne. "Accommodating Science." *Written Communication* 15.3 (July 1998): 330–50.

———. *Rhetorical Figures in Science.* New York: Oxford UP, 1999.

Fee, Elizabeth. "Science and the Woman Question 1860–1920." Diss., Princeton U, 1978.

Fellman, Anita Clair, and Michael Fellman. *Making Sense of Self: Medical Advice Literature in Late Nineteenth-Century America.* Philadelphia: U of Pennsylvania P, 1981.

Forster, Dora. "Jealousy and Violent Theorizing." *Lucifer, the Light Bearer* 7.8 (March 4, 1903): 57.

———. "The Passing Ideal and the Coming Ideal." *Lucifer, the Light Bearer* 7.2 (January 22, 1903): 10.

———. *Sex Radicalism as seen by an Emancipated Woman of the New Time.* Chicago: M. Harman, 1905.

———. "Varietism." *Lucifer, the Light Bearer* 6.48 (December 11, 1902): 381.

Foucault, Michel. *The History of Sexuality.* 3 vols. Trans. Robert Hurley. New York: Vintage, 1985.

Frankel, Simon. "The Eclipse of Sexual Selection Theory." *Sexual Knowledge, Sexual Science.* Ed. Roy Porter and Mikulas Teich. Cambridge: Cambridge UP, 1994. 158–83.

Freedman, Estelle. "Sexuality in Nineteenth-Century America: Behavior, Ideology, and Politics." *Reviews in American History* 10.4 (December 1982): 196–215.

Frisken, Amanda. "Sex in Politics: Victoria Woodhull as an American Public Woman 1870–1876." *Journal of Women's History* 12.1 (2000): 89–100.

———. *Victoria Woodhull's Sexual Revolution: Political Theater and the Popular Press in Nineteenth-Century America.* Philadelphia: U of Pennsylvania P, 2004.

Fye, W. Bruce. *The Development of American Physiology: Scientific Medicine in the Nineteenth Century.* Baltimore: Johns Hopkins UP, 1987.

Gabriel, Mary. *Notorious Victoria: The Life of Victoria Woodhull, Uncensored.* Chapel Hill, NC: Algonquin Books of Chapel Hill, 1998.

Galton, Francis. *Hereditary Genius: An Inquiry into its Laws and Consequences.* 2nd ed. London: Macmillan, 1892. Online ed., *Galton.org*, 2000. December 22, 2006. <http://galton.org/books/hereditary-genius/>.

Garraty, John A., and Mark C. Carnes. *American National Biography.* 24 vols. New York: Oxford UP, 1999.

Geison, Gerald L. *The Private Science of Louis Pasteur.* Princeton: Princeton UP, 1995.

Gillispie, Charles Coulston, ed. *Dictionary of Scientific Biography.* 18 vols. New York: Scribner's, 1974.

Gilman, Charlotte Perkins. *Herland.* New York: Pantheon, 1979.

———. *Women and Economics: The Economic Factor between Men and Women as a Factor Is Social Evolution.* New York: Harper and Row, 1966.

Goldsmith, Barbara. *Other Powers: The Age of Suffrage, Spiritualism, and the Scandalous Victoria Woodhull.* New York: HarperPerennial, 1998.

Gordon, Linda. *The Moral Property of Women: A History of Birth Control Politics in America.* Urbana: U of Illinois P, 2002.

———. "Voluntary Motherhood: The Beginnings of Feminist Birth Control Ideas in the United States." *Feminist Studies* 1.3/4 (Spring 1973): 5–22.

———. *Woman's Body, Woman's Right: A Social History of Birth Control in America.* New York: Penguin, 1977.

Gordon, Michael. "From an Unfortunate Necessity to a Cult of Mutual Orgasm: Sex in American Marital Education Literature, 1830–1940." *Studies in the Sociology of Sex.* Ed. James M. Henslin. New York: Appleton-Century-Crofts, 1971. 53–77.

Gove, Mary S. *Lectures to Women on Anatomy and Physiology with an Appendix on Water Cure.* New York: Harper & Brothers, 1846.

Gove Nichols, Mary. "Letter from Mrs. Gove Nichols." *Water-Cure Journal* 14.3 (September 1852): 67.

———. "Mrs. Gove's Experience in Water Cure." *Water-Cure Journal* 7.2 (February 1, 1849): 40.

———. "The Murders of Marriage." *Root of Bitterness: Documents of the Social History of American Women.* Ed. Nancy Cott. Boston: Northeastern UP, 1996. 303–8.

———. *A Woman's Work in Water Cure and Sanitary Education.* London: Nichols & Co., 1874.

———. "Woman the Physician." *Water-Cure Journal* 12.4 (October 1851): 73.

Gutierrez, Cathy. "Sex in the City of God: Free Love and the American Millennium." *Religion and American Culture* 15.2 (Summer 2005): 187–208.

Habegger, Alfred. "*The Bostonians* and Henry James Sr.'s Crusade against Feminism and Free Love." *Women's Studies* 15.4 (1988): 323–43.

Hall, Lesley. "Hauling Down the Double Standard: Feminism, Social Purity and Sexual Science in Late Nineteenth-Century Britain." *Gender and History* 16.1 (April 2004): 36–56.

Hall, Thomas S. *History of General Physiology: 600 B.C. to A.D. 1900.* 2 vols. Chicago: U of Chicago P, 1969.

Haller, John S. *A Profile in Alternative Medicine: The Eclectic Medical College of Cincinnati, 1845–1942.* Kent, OH: Kent UP, 1999.

Haller, John S., and Robin M. Haller. *The Physician and Sexuality in Victorian America.* Urbana: U of Illinois P, 1974.

Harman, Lillian. "The Age of Consent, Again." *Lucifer, the Light Bearer* 7.5 (June 21, 1895): 2.

———. "An 'Age-of-Consent' Symposium." *Lucifer, the Light Bearer* 11.46 (March 8, 1895): 1.

———. "An 'Age-of-Consent' Symposium: A Protest against Gratuitous Insults." *Lucifer, the Light Bearer* 11.48 (March 22, 1895): 1.

———. "Freedom of Choice, the Foundation Principle." *Lucifer, the Light Bearer* 1.8 (February 24, 1897): 58.

———. "From My Point of View." *Lucifer, the Light Bearer* 3.12 (April 1, 1899): 93.

———. "From My Point of View." *Lucifer, the Light Bearer* 4.1 (January 13, 1900): 5.

———. "From My Point of View." *Lucifer, the Light Bearer* 4.9 (March 10, 1900): 69.

———. "Good News from Voltairine de Cleyre." *Lucifer, the Light Bearer* 6.52 (January 8, 1903): 412.

———. *Marriage and Morality.* Chicago: M. Harman, 1900.

———. *Moses Harman.* Los Angeles, 1910.

———. "Not Natural Enemies." *Lucifer, the Light Bearer* 4.18 (May 11, 1900): 139.

———. "Our Brethren of Darker Hue." *Lucifer, the Light Bearer* 3.24 (June 24, 1899): 189.

———. "The Race Question." *Lucifer, the Light Bearer* 3.21 (June 3, 1899): 161.

———. "Radical Women—and Others." *Lucifer, the Light Bearer* 6.9 (May 22, 1902): 148.

———. "The Regeneration of Society." *Lucifer, the Light Bearer* 3.19 (May 20, 1899): 145–46.

———. "The Regeneration of Society." *Lucifer, the Light Bearer* 3.20 (May 27, 1899): 153–55.

———. "Some Common Objections Considered." *Lucifer, the Light Bearer* 1.41 (October 13, 1897): 325.

———. "Some Problems of Social Freedom." *The Adult: A Journal for the Advancement of Freedom in Sexual Relationships.* 1898. Reprinted in McElroy, *Freedom, Feminism, and the State* 119–27.

———. "What Shall I Say to My Child?" *Lucifer, the Light Bearer* 1.18 (May 5, 1897): 140.

Harman, Moses. "Freedom versus Marriage." *Lucifer, the Light Bearer* 4.29 (July 28, 1900): 229.

———. "Lois Waisbrooker." *Lucifer, the Light Bearer* 1.38 (September 22, 1897): 301.

———. "The Marriage Problem." *Lucifer, the Light Bearer* 5.3 (February 2, 1901): 20.

Hasian, Marouf Arif, Jr. *The Rhetoric of Eugenics in Anglo-American Thought.* Athens: U of Georgia P, 1996.

Haynes, April. "The Trials of Frederick Hollick: Obscenity, Sex Education, and Medical Democracy in the Antebellum United States." *Journal of the History of Sexuality* 12.4 (2003): 543–74.

Heywood, Angela T. "Body Housekeeping." McElroy, *Freedom, Feminism, and the State* 131–34.

———. "Body Housekeeping—Home Thrift." *The Word: A Monthly Journal of Reform* (March 1893): 3.

———. "The Ethics of Sexuality." *The Word: A Monthly Journal of Reform* (April 1881): 3. Reprinted in McElroy, *Individualist Feminism* 39–43.

———. "The Ethics of Touch—Sex Unity." *The Word: A Monthly Journal of Reform* (June 1889): 3.

———. "The Grace and Use of Sex Life." *The Word: A Monthly Journal of Reform* (June 1890): 3.

———. "Human Sex-Power—Fleshed Realism." *The Word: A Monthly Journal of Reform* (December 1892): 2.

———. "Men's Laws and Love's Laws." *The Word: A Monthly Journal of Reform* (September 1876): 1.

———. "Men, Women, and Things." *The Word: A Monthly Journal of Reform* (June 1883): 3.

———. "Men, Women, and Things." *The Word: A Monthly Journal of Reform* (December 1883): 2.

———. "The Morality of Free Love." *The Word: A Monthly Journal of Reform* (August 1876): 3.

———. "Penis Literature—Onanism or Health?" *The Word: A Monthly Journal of Reform* (April 1884): 2.

———. "Personal Attitudes—Plain Facts." *The Word: A Monthly Journal of Reform* (October 1887): 2.

———. "Personal Health—Social Propriety." *The Word: A Monthly Journal of Reform* (September 1887): 3.

———. "The Religion of Sexuality." *The Word: A Monthly Journal of Reform* (January 1884): 2.

———. "Sex-Nomenclature—Plain English." *The Word: A Monthly Journal of Reform* (April 1887): 2–3.

———. "Sex Service—Ethics of Trust." *The Word: A Monthly Journal of Reform* (October 1889): 2.

———. "Sex-Symbolism—The Attucks Shaft." *The Word: A Monthly Journal of Reform* (December 1888): 3.

———. "Woman's Love: Its Relations to Man and Society." *The Word: A Monthly Journal of Reform* (July 1876): 1.

———. "The Woman's View of It—No. 2." *The Word: A Monthly Journal of Reform* (February 1883): 2.

———. "The Woman's View of It—No. 3." *The Word: A Monthly Journal of Reform* (March 1883): 2–3. Reprinted in McElroy, *Individualist Feminism* 46.

———. "The Woman's View of It—No. 4." *The Word: A Monthly Journal of Reform* (April 1883): 2–3. Reprinted in McElroy, *Individualist Feminism* 46–47.

Higgins, Lisa Cochran. "Adulterous Individualism, Socialism, and Free Love in Nineteenth-Century Anti-suffrage Writing." *Legacy* 21.2 (2004): 193–209.

Hollick, Frederick. *The Marriage Guide or Natural History of Generation; A Private Instructor for Married Persons and Those about to Marry.* 1850. New York: Arno, 1974.

Holmes, Lizzie M. "Another View of Pre-Natal Influence." *Lucifer, the Light Bearer* 12.25 (December 6, 1895): 3.

———. "Fewer and Better Children." *Lucifer, the Light Bearer* 13.4 (July 3, 1896): 1.

———. "More of the Problem." *Lucifer, the Light Bearer* 4.43 (November 10, 1900): 342.

———. "The Population and Economic Question." *Lucifer, the Light Bearer* 3.29 (July 29, 1899): 229–30.

———. "Revising Our Opinions." *Lucifer, the Light Bearer* 5.1 (January 19, 1901): 3.

———. "The 'Unwomanly' Woman." *Our New Humanity* 1.3 (March 1896): 1–13.

———. "Woman's Freedom Is Human Freedom." *Lucifer, the Light Bearer* 3.42 (August 26, 1899): 260.

Hopwood, Nick. "Pictures of Evolution and Charges of Fraud: Ernst Haeckel's Embryological Illustrations." *Isis: An International Review Devoted to the History of Science and Its Cultural Influences* 97 (2006): 260–301.

Horowitz, Helen Lefkowitz. *Rereading Sex: Battles over Sexual Knowledge and Suppression in Nineteenth-Century America.* New York: Vintage, 2002.

———. "Victoria Woodhull, Anthony Comstock, and Conflict over Sex in the United States in the 1870s." *Journal of American History* 87.2 (2000): 403–35. <http://www.historycooperative.org/journals/jah/87.2/horowitz.html>.

Jackson, Margaret. *The Real Facts of Life: Feminism and the Politics of Sexuality c1850–1940.* London: Taylor and Francis, 1994.

Jacob, Kathryn Allamong. "The Mosher Report: The Sexual Habits of American Women, Examined Half a Century before Kinsey." *American Heritage Magazine* 32.4 (June/July 1981). March 5, 2007. <http://www.americanheritage. com/articles/magazine/ah/1981/4/1981_4_56_print.shtml>.

Johnson, Mary Florence. "Pioneer Chips: From the Private Correspondence of Rachel Campbell." *Our New Humanity* 1.1 (December 1895): 26–42.

Johnson, Nan. *Gender and Rhetorical Space in American Life, 1866–1910.* Carbondale: Southern Illinois UP, 2002.

Johnston, Johanna. *Mrs. Satan: The Incredible Saga of Victoria C. Woodhull.* New York: Popular Library, 1967.

Jordanova, Ludmilla. "Sex and Gender." *Inventing Human Science: Eighteenth-Century Domains.* Ed. Christopher Fox, Roy Porter, and Robert Wokler. Berkeley: U of California P, 1995. 152–83.

Keetley, Dawn. "The Ungendered Terrain of Good Health: Mary Gove Nichols's Rewriting of the Diseased Institution of Marriage." *Separate Spheres No More: Gender Convergence in American Literature, 1830–1930.* Ed. Monika M. Elbert. Tuscaloosa: U of Alabama P, 2000. 117–42.

Kent, Austin. "Socialistic: The Origin of Free Love." *Woodhull & Claflin's Weekly,* April 18, 1874, 5.

Kern, Stephen. *Anatomy and Destiny: A Cultural History of the Human Body.* Indianapolis: Bobbs-Merrill, 1975.

"Knowledge Better Than Faith." *Lucifer, the Light Bearer* 9.44 (October 7, 1892): 2.

Laqueur, Thomas. *Making Sex: Body and Gender from the Greeks to Freud.* Cambridge, MA: Harvard UP, 1992.

Leach, William. *True Love and Perfect Union: The Feminist Reform of Sex and Society.* New York: Basic, 1980.

Leavitt, Judith Walzer. "Gendered Expectations: Women and Early Twentieth-Century Public Health." Leavitt, *Women and Health* 612–33.

———, ed. *Women and Health in America.* Madison: U of Wisconsin P, 1999.

"Letters from Friends." *Lucifer, the Light Bearer* 4.40 (January 14, 1887): 4.

"Light Bearer Library, No. 8." *Lucifer, the Light Bearer* 4.39 (October 6, 1900): 39.

Linnett, Amy. "Continence and Contracepts." *Lucifer, the Light Bearer* 1.18 (May 5, 1897): 139.

Locy, William A. *Biology and Its Makers.* New York: Henry Holt, 1915.

Logan, Adella Hunt. "Hereditary and Prenatal Influences." S. Logan, *"We Are Coming"* 211–14.

Logan, Shirley Wilson. *"We are Coming": The Persuasive Discourse of Nineteenth-Century Black Women.* Carbondale: Southern Illinois UP, 1999.

———, ed. *With Pen and Voice: A Critical Anthology of Nineteenth-Century African-American Women.* Carbondale: Southern Illinois UP, 1995.

"Lucinda B. Chandler." *Lucifer, the Light Bearer* 6.2 (April 27, 1888): 3.

Maines, Rachel. *The Technology of Orgasm: "Hysteria," the Vibrator, and Women's Sexual Satisfaction.* Baltimore: Johns Hopkins UP, 1999.

Malthus, Thomas Robert. "An Essay on the Principle of Population as it Affects the Future Improvement of Society, with Remarks on the Speculations of Mr. Gowin, M. Condorcet, and Other Writers." London: J. Johnson, 1798. *The Library of Economics and Liberty.* December 19, 2006. <http://www.econlib. org/library/Malthus/malPoptoc.html>.

"Marriage Versus Freedom." *Woodhull & Claflin's Weekly*, November 5, 1870, 6.

Mattingly, Carol. *Appropriate[ing] Dress: Women's Rhetorical Style in Nineteenth-Century America*. Carbondale: Southern Illinois UP, 2002.

———. "Telling Evidence: Rethinking What Counts in Rhetoric." *Rhetoric Society Quarterly* 32.1 (Winter 2002): 99–108.

———. *Well-Tempered Women: Nineteenth-Century Temperance Rhetoric*. Carbondale: Southern Illinois UP, 1998.

Maudsley, Henry. "Sex in Mind and in Education." *Fortnightly Review* 15 (1874). Reprinted in Rowold 32–53.

Mayr, Ernst. *The Growth of Biological Thought: Diversity, Evolution, and Inheritance*. Cambridge, MA: Belknap, 1982.

———. *One Long Argument: Charles Darwin and the Genesis of Modern Evolutionary Thought*. Cambridge, MA: Harvard UP, 1991.

McAllister, Pam. "Women in the Lead: Waisbrooker's Way to Peace." *A Sex Revolution*. By Lois Waisbrooker. Philadelphia: New Society, 1985. 1–52.

McElroy, Wendy. "The Contagious Disease Acts." *iFeminists.com*. January 30, 2001. March 5, 2007. < http://www.ifeminists.com/introduction/editorials/2001 /0130.html>.

———, ed. *Freedom, Feminism, and the State: An Overview of Individualist Feminism*. New York: Holmes and Meier, 1991.

———, ed. *Individualist Feminism of the Nineteenth Century: Collected Writings and Biographical Profiles*. Jefferson, NC: McFarland, 2001.

McGarry, Molly. "Spectral Sexualities: Nineteenth-Century Spiritualism, Moral Panics, and the Making of U.S. Obscenity Law." *Journal of Women's History* 12.2 (2000): 8–29.

McGregor, Deborah Kuhn. *From Midwives to Medicine: The Birth of American Gynecology*. New Brunswick, NJ: Rutgers UP, 1998.

McKinley, Blaine. "Free Love and Domesticity: Lizzie M. Holmes, *Hagar Lyndon* (1893) and the Anarchist-Feminist Imagination." *Journal of American Culture* 13.1 (1990): 55–62.

———. "Holmes, Lizzie May Swank." *Women Building Chicago 1790–1900: A Biographical Dictionary*. Ed. Rima Lunin Schultz and Adele Hast. Bloomington: Indiana UP, 2001. 400–402.

McLaren, Angus. "Sex Radicalism in the Canadian Pacific Northwest, 1890–1920." *Journal of the History of Sexuality* 2.4 (April 1992): 527–46.

Miller, Carolyn. "*Kairos* in the Rhetoric of Science." *A Rhetoric of Doing: Essays on Written Discourse in Honor of James L. Kinneavy*. Ed. Stephen P. Witte, Neil Nakadate, and Roger D. Cherry. Carbondale: Southern Illinois UP, 1992. 310–27.

"Morality vs. Brute Instinct." *Woodhull & Claflin's Weekly*, April 18, 1874, 5.

Morantz-Sanchez, Regina Markell. *Conduct Unbecoming a Woman: Medicine on Trial in Turn-of-the-Century Brooklyn*. New York: Oxford UP, 1999.

———. "Female Science and Medical Reform: A Path Not Taken." Walters, *Scientific Authority* 99–115.

———. "Feminist Theory and Historical Practice: Rereading Elizabeth Blackwell." *History and Theory* 31.4 (December 1992): 51–70.

———. *Sympathy and Science: Women Physicians in American Medicine*. New York: Oxford UP, 1985.

Morrow, Prince Albert. *Social Diseases and Marriage*. New York: Lea Brothers, 1904.

Mosher, Clelia Duel. *The Mosher Survey: Sexual Attitudes of 45 Victorian Women*. Ed. James MaHood and Kristine Wenburg. New York: Arno, 1980.

———. *Personal Hygiene for Women*. Stanford, CA: Stanford UP, 1927.

———. *Woman's Physical Freedom*. New York: Woman's P, 1923.

"Motherhood in Freedom." *Lucifer, the Light Bearer* 13.16 (September 25, 1896): 2.

"Mrs. Waisbrooker's Case." *Lucifer, the Light Bearer* 12.28 (May 8, 1896): 2.

Needham, Joseph. *A History of Embryology*. New York: Arno, 1975.

Nichols, J. Ben. "The Eclectic Medical System." *Medical News* 66.14 (April 6, 1895): 370.

Nichols, T. L., and Mary Gove Nichols. *Marriage: Its History, Character, and Results; its Sanctities, and its Profanities; its Science and its Facts. Demonstrating its Influence, as a Civilized Institution, of the Happiness of the Individual and the Progress of the Race*. Cincinnati: Valentine Nicholson, 1854.

"Notes on Selections and Correspondence." *Lucifer, the Light Bearer* 13.4 (July 3, 1896): 2.

Oppenheimer, Jane M. "Embryology and Evolution: Nineteenth Century Hopes and Twentieth Century Realities." *Quarterly Review of Biology* 34.4 (December 1959): 271–77.

Otis, Laura. *Membranes: Metaphors of Invasion in Nineteenth-Century Literature, Science, and Politics*. Baltimore: Johns Hopkins UP, 1999.

Owen, Robert Dale. *Moral Physiology; or, A Brief and Plain Treatise on the Population Question*. London: Holyoake, 1859.

Passet, Joanne E. "Freethought Children's Literature and the Construction of Religious Identity in Late-Nineteenth-Century America." *Book History* 8 (2005): 107–29.

———. "Power through Print: Lois Waisbrooker and Grassroots Feminism." *Women in Print: Essays on the Print Culture of American Women from the Nineteenth and Twentieth Centuries*. Ed. James P. Danky and Wayne A. Wiegand. Madison: U of Wisconsin P, 2006. 229–50.

———. "Reading *Hilda's Home*: Gender, Print Culture, and the Dissemination of Utopian Thought in Late-Nineteenth-Century America." *Libraries and Culture* 40.3 (2005): 307–23.

———. *Sex Radicals and the Quest for Women's Equality*. Urbana: U of Illinois P, 2003.

Peavy, Linda, and Ursula Smith. *Pioneer Women: The Lives of Women on the Frontier*. New York: Smithmark, 1996.

Perelman, Chaim, and Lucie Olbrechts-Tyteca. *The New Rhetoric*. Trans. John Wilkinson and Purcell Weaver. Notre Dame, IN: U of Notre Dame P, 1969.

Perry, Michael, ed. *Free Lover: Sex, Marriage and Eugenics in the Early Speeches of Victoria Woodhull*. Seattle: Inkling, 2005.

———, ed. *Lady Eugenist: Feminist Eugenics in the Speeches and Writings of Victoria Woodhull*. Seattle: Inkling, 2005.

Piercy, Marge. *Sex Wars: A Novel of Gilded Age New York*. New York: HarperPerennial, 2005.

Pinto-Correia, Clara. *The Ovary of Eve: Egg and Sperm and Preformation*. Chicago: U of Chicago P, 1997.

Porter, Roy, and Lesley Hall. *The Facts of Life: The Creation of Sexual Knowledge in Britain, 1650–1950*. New Haven: Yale UP, 1995.

Porter, Roy, and Marilyn Ogilvie, eds. *The Biographical Dictionary of Scientists*. 3rd ed. 2 vols. New York: Oxford UP, 2000.

Potter-Loomis, Hulda. *Social Freedom: The Most Important Factor in Human Evolution.* Chicago: M. Harman, c. 1890.

Ratcliffe, Krista. *Rhetorical Listening: Identification, Gender, Whiteness.* Carbondale: Southern Illinois UP, 2005.

Ray, Angela G. *The Lyceum and Public Culture in the Nineteenth-Century United States.* East Lansing: Michigan State UP, 2005.

Richardson, Angelique. *Love and Eugenics in the Late Nineteenth Century: Rational Reproduction and the New Woman.* Oxford: Oxford UP, 2003.

Rossiter, Margaret. *Women Scientists in America, Volume 1: Struggles and Strategies to 1940.* Baltimore: Johns Hopkins UP, 1982.

Rowold, Katharina, ed. *Gender and Science: Late Nineteenth-Century Debates on the Female Mind and Body.* Bristol, Eng.: Thoemmes, 1996.

Russett, Cynthia Eagle. *Sexual Science: The Victorian Construction of Womanhood.* Cambridge, MA: Harvard UP, 1989.

Sanger, Margaret. *What Every Girl Should Know.* Springfield, IL: United Sales, 1920.

"Says 'Boston Ideas'—." *Lucifer, the Light Bearer* 5.25 (July 6, 1901): 198.

Schneir, Miriam, ed. *Feminism: The Essential Historical Writings.* New York: Vintage, 1992.

Scudder, John M. *On the Reproductive Organs, and the Venereal.* 1873. 3rd ed. Cincinnati: John M. Scudder, 1890.

Sears, Hal D. *The Sex Radicals: Free Love in High Victorian America.* Lawrence: Regents P of Kansas, 1977.

Severance, Juliet H. *A Discussion of the Social Question between Juliet H. Severance, M.D. and David Jones, Editor of the "Olive Branch."* Milwaukee: National Advance, 1891.

———. "Dr. Severance on Ownership." *Lucifer, the Light Bearer* 3.43 (January 22, 1886): 3.

———. "Farmers' Wives." *Transactions of the Wisconsin Agricultural Society XXIV.* Madison: Democrat Printing, 1886. 273–83. <http://content.wisconsinhistory.org/u?/tp,22364>.

———. "From Dr. Severance." *Lucifer, the Light Bearer* 4.38 (December 24, 1886): 3.

———. *A Lecture on Life and Health, or How to Live a Century.* Milwaukee: Godfrey and Crandall, 1881.

———. *A Lecture on Religious, Political, and Social Freedom.* Milwaukee: Godfrey and Crandall, 1881.

———. *A Lecture on the Philosophy of Disease, and How to Cure the Sick Without Drugs, with an Explanation of Magnetic Laws.* Milwaukee: Trayser Bros., 1876.

———. *Marriage.* Chicago: M. Harman, 1901.

———. "Sex Hypnotics." *Lucifer, the Light Bearer* 9.51 (November 25, 1892): 1.

Showalter, Elaine, and English Showalter. "Victorian Women and Menstruation." Vicinus 38–44.

Shuttleworth, Sally, Gavin Dawson, and Richard Noakes. "Women, Science and Culture: Science in the Nineteenth-Century Periodical." *Women: A Cultural Review* 12.1 (2001): 57–70.

Silver-Isenstadt, Jean L. *Shameless: The Visionary Life of Mary Gove Nichols.* Baltimore: Johns Hopkins UP, 2002.

Skinner, Carolyn. "'The Purity of Truth': Nineteenth-Century American Women Physicians Write about Delicate Topics." *Rhetoric Review* 26.2 (2007): 103–19.

———. "'She Will Have Science': Ethos and Audience in Mary Gove's *Lectures to Ladies*." *Rhetoric Society Quarterly* 39.3 (Summer 2009): 240–59.

Slenker, Elmina Drake. "Borning Better Babies." *Lucifer, the Light Bearer* 4.9 (May 28, 1886): 3.

———. "Dianism." *Lucifer, the Light Bearer* 13.21 (October 30, 1896): 3.

———. "Dianism." *Lucifer, the Light Bearer* 1.15 (April 14, 1897): 117.

———. "Dianism." *Lucifer, the Light Bearer* 1.22 (June 2, 1897): 174.

———. "Dianism." *Lucifer, the Light Bearer* 4.25 (June 30, 1900): 198.

———. "Dianism and Right: An Open Letter to Mr. W." *Lucifer, the Light Bearer* 11.43 (February 15, 1895): 4.

———. "Dianism Further Explained." *Lucifer, the Light Bearer* 3.9 (March 4, 1899): 9.

———. "Divorce." *Lucifer, the Light Bearer* 1.45 (November 10, 1897): 355.

———. "Free Love." *Lucifer, the Light Bearer* 2.1 (January 5, 1898): 422.

———. "Karezza." *Lucifer, the Light Bearer* 13.7 (July 24, 1896): 3.

———. "Letters." *Lucifer, the Light Bearer* 4.41 (October 20, 1900): 322.

———. "Listen!" *Lucifer, the Light Bearer* 2.42 (October 22, 1898): 42.

———. "Marriage and Divorce." *Lucifer, the Light Bearer* 2.47 (November 26, 1898): 379.

———. "The Old and the New Ideal." *Lucifer, the Light Bearer* 1.1 (January 6, 1897): 8.

———. "Superiority of the Female." *Lucifer, the Light Bearer* 4.48 (May 18, 1887): 3.

———. "The Woman Who Does." *Lucifer, the Light Bearer* 2.22 (June 5, 1898): 174.

Smith-Rosenberg, Carroll. *Disorderly Conduct: Visions of Gender in Victorian America*. New York: Oxford UP, 1985.

Smith-Rosenberg, Carroll, and Charles E. Rosenberg. "The Female Animal: Medical and Biological Views of Woman and Her Role in Nineteenth-Century America." Leavitt, *Women and Health* 111–30.

"Social Evils: Regeneration a Necessity of Proper Generation." *Woodhull and Claflin's Weekly*, September 17, 1870, 8.

Spencer, Herbert. *Herbert Spencer on Social Evolution: Selected Writings*. Ed. J. D. Y. Peel. Chicago: U of Chicago P, 1972.

———. *The Study of Sociology*. New York: Appleton, 1874.

Spongberg, Mary. *Feminizing Venereal Disease: The Body of the Prostitute in Nineteenth-Century Medical Discourse*. New York: New York UP, 1997.

Spurlock, John C. *Free Love: Marriage and Middle-Class Radicalism in America, 1825–1860*. New York: New York UP, 1988.

———. "The Free Love Network in America, 1850 to 1860." *Journal of Social History* 21.4 (Summer 1988): 765–79.

Stepan, Nancy Leys. *The Hour of Eugenics: Race, Gender, and Nation in Latin America*. Ithaca, NY: Cornell UP, 1991.

Stern, Madeleine B., ed. *The Victoria Woodhull Reader*. Weston, MA: M & S, 1974.

Stoehr, Taylor, ed. *Free Love in America: A Documentary History*. New York: AMS, 1979.

Storer, Horatio Robinson. "The Mutual Relations of the Medical Profession, its Press, and the Community." *Chicago Medical Examiner* 12.6 (June 1871): 350–59.

Studebaker, M. L. "Is *Lucifer* Growing Conservative?" *Lucifer, the Light Bearer* 4.18 (May 11, 1900): 139.

Sutherland, Christine Mason. "Feminist Historiography: Research Methods in Rhetoric." *Rhetoric Society Quarterly* 32.1 (Winter 2002): 109–22.

Tange, Andrea Kaston. "Constance Naden and the Erotics of Evolution: Mating the Woman of Letters with the Man of Science." *Nineteenth-Century Literature* 61.2 (2005): 200–240.

Taylor, Lloyd C., Jr. *The Medical Profession and Social Reform, 1885–1945*. New York: St. Martin's, 1974.

Theriot, Nancy M. "Gender and Medicine in Nineteenth-Century America." *NWSA Journal* 15.2 (Summer 2003): 144–53.

———. "Negotiating Illness: Doctors, Patients, and Families in the Nineteenth Century." *Journal of the History of Behavioral Sciences* 37.4 (Fall 2001): 349–68.

———. "Women's Voices in Nineteenth-Century Medical Discourse: A Step toward Deconstructing Science." *Signs* 19.1 (Autumn 1993): 1–31.

Tomes, Nancy. "Germ Theory, Public Health Education, and the Moralization of Behavior in the Antituberculosis Crusade." Warner and Tighe 257–64.

———. *The Gospel of Germs: Men, Women, and the Microbe in American Life*. Cambridge, MA: Harvard UP, 1998.

———. "Spreading the Germ Theory: Sanitary Science and Home Economics, 1880–1930." Leavitt, *Women and Health* 596–611.

Toulmin, Stephen. "From the Uses of Argument." *The Rhetorical Tradition: Readings from Classical Times to the Present*. Ed. Patricia Bizzell and Bruce Herzberg. Boston: Bedford/St. Martin's, 2001. 1413–28.

Trall, Russell. *Sexual Physiology: A Scientific and Popular Exposition of the Fundamental Problems in Sociology*. 1866. New York: Arno, 1974.

Tuchman, Arleen Marcia. "'Only in a Republic Can It Be Proved That Science Has No Sex': Marie Elizabeth Zakrzewska (1829–1902) and the Multiple Meanings of Science in the Nineteenth-Century United States." *Journal of Women's History* 11.1 (1999): 121–42.

Underhill, Lois Beachy. *The Woman Who Ran for President: The Many Lives of Victoria Woodhull*. Bridgehampton, NY: Bridge Works, 1995.

"Various Voices." *Lucifer, the Light Bearer* 3.24 (June 24, 1899): 191.

"Various Voices." *Lucifer, the Light Bearer* 3.30 (August 5, 1899): 239.

Vicinus, Martha, ed. *Suffer and Be Still: Women in the Victorian Age*. Bloomington: Indiana UP, 1972.

Waisbrooker, Lois. *Alice Vale: A Story for the Times*. Boston: William White, 1869.

———. *Anything More, My Lord?* Topeka: Independent, 1895.

———. *Eugenics; or, Race Culture Lessons*. Chicago, 1907.

———. "First Freedom, then Peace." *Lucifer, the Light Bearer* 2.26 (July 2, 1898): 202.

———. *The Fountain of Life, or the Threefold Power of Sex*. Topeka, 1893.

———. *From Generation to Regeneration; or, The Plain Guide to Naturalism*. Los Angeles, 1879.

———. *From Generation to Regeneration: The Plain Guide to Naturalism; The Sex Question and the Money Power; and The Tree of Life Between Two Thieves: Three Pamphlets on the Occult Forces of Sex*. New York: Murray Hill, 1890.

———. "From Lois Waisbroker [*sic*]." *Lucifer, the Light Bearer* 4.40 (June 14, 1887): 2.

———. *Helen Harlow's Vow*. Boston: William White, 1870.

———. "A Last Word." *Lucifer, the Light Bearer* 1.19 (May 12, 1897): 150.

———. "Letter from an Old Contributor." *Lucifer, the Light Bearer* 1.3 (January 27, 1897): 30.

——. *Mayweed Blossoms*. Boston: William White, 1871.

——. *Nothing Like It, or Steps to the Kingdom*. Boston: Colby & Rich, 1875.

——. "The Rainstorm Duck." *Lucifer, the Light Bearer* 2.4 (January 26, 1898): 446.

——. *The Sex Question and the Money Power: How Should This Power be Made to Serve Instead of Ruling Us? A Lecture Delivered by Lois Waisbrooker, at Jackson, Mich., Sunday December 14, 1873, and Published at the Time by Request*. Waisbrooker, *From Generation . . . Three Pamphlets*, 61–91.

——. *A Sex Revolution*. 1893. Philadelphia: New Society, 1985.

——. "Sexual Morality." *Lucifer, the Light Bearer* 1.46 (November 17, 1897): 365.

——. *Suffrage for Woman: The Reasons Why*. St. Louis: Clayton & Babington, 1868.

——. *The Temperance Folly; or, Who's the Worst*. N.p., c. 1900.

——. "Things as I See Them." *Lucifer, the Light Bearer* 1.51 (December 22, 1897): 407.

——. *The Tree of Life Between Two Thieves*. Waisbrooker, *From Generation . . . Three Pamphlets*, 93–129.

——. "Voluntary, Not Authoritarian." *Lucifer, the Light Bearer* 13.9 (August 7, 1896): 2.

——. "The Wail of Ignorance." *Lucifer, the Light Bearer* 4.8 (March 3, 1900): 59.

——. "Who Protects the Wife?" *Lucifer, the Light Bearer* 2.48 (December 3, 1898): 385.

——. "Woman and Economics." *Lucifer, the Light Bearer* 3.30 (August 5, 1899): 238.

——. "Woman's Power." *Lucifer, the Light Bearer* 1.16 (April 21, 1897): 125.

——. "Woman's Source of Power." *Lucifer, the Light Bearer* 2.16 (April 20, 1898): 125.

——. "A Word to Lillian Harman." *Lucifer, the Light Bearer* 3.43 (September 2, 1899): 269.

Walker, Santiago. "Love is Not Dead." *Lucifer, the Light Bearer* 4.33 (August 25, 1900): 261.

Waller, John. *The Discovery of the Germ: Twenty Years That Transformed the Way We Think about Disease*. New York: Columbia UP, 2002.

Walters, Ronald G. *Primers for Prudery: Sexual Advice to Victorian America*. Baltimore: Johns Hopkins UP, 2000.

——, ed. *Scientific Authority and Twentieth-Century America*. Baltimore: Johns Hopkins UP, 1997.

Warner, John Harley, and Janet A. Tighe, eds. *Major Problems in the History of American Medicine and Public Health*. Boston: Houghton, 2001.

Warner, Michael. *Publics and Counterpublics*. New York: Zone, 2002.

Weismann, August. *Essays upon Heredity and Other Kindred Biological Problems*. Trans. and ed. Edward B. Poulton, Selmar Schonland, and Arthur E. Shipley. Oxford: Clarendon, 1889. December 15, 2006. <http://www.esp.org/books/weismann/essays/facsimile/>.

Weiss, Harry B., and Howard R. Kemble. *The Great American Water-Cure Craze: A History of Hydropathy in the United States*. Trenton, NJ: Past Times, 1967.

Wellman, Kathleen. "Physicians and Philosophes: Physiology and Sexual Morality in the French Enlightenment." *Eighteenth-Century Studies* 35.2 (2002): 267–77.

Wells, Susan. *Out of the Dead House: Nineteenth-Century Women Physicians and the Writing of Medicine*. Madison: U of Wisconsin P, 2001.

"What They Think of the Controversy." *Lucifer, the Light Bearer* 1.22 (June 2, 1897): 171.

White, Lillie D. *The Coming Woman*. Chicago: M. Harman, 1900.

——. "Does Liberty Slay Love?" *Lucifer, the Light Bearer* 3.14 (April 15, 1899): 109.

——. "Greeting." *Lucifer, the Light Bearer* 4.44 (October 7, 1892): 2.

———. "Love and Finance." *Lucifer, the Light Bearer* 3.41 (August 19, 1899): 250.

———. "The Old and the New." *Lucifer, the Light Bearer* 4.9 (March 10, 1900): 70.

———. "Playing at Love." *Lucifer, the Light Bearer* 4.30 (August 4, 1900): 234.

———. "Population and Economics." *Lucifer, the Light Bearer* 1.15 (April 14, 1897): 115.

———. "Progress Does not Depend on Martyrdom." *Lucifer, the Light Bearer* 4.16 (April 28, 1900): 122.

———. "Rights of Fathers." *Lucifer, the Light Bearer* 3.41 (October 21, 1899): 322.

———. "Shall We be Happy by Being Deceived?" *Lucifer, the Light Bearer* 6.14 (April 17, 1902): 106.

———. "Woman's Dangerous Friends." *Lucifer, the Light Bearer* 9.44 (October 7, 1892): 3.

———. "Woman's Work." *Lucifer, the Light Bearer* 10.8 (January 27, 1893): 2.

Whitehead, Celia. "Mrs. Whitehead to Elmina." *Lucifer, the Light Bearer* 4.13 (June 25, 1886): 3.

Willard, Frances. "Address of Frances E. Willard, President of the Woman's National Council of the United States . . . at its First Triennial Meeting, Albaugh's Opera House, Washington, D.C., February 22–25, 1891." *Votes for Women: Selections from the National American Woman Suffrage Association Collection, 1848–1921.* Library of Congress. July 22, 2006. <http://memory.loc.gov/ammem/naw/nawshome.html>.

———. "A White Life for Two." *Key Texts of the Early Feminists.* Volume 2 of *Man Cannot Speak for Her.* Ed. Karlyn Kohrs Campbell. NY: Greenwood, 1989. 317–38.

Williams, Perry. "The Laws of Health: Women, Medicine, and Sanitary Reform, 1850–1890." *Science and Sensibility.* Ed. Marina Benjamin. Oxford: Basil Blackwell, 1991. 60–88.

Williams, Trevor. *Biographical Dictionary of Scientists.* Glasgow: HarperCollins, 1994.

"A Woman's Number." *Lucifer, the Light Bearer* 10.24 (May 19, 1893): 2.

"Woman's Responsibility." *Lucifer, the Light Bearer* 1.16 (April 21, 1897): 124.

Wood, Janice. "Prescription for a Periodical: Medicine, Sex, and Obscenity in the Nineteenth Century, as Told in *Dr. Foote's Health Monthly*." *American Periodicals* 18.1 (2008): 26–44.

Woodhull, Victoria. *"And the Truth Shall Make You Free": A Speech on the Principles of Social Freedom.* New York: Woodhull, Claflin, 1871.

———. *The Correspondence between the Victoria League and Victoria C. Woodhull.* N.p., 1871.

———. *The Elixir of Life; or, Why Do We Die?* New York: Woodhull and Claflin, 1873.

———. *The Human Body the Temple of God; or the Philosophy of Sociology.* London: Hyde Park Gate, 1890.

———. *A Lecture on Constitutional Equality, Delivered at Lincoln Hall, Washington, D.C., Thursday, February 16, 1871, by Victoria C. Woodhull.* New York: Journeymen, 1871.

———. *The Scare-Crows of Sexual Slavery: An Oration.* New York: Woodhull and Claflin, 1874.

———. *Tried as by Fire; Or, The True and the False Socially.* New York: Woodhull and Claflin, 1874.

Woodhull Martin, Victoria. *The Rapid Multiplication of the Unfit.* London, 1891.

———. *Stirpiculture; or, The Scientific Propagation of the Human Race.* London, 1888.

Wynn, James. "Alone in the Garden: How Gregor Mendel's Inattention to Audience May Have Affected the Reception of His Theory of Inheritance in 'Experiments in Plant Hybridization.'" *Written Communication* 24.1 (January 2007): 3–27.

Zaeske, Susan. "The Promiscuous Audience Controversy and the Emergence of the Early Women's Rights Movement." *Quarterly Journal of Speech* 81 (1995): 191–207.

abolition, 1, 4, 34, 40, 46; of marriage, 2, 3, 5, 16, 44, 73, 126, 194

abortion, 32, 53, 54, 112, 138–39, 149, 151–52, 231

abuse, spousal, 3, 33, 37, 52, 154

Acton, William, 85, 96, 230

Adult, The, 42, 165

agency, 5, 58, 61, 75, 78, 116, 121, 139, 145–46, 147, 150, 152, 156, 159, 165, 173, 181, 193, 209–10, 226, 229

age of consent, 42, 44, 121, 125, 126, 136, 185

Alcott, William, 80

allopath, 85, 86, 87, 228, 230

American Journal of Eugenics, 11, 40, 201, 206

American Social Hygiene Association, 122

anarchism, 34, 44, 47–48

anarchists, 18, 19, 22, 30, 34, 37, 39, 40, 41, 42, 47–49, 51, 54, 135, 165, 166, 198, 213, 225

"anarchist eugenics," 213

anatomy, 23, 25, 35, 53, 80, 83, 88, 94, 143, 146, 148, 210, 227

Anderson, Elizabeth Garrett, 227

Andrews, Stephen Pearl, 10, 17, 27–28, 69, 199, 222; and Victoria Woodhull, 27–28, 222

Anthony, Susan B., 27, 225

antifeminism, 6, 59–60, 63, 74, 77, 82, 90, 101, 103, 104, 108, 110, 228, 231, 232; and science, 6, 59–60, 77

Aristotle's Master-piece, 84

Athey, Stephanie, 182, 186, 187, 213

bacteriology, 5, 8, 13 112–40, 142, 179, 182, 185

"bacteriomania," 13, 124

Baer, Carl Ernst von, 142, 143, 144, 147, 148

Barry, Francis, 22, 34, 47, 50

Beecher, Henry Ward, 28, 29, 30, 222

Beecher-Tilton scandal, 28, 29, 30, 222

Berlin Heights, 17, 47, 49, 221

Besant, Annie, 200

Bichat, Marie-Francois-Xavier, 82

birth control, 16, 30, 32, 35, 41, 47, 52, 53–54, 67, 80, 84, 88, 92, 99, 153, 200–201, 207, 216, 224, 229, 230. *See also* contraception

birth defects, 122, 125

Bitzer, Lloyd, 7, 87

Blackwell, Elizabeth, 44, 82, 93–94, 97, 101, 104, 105, 106, 117, 119–21, 122, 126, 133, 179, 181–83, 184, 185, 192, 201, 202, 211, 212, 214, 230

Blood, James Harvey, 27, 28, 29, 30, 222

Buchanan, Lindal, 4, 216, 222–23

Burke, Kenneth, 7

Butler, Josephine, 120

Campbell, Karlyn Kohrs, 4, 210, 216

Campbell, Rachel, 36–39, 97–99, 103, 105, 119, 127–29, 130, 131, 132, 137, 141, 154, 224

cells, 78, 146–47, 148, 152, 161–62, 173, 174

censorship, 52, 110, 138, 225

Challis, Luther, 28, 30

Chamberlain, Edward, 41

Chandler, Lucinda, 15, 45–46, 61, 160–61, 199, 204, 224–25

chastity, 28, 31, 96, 136, 228

childbirth, 96, 149, 170

Claflin, Tennessee (Tennie C.), 10, 17, 20–21, 22, 29, 30–32, 45, 52, 54, 63–66, 92, 101, 131–35, 136, 137, 156–60, 162, 164, 165, 166, 167, 188, 196–99, 214, 223

Clarke, Edward, 83, 85–86, 227, 228

venereal disease testing, 122, 125–26, 135, 185, 231
Venette, Nicolas, 84, 146, 228
"Victorian prudery," 6, 9, 14, 211, 228, 229
virtue, 29, 31, 33, 38, 72, 96, 101, 112, 128–29, 130, 131, 132, 136, 137–38, 230–31
vitalism, 81–82, 83, 90, 106, 212
voluntary motherhood, 44, 66, 67, 179, 186

Waisbrooker, Lois, 3, 10, 15, 18, 21, 29, 39–41, 44, 46, 47, 49, 50, 52, 53, 54, 67, 68, 69–71, 78, 103, 105–7, 129–31, 136, 137, 141, 142, 147, 157, 160, 162–64, 167, 168, 170, 199–202, 203, 204, 206, 207, 211, 212, 221, 224, 231, 233
Walker, Edwin, C., 2, 42, 43, 61, 221
water cure, 23–24, 25, 32, 85, 86, 89, 90, 91, 95, 221, 228, 232; and women's rights, 25, 90, 91
Water-Cure Journal, 25, 46, 225
Weismann, August, 139, 173–74, 175, 178, 183, 184, 185, 190, 207
Wells, Ida, 42
Wells, Susan, 7, 111, 179

Wesselhoeft, Robert, 24
White, Lillie D., 15, 18, 22, 40, 41, 49–51, 55, 56–57, 78, 110, 204–5, 206, 225; as editor of *Lucifer*, 18, 40, 49
Whitehead, Celia, 15, 47, 52
Willard, Frances, 44, 126–27, 136, 170, 186, 214
Wingate, Charles, 137
Wolbarst, Abraham, 125
Woodhull, Canning, 27, 29, 30
Woodhull, Victoria Claflin, 1, 5, 7, 10, 17, 20, 26–31, 32, 34, 39, 44, 45, 46, 50, 53, 61–63, 64, 65, 78, 86, 92, 99–103, 106, 107, 108, 135–36, 137, 140, 155–56, 162, 163, 164, 165, 167, 170, 188, 194–96, 197, 209, 210–11, 212, 214, 216, 221, 222–23, 225, 231, 233; authorship of speeches, 27–28, 222–23
Woodhull & Claflin's Weekly, 10, 17, 28, 32, 199, 222
Word, The: A Monthly Journal of Reform, 10, 17, 35, 53, 68, 138, 199, 224
Wright, Fanny, 17

Zaeske, Susan, 4

Wendy Hayden is an assistant professor of English at Hunter College of the City University of New York. Her work has been published in *Rhetoric Review*.

Studies in Rhetorics and Feminisms

Studies in Rhetorics and Feminisms seeks to address the interdisciplinarity that rhetorics and feminisms represent. Rhetorical and feminist scholars want to connect rhetorical inquiry with contemporary academic and social concerns, exploring rhetoric's relevance to current issues of opportunity and diversity. This interdisciplinarity has already begun to transform the rhetorical tradition as we have known it (upper-class, agonistic, public, and male) into regendered, inclusionary rhetorics (democratic, dialogic, collaborative, cultural, and private). Our intellectual advancements depend on such ongoing transformation.

Rhetoric, whether ancient, contemporary, or futuristic, always inscribes the relation of language and power at a particular moment, indicating who may speak, who may listen, and what can be said. The only way we can displace the traditional rhetoric of masculine-only, public performance is to replace it with rhetorics that are recognized as being better suited to our present needs. We must understand more fully the rhetorics of the non-Western tradition, of women, of a variety of cultural and ethnic groups. Therefore, Studies in Rhetorics and Feminisms espouses a theoretical position of openness and expansion, a place for rhetorics to grow and thrive in a symbiotic relationship with all that feminisms have to offer, particularly when these two fields intersect with philosophical, sociological, religious, psychological, pedagogical, and literary issues.

The series seeks scholarly works that both examine and extend rhetoric, works that span the sexes, disciplines, cultures, ethnicities, and sociocultural practices as they intersect with the rhetorical tradition. After all, the recent resurgence of rhetorical studies has been not so much a discovery of new rhetorics as a recognition of existing rhetorical activities and practices, of our newfound ability and willingness to listen to previously untold stories.

The series editors seek both high-quality traditional and cutting-edge scholarly work that extends the significant relationship between rhetoric and feminism within various genres, cultural contexts, historical periods, methodologies, theoretical positions, and methods of delivery (e.g., film and hypertext to elocution and preaching).

Queries and submissions:
Professor Cheryl Glenn, Editor
    E-mail: cjg6@psu.edu
Professor Shirley Wilson Logan, Editor
    E-mail: slogan@umd.edu

Studies in Rhetorics and Feminisms
Department of English
142 South Burrowes Bldg.
Penn State University
University Park, PA 16802-6200